From Bevan to Blair

Also by Geoffrey Goodman

The Awkward Warrior:
Life and Times of Frank Cousins

The Miners' Strike, 1984/85

The State of the Nation:
The Political Legacy of Aneurin Bevan

From Bevan to Blair

Fifty Years' Reporting from the Political Front Line

Geoffrey Goodman

Pluto Press

LONDON • STERLING, VIRGINIA

First published 2003 by Pluto Press
345 Archway Road, London N6 5AA
and 22883 Quicksilver Drive, Sterling, VA 20166-2012, USA

www.plutobooks.com

British Library Cataloguing in Publication Data
A catalogue record for this book is available from
the British Library

ISBN 0 7453 2178 X hardback

Library of Congress Cataloging in Publication Data
Goodman, Geoffrey.
    From Bevan to Blair : fifty years' reporting from the political
front line / Geoffrey Goodman.
        p. cm.
Includes index.
    ISBN 0–7453–2178–X (hardback)
    1. Goodman, Geoffrey. 2. Journalists—Great Britain—Biography. I.
Title.
    PN5123.G59A3 2003
    070.92—dc21

10   9   8   7   6   5   4   3   2   1

Designed and produced for Pluto Press by
Chase Publishing Services, Fortescue, Sidmouth, EX10 9QG, England
Typeset from disk by Stanford DTP Services, Towcester, England
Printed and bound in the European Union by
Antony Rowe, Chippenham and Eastbourne, England

Contents

Acknowledgements

It is hard for me to grasp that this book has been in preparation, in one way or another, for some ten years. Of course, there have been large gaps in my attention to it and, still more, moments when I reflected that the whole thing should be put on a shelf and forgotten. That it was not dumped into the notorious dustbin of history is frankly due, largely, to the persistent encouragement from so many friends and old colleagues who insisted that I must not allow it to be pushed into that hungry maw. It is to them that I turn to express my gratitude – and the hope that the completed product will not disappoint them too much.

Their names are too numerous to catalogue here, and I also know that most of them would prefer to remain anonymous, no doubt wisely – albeit below I will make two exceptions to this rule. There are, of course, those to whom I owe an enormous debt of thanks not only for their persistent encouragement but also their sustained practical help. At the head of this list are my wife, Margit, and our children, John and Karen, whose love and support has always been unstinting as well as vital to me. They know full well the sacrifices a journalist's family is called on to make to keep a newspaperman on the road. To them goes my eternal gratitude. I also want to pay particular tribute to my son John Goodman who compiled the index.

Then come my dear friends the McCarthys – Bill and Margaret, Lord and Lady McCarthy of Headington, Oxford. Bill, a distinguished Emeritus Fellow of Nuffield College, Oxford, arranged for me to continue a long association with the College, which he originally had inspired some thirty years ago. It was in Oxford at Nuffield, over the years, that much of this book was written. It was there that I received hospitality, a vast amount of intellectual stimulus, support and creative criticism from many friends and Fellows of the College, not least successive Wardens including the current one, Sir Tony Atkinson. I owe them all a great debt.

There are also those who stand in the shadows and without whose help and support a construction of this kind could never have been built. In particular I want to mention my former secretary at the *Daily Mirror*, Mrs June Hoile, whose devoted asssistance played a notable role in the early foundations of this book.

Then the two notable exceptions I referred to above. First, my dear friend of over fifty years, Leo Abse, whose 29 years as a Labour MP established him as the most distinguished backbench legislator of the twentieth century. Second, to my equally dear friend of half a century, Michael Foot, whose political, professional and personal friendship has been priceless. To all of them – my thanks. I also wish to add the name of Professor Richard Hoggart the distinguished writer whose encouragement and friendship has been an invaluable asset.

And finally, beyond the normal routine of acknowledgements I want to dedicate this book to the memory of a number of outstanding journalists whose personal friendship and professional inspiration it has been my privilege and good fortune to enjoy. They are no longer with us but, beyond question, they are woven into the fabric of the story that now unfolds. Their names, in alphabetical order, are: Tom Baistow, James Cameron, Robin (Robert James) Cruickshank, Hugh Cudlipp, Trevor Evans, Harold Hutchinson, Sydney Jacobson, Ian Mackay, Patrick (Paddy) Monkhouse, Laurence Thompson and the cartoonist-exceptional, Vicky (Victor Weisz).

All were an integral part of what has contributed to build a work of this character. To all of them and to the unmentioned names, my salutes and profound thanks.

Geoffrey Goodman
July 2003

Preface

Being a journalist is a kind of alternate for a job in an entire range of semi-skilled, perhaps even unskilled, trades. I am thinking especially of jobs such as the secret intelligence services – incidentally, a much overrated occupation; a bookmaker (much underrated), managing a casino, becoming a politician, which has increasingly developed into a job akin to running a casino; and, to be sure, pretending to be an academic, preferably one occupied with psychology or, maybe still more appropriate, 'modern communications'. Any one of these trades, in my view, can be regarded as interchangeable with journalism. Come to think of it, you could add a few more – being a beachcomber, a coastguard on a lighthouse overlooking a particularly rugged coastline or island or, if things became really difficult, a brothel keeper.

I am quite sure it would be easy to think of other alternates; or perhaps a permutation of various of these splendid categories rolled into one inglorious amalgam of chance, circumstance, fortune and probably ill-luck, much of which is always lurking around. So, briefly, I felt tempted to give this book a title of:

IT'S ONLY TOMORROW'S FISH AND CHIPS.

It was a description offered to me many years ago by a brilliantly perceptive colleague on the *Daily Mirror* (dear long-dead Len Jackson), who, after my outburst of outrage and frustration at the way a piece of mine had been mishandled in the paper that day, once reminded me: 'Just remember, old chap,' he solemnly consoled, 'it'll all be forgotten in a couple of days when the paper is being used to wrap up six-penn'orth of fish and chips. It's only tomorrow's fish and chips we are talking about ...' They were the days when almost all fish and chip shops used newspaper pages to wrap round their delectable cod and two-penn'orth of chips. Sadly, in my nostalgia, I fear that this crude but workmanlike practice has faded from our clean-food culture. Fish and chips are no longer wrapped in yesterday's newspapers, though, who knows, perhaps in some remote corner the heritage continues. So the original title of this book has taken on fresh tokenism.

At any rate I am not sure why I ever regarded my range of skills, or lack of them, as qualifying me to become a newspaperman. Maybe it was pure romanticism. Perhaps I saw too many cheap films as a kid. More likely there was nothing better to do in the days when I was beginning to consider the forbidding prospect of a lifetime at work. I well remember the retirement speech made by an old *News Chronicle* colleague, a great Parliamentary reporter of that paper (those were days when every national morning paper had its own reporter in the press gallery of the House of Commons) – E. Clepham Palmer ('Cleph'). Upon receiving the beneficent retirement gesture from the Cadburys, who then owned the paper, Cleph observed in his dry, drawn-out East Anglian tones:

> It's been a wonderful life. It's paid my mortgage, helped educate my children, kept me in food, drink, tobacco and clothing; assisted me to see something of the world at someone else's expense and has provided me with a platform to address the nation at large ... what other job would have provided me with such an opportunity? What other form of work could have given an unskilled labourer, which is what I am, such good fortune?

Dear Cleph meant every word of that as he retreated to somewhere in his old native heath to enjoy the fruits of retirement from the Cocoa Press. He was not alone with such sentiments about the advantages of being in the newspaper trade. Ian Mackay was another labourer in that vineyard. The Great Bohunkus, as he was affection-ately labelled by his chums, would frequently reflect on his good fortune. As a young boy in Wick he started working life at the age of 14 humping coal for a local merchant at two *old* pennies a day. He got up at 6 am every morning to qualify in the grime trade before he dusted his hands and landed a job as a messenger boy for a local paper. That was how Mackay started along the road to becoming one of the outstanding diarists and essayists to grace Fleet Street in the twentieth century. He died, aged 54, still full of zest and brilliance, at the peak of his form, a pure Mozart of journalism, and still amazed at his good fortune at being able to spend his later life reading books and absorbing knowledge about the world, then writing about all this – subsidised, as he was fond of observing, by Mr Cadbury's bars of milk chocolate.

It is not a bad way of avoiding work, though some people have clearly discovered still better methods. Not that there was much money in the trade in those days – unlike modern media cash registers. Most of the best journalists of my time seemed to end up with a mere handful of loose change and large debts, which they could scarcely understand, let alone pay off. All that has changed. The modern generation of Media men and women are very well paid – at least by comparison – and some are among the more privileged earning groups in society. So they should be: the job is far more demanding than it ever was as well as demanding far greater skills of invention.

*   *   *

So why this book? Why bother with yet another kind of memoir about a trade that has had its over-share of nostalgic inner reflection? I have only one strong reason – I believe the picture I am presenting here is different. This story is a picture reflection of the century we have just left behind: a reflection of life for a working-class, under-educated, certainly under-privileged boy who, through the Depression years and the Second World War, somehow found a pathway into journalism and political life. The interweaving of life as a journalist and its contact with political power is a fascinating reflection of power throughout the ages. It always has been – though arguably more so today than ever. Northcliffe would be amazed if he returned to his old scene to witness how his own Citizen Kane role during the first two decades of the twentieth century has been dwarfed by contemporary moguls of media power.

The book is also a testimony to a generation, my generation, the children born in the wake of the First World War. It is, of course, the experience through one eye: an eye that has seen an extraordinary transformation at every level across the spectrum of time. It encapsulates the story of an ordinary child of the century, born and reared in a north of England working-class home of Jewish immigrants from Russia and Poland. There were no privileges except those bestowed from the natural ferment of a home, encompassing a large family, which generated turbulent spirits that erupted naturally from the insecurity and uncertainties of immigrant life. I count all this not as a disadvantage but as a privilege, a huge gain, since it contained the stimulus, the vibrancy, the drive to establish roots and identity. It was a fight to survive from unpromising beginnings.

There are, of course, wider considerations that the book will try to reflect. I grew up in the slipstream of vast political and social upheaval, indeed of revolution. All over the world, following the 1914–18 Great War, there came an earthquake of change. The great melting pot of the twentieth century was being moulded: socialism and communism were being hailed as the 'New Religion'. Fascism was breeding on the carcase of decaying ancient regimes. When my father returned from the filth, death and destruction of the trenches across the Channel in 1918 and eventually emerged from a recovery unit in an Edinburgh hospital, he went in search of work. Work? Ah, that was another story. He always told me his story with considerable reluctance and a brevity that matched his modest outlook on life. He had emerged alive from the trenches – which surprised him; he had a few dreams and was a great Lloyd-George fan; he wanted to believe that a new world was beckoning. Armed with those hopes, those dreams, he began looking for a job, found one briefly but then joined the long queue of broken dreamers. That was the crucible in which my earliest memories were formed.

Growing up in the 1920s and 1930s was an outcrop of that time warp. Yet it was more complex than that. In the immortal phraseology of Maxim Gorky, those years were in fact 'My University'. In that crucible all future life was shaped, unconsciously but no less real. Feelings, passions, prides, prejudices, rights and wrongs, dreams and poetry – they all emptied into the crucible, shaping my ignorance as well as my knowledge. Such things are not open to choice, they simply happen. Like Everest, they are there, dominating the landscape of one's life. For those people who grew up at the same time and yet remained outside that kind of ambience, which was essentially a zone of protest and revolt, the world clearly looked very different. Yet among my own contemporaries there were very few who were not involved, at one stage or another, in 'trouble making' – politically, socially, or just for the sheer hell of it to break the monotony of orthodoxy. And since we were not protected by wealth, or the kind of class background that, by definition, provided its own immunisation from reality, our options were limited – albeit no less attractive in a negative sort of way.

So I came to inherit the socialist dream as part of the accepted litany of any sensible life. Gradually the message grew more sophisticated, more complex but also acquired a deeper logic. It was a kind of new, or different, divinity, offering idealised thoughts on the future of mankind and all that. It also provided an avenue of escape from the more conventional themes of organised mysticism and absurdities manifest in routine religious belief as practised in church, synagogue or mosque. Aneurin Bevan, whom I came to know so well in later years, once described socialism to me as a 'natural biological development'. He believed that the species would ultimately come to it in pursuit of its own self-interest rather than routed via pure idealism. Bevan saw this as the 'civilising process' – which, I still believe, is what drew so many of my generation to the concept. That indeed was our twentieth-century dream.

Even now it is still impossible to predict how influential, or superfluous, that concept may prove to be in fashioning and moulding the illusions of this new twenty-first century. Darwin once observed that it is always easier to prophesy for a million years ahead than for the next fifty. Even so it is a reasonable assumption that many of the features of the new society that is now in embryo will, in fact, come to resemble some of the dreams that we, in our time, allowed to dominate much of our lives.

All this and newspapers too … well, it has been frequently claimed that journalism is the 'first draft of history': that somewhat presumptuous claim can be placed against my original and, I fear, more modest, sceptical offering – 'Tomorrow's fish and chips'. And although it is not the title of this book, I have a feeling at the far end of my mind that the truth might still fit, even if uneasily, somewhere between each.

1   1945: Footsteps in the Dark

Looking back, I like to think of 1945 and the decade that followed as something akin to my treading footsteps in the dark. It was a strange beginning to adult life – an adult life that had already matured through war but was still absurdly ill-suited to growing up away from the sound of gunfire.

None of us really knew where we were going, though we did seem to know we wanted to get there. Everything was a period of self-discovery insofar as any of us ever really discover ourselves. It was a course in adult-awareness. We were, I am sure of this, all pioneers in the infancy of adulthood. A bit like the discovery of sex.

They were, to be sure, years of considerable emotional difficulty and even pain as we reflected on those who were no longer with us: beloved friends now dead. Yet in a very curious way I don't recall ever feeling consciously fortunate to be alive and having survived. The footsteps simply took over, and all movement seemed to be equally in the dark.

Hardly anyone who had been actively involved in the war of 1939–45 – and inevitably, by that, I mean in the armed forces – found it easy to adjust to the ambience of those immediate postwar years. Jobs that had been kept open for returning servicemen – as required by wartime legislation – were often not taken up. The reasons are obvious: men had grown out of the jobs they began as mere boys or even as young men. That world of the past seemed utterly remote. Wartime experiences catapulted boys into manhood. They disdained the very thought of returning to the kind of work they were doing before. For the first time in their life the element of choice appeared on the agenda of living. It was all very strange, new and unclear. Yet at the same time millions of men and women who either had no job at all before the war or at best a tenuous connection with secure work were now being rehabilitated (as the official phrase-book explained) into civilian life. Civvy street beckoned and the mist descended.

To begin a life story at this point is a purely arbitrary choice. A story like this could start at any point. But I choose this bridgehead for very clear reasons: it was for me, as for millions of others of my generation, the true starting point.

The supreme task facing the newly elected Labour Government of Clement Attlee was to 'rehabilitate' the nation: to transform it from a people at war, in or out of uniform, to a people at peace; to rebuild and reshape; to cope with dreams. Even to state the problem gives some clue to the Herculean nature of that task. This was to provide a role in civilian life for five or six million people, many of whom had no previous experience, certainly no substantial understanding of what 'civilian life' involved; or, if they had then it was about a civilian life that had effectively ceased to exist. The miracle was that this was achieved at all without far greater social turmoil and emotional upheaval.

I am thinking back. Everywhere there were shortages – of food, clothing, houses; of materials with which to begin the enormous task of rebuilding the towns, the cities, the streets damaged by bombing, and often combined with the neglect of those prewar years when depression and deprivation stalked the streets before they were bombed. Then there was that dream – that vision of a New Jerusalem; that image which danced so capriciously within the minds of a generation released into a future they could scarcely conceive. Such was the inheritance from six years of war that had engulfed practically all of us; that had been 'total', as the cliché assured. For once the cliché was correct, even precise.

Within a year of taking office the Attlee Government was already struggling. Not so much for its own survival – since it possessed an overwhelming Parliamentary majority, the first of its kind in Labour's history, but for the survival of the postwar dream. They are so fickle, these dreams; but they are also deeply persistent.

Consider the backdrop from that Attlee election victory of July 1945, less than three months after the war in Europe ended and before Japan had finally surrendered to the atomic bomb. For myself I was stumbling around in Germany, hovering between Hamburg and Berlin, amid the unforgettable rubble of post-Nazi Germany, wondering what the hell was going to emerge from all this. When I returned to England in 1946 the first crisis was all too visible – the financial aftermath. The dollar crisis, as it came to be known throughout the Attlee years, had hit the new government when the Americans cut off the wartime Lease-Lend arrangement that provided a beleaguered Britain with a desperately needed economic prop. The effect of Lease-Lend as Roosevelt had originally organised it was to allow Britain to lean, almost totally, on US economic assistance in return for leasing off parts of the old British Empire to the United

States. That deal, signed on 11 March 1941, ensured that we had a steady flow of arms, food and materials to keep us alive and kicking.

That was brought to an abrupt stop at the end of the war, and we were in real trouble. In fact, almost as soon as the Attlee Government took office in the summer of 1945 John Maynard Keynes – still in his role as the government's chief economic adviser – warned Attlee and the Cabinet that Britain faced 'a financial Dunkirk' as a result of the United States cutting off Lease-Lend so swiftly. Attlee sent Keynes to Washington to negotiate a survival package. Franklin Roosevelt had just died, and Harry S. Truman was sitting in the White House. The Americans were far from keen to help a British government now run by socialists like Attlee and Co. rather than Winston Churchill. The negotiations were tough for Keynes and hard for Britain. The price was high: for the loan of $3,750 million Britain was compelled to accept the convertibility of sterling. That meant a huge drain on UK resources and therefore a severely limiting factor on the Attlee Government's plans to reconstruct postwar Britain. It was the foundation stone on which postwar British policy would be shaped – especially the relationship with the United States.

The dollar shortage caused food rations to be cut below even the wartime level, and the Minister of Food, John Strachey – one of the outstanding radical socialist minds of his generation – was forced to introduce bread rationing in July 1946, which was something that had not been necessary even in the darkest days of wartime Britain. Throughout the country a war-wearied nation felt the ever tighter pinch of austerity. All 'luxury' goods were marked 'For Export Only', which, of course, led to a black market to supply those at home with access to loads of available cash anxious to collect their nylons, whisky and even chocolate, which were for export only. So the gloom descended, the screw tightened and the critics of the Attlee Government began to emerge from their dug-outs to mock the socialists' attempt to build this much-vaunted New Jerusalem. Mocking came easy, especially to a largely Conservative-dominated, and -owned, national press. For there was no television to offer a balancing glimpse; no commercial radio to challenge the BBC radio monopoly, which, good as it was in so many areas of broadcasting quality, was nonetheless seriously handicapped to offset the mocking taunts that came from most daily newspapers. That was the atmosphere into which so many of us were finally demobbed.

Yet, somehow, the miracle continued. Despite all these tribulations the Attlee Government managed to sustain its own spirit and a remarkable degree of dedication. So much so that even against the catalogue of disasters that still greatly underestimated government embarked on a most astonishing social and economic revolution – the Welfare State, as outlined by Beveridge; a National Health Service (1948) brought to the statute book by Aneurin Bevan against bitter and prolonged protest from the Conservative Opposition and the vested interests of the medical world; a National Insurance Scheme compiled by the former Welsh miners' leader Jim Griffiths; the nation-alisation of the coal mines, the railways, the Bank of England, gas, electricity. Even to recite the list in today's climate of political cynicism can bring shudders of incomprehension. Even then it seemed like an age of miracles had dawned.

*   *   *

As we returned in our demob suits we collected our ration books and clothing coupons. If you were fortunate enough to have a home or to have been allocated one – often a pre-fab temporary house to accommodate the homeless and bomb-victims – it was then necessary to gather a bit of furniture. For most people this was known as 'Utility' furniture – a kind of make-do product, hardly designer-friendly to the artist's eye but exceptionally robust, well made, durable and remarkably utilitarian (hence the label); I still have some of that splendid stuff, which looks rather better than various items of modern furniture. So although it was not yet Jerusalem it was certainly not purgatory; there was a job, a modest flat or pre-fab house equipped with a Utility bed, table and chairs – better than so many other places across a ravaged war-torn Europe.

Indeed there was even much laughter emerging from the simple pleasures of a simple life; or perhaps it wasn't quite as simple as we then imagined. The Old Vic Company presented *King Lear* at the New Theatre in October 1946, produced by Laurence Olivier, who also played Lear. It was a stupendous performance and a notable event in the postwar theatre, which, I now realise far more than I appreciated at the time, also reflected the *Zeitgeist*. Then there was cricket, of course: Wally Hammond, the great and legendary man from Gloucester, the first professional to captain England, leading the MCC team to Australia in 1946/7 in the first postwar Test series. The Aussies won that series and the Ashes. Even so I think we felt that things were beginning to return to 'normal' – except I doubt we knew what 'normal' meant. We were in fact creating our own new normality, slowly fashioned from those footsteps in the dark. A little light was starting to glow. Not much but enough to enable us to see in the dark.

There was trouble in Greece, in Palestine and with Uncle Joe Stalin's Russia. Peace was still slow, unbearably slow, to uncoil. Allies were becoming labelled as new enemies, old enemies as new allies. What madness it all seemed. How was it possible to even think of regarding this scene as 'normal'? The meat ration fell to 1s 2d worth a *week* (about 6p in current terms). Snow blanketed the country in the winter of the big freeze, 1946/7, paralysing large tracts of the land. There was insufficient coal to feed the power stations and fuel was rationed. Hugh Gaitskell, then a Minister of Fuel, told us not to have a bath because it might waste too much energy. Unemployment rose, briefly, to over 2,500,000 because the big freeze simply refrigerated work and closed factories. Exports fell to practically nil, which meant that all those 'luxury' goods found an even bigger black market for those few who still had the cash to corrupt. Clem Attlee, who always signed himself as C.R. Attlee, proclaimed to this New Jerusalem: 'We are engaged in another Battle of Britain.'

Life was no great fun and yet people, while grumbling of course, were not bitter with discontent. There remained throughout this period of the late 1940s and even into the early 1950s a strong residual feeling of wartime community spirit, which somehow acted as a protective cushion to the external battle for existence. The favourite music hall chant went, in Flanagan and Allen's memorable script, 'Blimey, if this was winning the war what would bloody defeat have meant?' The house rocked with self-mocking laughter. But it was a serious question.

In the middle of 1947, just as the country slithered out of the big freeze with bursting pipes in most homes, the United States recognised that the economic crisis that was affecting the entire European continent – in which Britain was certainly not the worst affected – was itself laying the foundation of a new political crisis in which the Soviet Union, through the Communist parties in every European country, was gaining massive influence. Truman and his advisers sensed danger; they were urged on by Britain's Foreign Secretary Ernest Bevin whose long-standing anti-Soviet views were now reinforced by Stalin's policies. The Marshall Plan was born. It changed the face of Europe, set down the cornerstone of postwar American policy in Europe and put in motion the wheels of the Cold War. The truth about the Marshall Plan, in which Bevin played a

crucial role both in public and behind the scenes, is now plain to
see; it was the American response to what had already been perceived
as the postwar Soviet challenge. But it was less clear at the time, and
deeply divisive both in Britain and throughout an increasingly
divided Europe. In Britain it divided the Labour Party and even
members of the Attlee Government; the Conservative Opposition
welcomed it in public but reserved private doubts about American
longer-term intentions – the suspicion always lurked that the United
States was already replacing Britain as a world imperial power. But
Winston Churchill had no doubts; the Marshall Plan echoed all his
own querulous tones as expressed in his famous Fulton speech about
an 'Iron Curtain descending across Europe'.

It is also true as we now know from the disclosures of the secret
Soviet files that a number of Eastern European Communist countries
wanted to accept the Marshall Plan – until Stalin stopped them. It was
perhaps Stalin's most serious postwar error of political judgement.
Had he shrewdly and, of course, cynically accepted Marshall's
proposals the Soviet bloc could have put the Americans on the spot.
We shall never know.

In any event it took time for the Marshall Plan to work its way
through the frozen veins of the European economies. In Britain the
convertibility of sterling was suspended and drastic cuts made in UK
imports of tobacco, petrol and newsprint. The price of a packet of
20 fags rose from 2s 4d to 3s 4d (from about 12p to around 17p) –
which was a big increase in average wage packets of around £5 a
week. Yet in August of that same year – 1947 – the Attlee Government
gave India self-government, with Lord Louis Mountbatten as the last
Viceroy – an extraordinary act of principle and in defiance of the
economic crisis, dire warnings from the Conservatives, deep
misgivings within the entire British Establishment and the
imminence of civil war between Mahatma Mohandas Gandhi's India
and Mohammed Ali Jinnah's Pakistan. The great British Empire was
unwinding as America's world dominance became increasingly a fact
of life. At the end of that year of so much turmoil the bells rang out
for the wedding of Princess Elizabeth, heir to the throne, to the young
Greek-born naval lieutenant, Philip Mountbatten RN. A nation
starved of pageantry loved it: the fairy Princess and the handsome
sailor. It was pure Hollywood. But it was more than that – it was
British and it was happening in real life.

By the summer of 1948 the foundations of the Welfare State were
firmly laid through a series of Acts of Parliament. Three years after

taking office the Attlee Government, in the face of all its mountainous problems, could justly claim to have taken fundamental steps to abolish poverty. Not yet achieved – but the first few rungs of the ladder were being climbed. Full employment was established – indeed, some of the classical school of economists complained that it was 'too full' and would lead to inflation and labour indiscipline; new houses were being built to higher standards of quality than any previously set by local authorities; New Towns began to spring up in unlikely places like Harlow. Rationing remained severe though just tolerable as bread came off the ration book in July 1948 to coincide with the launching of Aneurin Bevan's National Health Service.

It was all happening in a strange ambience. The political fanfares were loud though never overbearing: people slipped into the new habits with little fuss and, it has to be said, with no overwhelming sense of liberation. It was another footstep on the road to that postwar dream of 'something better'; that was the key phrase of the age. People believed, indeed were convinced, that the nation deserved 'something better' than what they remembered from prewar, and 'something better' was beginning to happen. Not too much drama; not too much bullshit propaganda either; just the voice of this or that minister explaining the significance of it all in an occasional radio broadcast (still no television for the masses, remember) and the rather smuggy feeling one had that we were in fact living in a rather civilised country. Subsidised milk and orange juice were provided for children of families who, at first, viewed these 'luxuries' with a dubious eye. 'Free orange juice for the kids?' mothers would query; 'can the Government afford this?' they asked, like professors of economics. But it was there.

Britain had, in truth, started to build a new postwar generation, the 'free milk and free orange juice children'; a healthier breed. Rickets, the scourge of the undernourished children of prewar poverty denied the vital vitamin D, was on the way out. That appalling disease of the unequal society, from which a cousin of mine died, aged 9, was killed off by Attlee's Welfare State. It brought back memories of what was missing from so much of our lives in prewar Britain. It is easy now to reread Orwell's *Road to Wigan Pier* (first published by Victor Gollancz's Left Book Club in 1937) and scoff at its far-away descriptions of poverty, squalor, mass unemployment, hunger, ill health and appalling slum housing. Yet those *were* the conditions of the period in which I grew up. Orwell dramatises but he does not exaggerate. There was no National Health Service. If you could afford a few pennies a week – and for many that was a genuine burden – you could buy into primitive health insurance schemes to escape a pauper's experience in hospitals. The local doctors' 'panel' was often restricted both in numbers and availability. The inequalities were grotesque – albeit accepted by an underclass (that phrase was not then in use) as *their lot*. The war, 1945, and what followed changed that scene.

*   *   *

For the generations of more recent years, bred in a different climate of cynical disbelief, of broken dreams or even half-formed dreams, the mere concept of a New Jerusalem probably sounds like a refrain from a Never-Never Land. Yet it *did* exist in that postwar ambience. It actually blossomed in the hearts and minds of millions of people who had travelled through the war years and, still more crucial, had grown up through the prewar years of the 1930s that did so much to design the mood and emotions of the generation that fought the Second World War.

My generation was the product of births in the wake of the 'other' World War, that of 1914–18, but still more the product of a quite exceptional period of the century, the 1920s and 1930s. It was this epoch that set the tone, the anguish, the despair and, ultimately no doubt, the disillusion of the century. This was the time-span in which the socialist idea seemed to be validated beyond reasonable doubt; the period in which capitalism failed to answer the human dilemma; the period in which Soviet Communism came of age to influence the entire perspective of a feasible future; when great intellects were drawn to the belief that a formula had been found, however rough-hewn at that point, to resolve the global conflict and to bridge the gap between the gruesome past and the dawn of a new civilisation. It was mostly a message of hope. Darkened, to be sure, by the emergence of fascism in Europe with the rise of Mussolini in Italy and Hitler's Third Reich. Threatened, of course, by Oswald Mosley's blackshirts rampaging through the streets, chanting their own slogans to herald their own concepts of a future fascist state. But our signposts had begun to be set in stone before Mosley's banner was unfurled. Growing up in the 1920s assured that. The real mould had been formed a long way back.

Long before I left a demob station in the Midlands early in 1946 with a set of civilian clothes – most of which, to my amazement, appeared to fit; long before my war years in the RAF; long before I volunteered for service in the early months of 1940 at the RAF recruiting station tucked, obscurely, behind the wonderful Inigo Jones Euston Church, the signposts were already engraved on my mind. Subconsciously, no doubt; not readily identified at the time; scarcely thought about in serious terms; but embedded in the recesses of my collected subconscious experiences, all of them oddly assorted, ill-formed and hugely lacking in educated awareness. But some kind of dream had been invested. Of that I knew.

If such idealism now sounds like simplistic naivete to the modern cynic, as it probably does, let me try to open up a few doors to the past, the kind of past of my own experience and of my contemporaries. It was by any standards a remarkable crucible. It is true that the tales from earlier generations inescapably tend to sound like fables from a primeval age, and this is almost certainly how any description of life in working-class Britain, circa the 1920s and 1930s, is likely to be perceived. The speed of social and technological change in the last thirty years has been so great that it is very difficult for today's generation to imagine what ordinary life was like in the 1960s; how much more so then to consider the social and economic scene of sixty or seventy years ago.

I grew up in the 1920s and 1930s. That was before television; radio was still in a primitive state; the aeroplane and even the motor car were still in their infancy of development. As a schoolboy I knew no one who owned a car or, come to that, ever imagined they would be in a position to own one. The telephone in the home was a mark of belonging to a privileged, rather special, minority. Communal life was based on small, largely immobile groups – even in the urban areas of north-west England and still more so in the rural districts. Gas lighting was still the common factor in the streets, and electricity in our homes was just beginning to be switched on, tentatively and slowly. Nor am I now describing a scene from Dickens; this was England, my England, in the year 1930 when at the age of 9 I began to look around at my environment; when the world beyond our garden fence, let alone beyond the county or national frontiers, was as remote as outer space may have seemed to yesterday's children. Most of the scientific and technological innovation that we now take for granted has been developed, if not actually invented, in my lifetime. In something like sixty years or so we have discovered and, maybe one might say, inflicted on society, a range of technological advances that might realistically have taken previous generations around 500 years to introduce and certainly to absorb. This is one reason why the literature, and even the updated experiences, from the 1930s may seem like medieval fantasies being played out to a contemporary audience. Indeed, they often appear that way to those of us who lived through the period.

My generation, certainly all the friends and acquaintances on my list, were liberated by the Second World War. We grew up and were at school surrounded by depression, mass unemployment and the ambience of wars just experienced and wars to come. The rise of fascism in Europe came first under Mussolini in Italy, and then as Hitler took power in Germany from January 1933 came Nazism. Mussolini set the pattern that many of those in high social and political circles throughout Europe (including Britain) wanted to follow. Most of them preferred fascism to the other option on the agenda pad – socialism or communism. As Mussolini moved into North Africa, bombing his way across Abyssinia (Ethiopia) and sending what the Italian propaganda machine then described as 'primitive natives' scurrying into their sandy hovels of death, Roman culture was brought to the streets of Addis Ababa to the approval of influential circles in Europe. General Franco launched his 'Christian crusade' (for that is what he called it) against the elected Republican government of Spain to start the Spanish Civil War. That indeed was the critical watershed of the 1930s. It aroused the passion and anger of the liberal and civilised world as no other single event had done, or subsequently did, between the two world wars. At about the same time the Japanese armies spread themselves across China, decimating and raping Nanking and any other Chinese city that lay in the path of Tokyo's 'Operation Co-prosperity' – designed to spread Japan's modern message throughout the Pacific zone.

In Britain, and especially in England, Sir Oswald Mosley took up the argument for fascism and used Mussolini's template and example. He dressed his followers in black shirts, like his Italian mentor, and paraded the streets of London, Manchester, Leeds, Liverpool and other places with slogans, echoing first the rantings of Mussolini and later with the anti-semitic poison of Hitler and Goebbels. To be brought into one's teens as all this was happening around our ears, and eyes, was an experience that etched certain messages into our still-untutored minds. None of this could be picked up from our school books and only faintly from the puzzled whispers of our elementary school teachers, though in this respect I reckon I was more fortunate than many.

I was not conscious, at the time, of the smell of decay. I do not recall having had the gift of any nostril-measure to identify the effect of living, growing up, in such an ambience. Just a vague sense that there was no particularly significant future to look forward to except, no doubt, the prospect of another war. My headmaster at the time, Tommy Humbles, forever insisted that we, the children of the First World War, were destined to follow the death and/or glory steps of our fathers. He was right – though he offered us his view of the future without excitement, just a grim menace.

That was the ethos I still recall so vividly. Fifty or sometimes even sixty children to each classroom: assembling for prayers in the morning under the arched oak-beams of a huge cavernous school-hall, which looked a bit like a converted church and may well have been. Some 500 children packed shoulder-to-shoulder lined up military-style each morning at 8.30 am to burble, absent mindedly, allegiances to conventional mythology. The smell of Plasticine on sweaty woolly jersies mingled with the whiff of juvenile farting as we chanted the Lord's Prayer. The atmosphere had a special flavour of the sour times. I glanced shyly at the legs of a freckled-faced flaxen-haired girl and slowly up her bodyline without quite realising the promptings of sensual feelings. It was more important to think about other things – such as being chosen to play for the school football (soccer, of course, not rugby) on a Thursday. It was a nice thought to have even when you knew it was unlikely because you simply weren't good enough for the first team. Always there hovered in my mind, and no doubt the chums around me, that feeling of failure and the sense of hopeless search; that feeling, too, of the failure of our teachers to comprehend, let alone tolerate, our pitiful inadequacies. Fear mingled with an infant despair.

Tommy Humbles made a practice of walking round the classrooms with a bamboo cane, a short stick, which he proudly exhibited as his tool of the trade. Tommy Humbles: how well I see him in my eye – tallish, devilishly thin, with swept-back greying hair and steel-rimmed spectacles across his chalky-white face, lined heavily with the sufferings of his war, the subject about which he was unerringly and unhealthily obsessed. He would stroll into any classroom, arbitrarily selected, carrying his bamboo cane, lay it on the desktop and look around the room, arms folded. His steely glint carried its own special menace, which, in later years, I would reflect on and compare with a Gestapo *Ubersturmbandfuhrer* surveying his victims. There was always total silence in the classroom as Tommy's glance crept across the heads of children in fear. His mere presence evoked fear. No matter what the subject was – history, geography, even algebra – Tommy would somehow bring it all round to war, the one just passed and the next one in line, and re-echo his prophecy, which he clearly relished, that we would all – except the girls, of course – become fodder to the guns of what would shortly happen all over again. It was very clear to Tommy. Then he would smile, thinly, pick up his cane and arch it between outstretched hands, nod to the class teacher (who seemed as intimidated by him as we were) and slip out of the door as snake-like as he had glided in.

We grew up slowly, absurdly ill-equipped for anything but lectures on pessimism and a life of humdrum uncertainty. In that northern elementary school of no particular quality or distinction heaven was kicking a ball around in a concreted playground or bowling at 'wickets' chalked on the bricks of the lavatory wall. What you have read in Orwell's *Road to Wigan Pier* was not fiction but brilliant, investigative reporting, circa 1937. Somehow we came to life under the plinth of unemployed fathers, mothers trying to feed families on scraps and teachers heroically clinging to their conviction that most kids under their influence were better off in their classrooms than at home. They were – despite the Tommy Humbles of the epoch.

We all sang programmed praises to that dying age and saluted the flag. Yet there was one man who raised my sights above those dismal ramparts and, perhaps, for all I know, performed similar miracles for other kids. He was a large, rounded figure who appeared, at times, to fill the whole of the space in front of the blackboard. His fair-to-blondish hair was thinning and starting to show signs of greying at the sides as it brushed back. He wore large glasses wrapped in a kind of pinkish frame, which seemed to produce a peculiar refracted light from the beams of occasional sunlight that sliced across the classroom as they entered the long dormer-style windows, which relieved the monotony of the red-bricked outer walls of our school.

He was Leonard Charles Cookson, and he was a sort of Jesus Christ with chalk and blackboard and we were his disciples. 'Cookie' did not believe in the practice of intimidating his children; nor did he much approve of lectures in gloom and pessimism. He clearly disliked Tommy Humbles, not merely because of the Humbles' syndrome of destruction-ahead but, we all guessed, because he simply didn't like the fellow. 'Cookie' – and none of us called him anything else behind his back – sought to control – no, I think I prefer 'influence' to 'control' – the unruly motley that we were with a mixture of superb teaching qualities, a moral and religious zeal, and a degree of patient sensitivity and understanding that even our untutored minds recognised as 'special'. He would stand there, roly-poly in his large grey suit, smiling over his specs and, I am certain, winking at our idiocies without ever betraying a muscle of his eyes.

More than any other man from my childhood 'Cookie' provided me with parameters; he was pre-eminently someone who taught us to appreciate a system of values. His own brand of religious commitment was to the Christadelphians (a sect sometimes described as the Brethren of Christ, who look for a return of Christ to earth to reign over the restored twelve tribes of Israel. Their 'prophet' was John Thomas, a Brooklyn revivalist preacher, circa 1805–71).

This allegiance explained a great deal about 'Cookie', and especially his unusually high regard for Jewish people. He admired the Jewish philosophy of life as virtually his own and regarded the sons of Israel as possessing some special quality. In his eyes he did not question their status as 'The Chosen People', and in that context seemed to adopt me as a kind of infant prodigy. By the same token I clearly adopted him as my mentor, and he remained, till his death, a person of special significance to me. He was without question the most powerful influence during my boyhood years. In fact, Leonard Charles Cookson, man of Lancaster, and certainly a man of God, was to me above all a kind of surrogate father; he was a man for all my seasons of childhood, and even as I grew up – a disbeliever, a socialist and an atheist – we never lost touch. There is no way I could ever underestimate his role in my life.

2   Early Life: Buttonholes and Cornerstones

Learning never came easily to me. There was no natural talent that I could depend on to carry me through the awkward reefs of growing up. I knew numerous other boys among my chums who seemed to stride effortlessly through various subjects, particularly maths and the sciences. I was always well behind in those areas. Most learning, to me, was a hard grind. Nothing came with a natural glow, except perhaps history and geography for which I did seem to have an instinctive interest. Nor were there rows of bookshelves at home from which my parents could draw or books to leave lying around for me to casually pick up. Neither my mother nor father were equipped to teach me to love books or to open doors of awareness. They tried in their loving and committed way to apply the moral and religious precepts of their own Jewish background, and my father especially would consistently point toward the Talmud. But their circumstances were dire; there was no money and my father was mostly out of work, which is why my earliest childhood was spent in the home of my maternal grandparents. We couldn't afford the rent for a home of our own after my father became one of the unemployment statistics of the early 1930s.

The truth is that I learned as much in the streets of Stockport as I did at home. Very quickly I realised it was a serious handicap to be a Jew in a small, Anglicised community where religion, whether Church of England or Catholic, was less important in itself but crucial to the bonding against an 'outsider' religion like Judaism. I learned, too, from my maternal grandfather, a great bearded Russian Jew, who bade me sit by him on a low stool at meal times in my grandmother's home (Grandmother Rebecca was the matriarch of the family, the genuine Yiddisha Momma who never seemed to stop cooking, washing up, managing the family and keeping a sharp eye on all her grandchildren's habits). That is where I spent my formative years. It was a wonderful ambience of warmth and emotional protection, a barrier against the outside world. My grandfather Davidovitch Bowman was the shining light in my life up till the age of 6 when he died and I fell into a mood of child-like despair, crying inconsolably when, for the first time, I realised what death really meant – that the people you loved suddenly disappeared from your life and were from then on beyond your reach for all time.

I suppose that apart from Leonard Cookson it was Grandfather Bowman who laid some kind of foundation to my life that I have never fully understood – except that it is there. He would recite Hebraic fables to me, stories of moral heroism that lifted the spirits of people; in his soothing murmur he would reflect on his childhood in Czarist Russia and occasionally use the cursed name of 'The Cossacks' as an example of undiluted evil – since they were, in his eyes, the instrument of Czarist anti-Jewish pogroms. He would reflect on life in his Shtetl, somewhere near Minsk. It all came, like wine pouring from a jug, while Grandma Rebecca was disbursing the pickled herring and chopped liver. I imbibed it all. Abraham and Isaac were served with the gefilte fish. I simply could not, did not, comprehend the meaning of death until one day they told me that Davidovitch had gone and never again would he put his hand on my head and tap it gently with his long index finger. Strange how such a forceful feeling remains so powerfully with one as the ageing process develops.

My grandparents' home – my home – was in fact a tailors' business. Two rooms on the ground floor of that large, three-storey corner house had been turned into a tailors' workroom, with a cloth store room tucked behind the tailoring room where my grandfather presided. His youngest son, Abraham 'Scotty' Bowman, handsome, gifted as a brilliant pianist who couldn't read music, was grandfather's apprentice. He eventually inherited the role of master tailor. The eldest son, my Uncle Joe – the only one of my mother's siblings born in Russia before they fled from the great pogroms of 1881 – worked the old Singer sewing machine and, to break the monotony, did the rounds as a part-time insurance salesman for the Pearl. My mother, needing to offer some token for the shelter we were receiving, was the chief buttonhole and seam feller assistant to Grandfather David, and a very good buttonhole she made, too. So the influence of cotton thread, the smell of tailors' heavy soap, the large tailors' iron running over damp cloth and that rich mustiness of rolled cloth have always stuck in my senses. I cannot enter a clothing store without a spasm of recall passing across my mind.

In that same house-cum-tailors' shop at the corner of a busy, albeit still unmade side road I would, even then, ponder on all this as I looked out from a bedroom window at the workhouse across the street. All through the year, every day, the tramps (vagrants, as they were less pejoratively called) would line up against the workhouse wall in the late afternoon and early evening. The queue became a straggling line in search of a night's sleep and food. They edged slowly through a small door at the top of Flint Street (as the side road was so aptly named) and then disappeared into the maw of a so-called reception hall where they were checked for lice and other possessions. During the day, starting in early morning before I went to school, women shrouded in black shawls draped over their heads wheeled prams or, more likely, orange boxes fixed to small cart-wheels, which housed anything from children to their worldly goods. They moved into the workhouse main building like silent shadows, rarely glancing one way or the other. Once inside they collected bread and the iron rations of subsistence from the Poor Law hand-out system. There was nothing else. That was the system, which gave a token, somewhat grudging, recognition to life.

The workhouse warden, one John Burgess – I think his name was John – would prowl on the steps of his establishment looking down on this scene of social desolation with the eye of a military commander surveying enemy captives. His lips would curl and twitch with contempt. Occasionally he would bark a command at the shawled women to order the queue to 'get a move on'. It was as if the mere sight of this pauperised pack evoked a physical and emotional upheaval in the warden. I never liked Burgess. I would often catch his eye when I happened to kick a ball in his direction having misdirected my aim. We developed a hearty dislike for each other – me the street urchin with a ball, him the evil monster wielding authority. Sometimes when my ball disappeared into the wen of the workhouse I would ask him to return it – a request he clearly regarded as beneath his station and dignity to respond to.

So I would complain to Grandmother Rebecca who smiled at me with her warming benevolence: 'Don't worry, *mein kind*, he'll give back your ball.'

Burgess and I could never be soul mates. I grew to loathe him and even to fear his lurking presence under the shadow of that appalling workhouse edifice, a red-brick mountain of charitable terror that came to represent, in my mind, a corner of life's horrors. Both Burgess and his charge were manifestations of something that was not right about the way of things. It occurred to me even then that there are at least two worlds: the world within which I was protected and from which I saw strong men being fitted out with smart suits and immaculate buttonholes and seams felled by my mother, and the other world, across the unmade street, where those haunting shadows of women and children begged for bread.

*   *   *

When my father, already a victim of a First World War wounding to his legs and feet, was laid low with severe injuries following a car accident in which the vehicle ran over his suffering legs, we were in some desperation as a family unit. My mother's attempts to find part-time work in the local markets were unrewarded and we were largely dependent on help from my grandparents and extended family aid. Good luck seemed to play no part in our lives. The town of Stockport, on the edge of south Manchester, was a town deep in depression, with one in three of the men out of work. There is no need to recite the minutiae of that depression since they are engraved on the history of Britain in the twentieth century. Yet it was a period so full of paradox. Spontaneous generosity came with every morning light; the community spirit of what was later to be experienced in wartime was the norm of life; front and back doors were left open without anyone pinching the ironing board or even the food; the Bobby on the Beat would stand at the corner, under the lamp post, chatting to the neighbourhood – though always ready to kick the arse of an unruly urchin. The local Co-op shop provided basic groceries 'on tick' until your father drew his dole money; it was a mad, uneven, unjust, grotesquely unequal world of warm humanity in a kind of shared poverty. And Stockport, circa 1929–31, was no worse, in some ways a lot better, than many other places in Britain.

Such was the ethos, if that term can be used in this context, in which I began to hear such names as the Labour Party, the Liberals, the Conservatives and all that; when phrases like 'general election' were mentioned and people were called on to vote; when schools were turned into polling stations and grown men – though rarely women – moved about the streets wearing huge rosettes the size of cabbages. The Labour Party in the north of England then had clumps of yellow ribbon hanging on their lapels; the Liberals carried red, and the Tories always kept to their same deep rich and heavy blue. I remember hearing the names of strange, far-away improbable figures with odd titles that seemed devoid of any meaning to one's life.

There was Lloyd-George, of course. Father was always talking about him with a great deal of relish: 'born in Manchester, you know' father would inform me with pride. He felt that being born in Manchester – as he had been – was a mark of some distinction. I heard L-G's voice on the old 'cat's whiskers' wireless (it was unlikely to be called a 'radio' at that time). His strong Welsh undertone came through the wires of a strange-looking wooden box that had large control knobs on the outside. I recall looking for Lloyd-George inside that box, which was easily opened at the top. Stanley Baldwin was the prime minister at that time. No one in our house liked him. 'Not for us', the family would proclaim. Ramsay MacDonald was the Labour chap. They all spoke kindly of MacDonald though, as far as I can remember, they didn't vote for him. The family called themselves 'Liberal'. 'What's a Liberal, Dad?' I enquired. Whatever he replied, I forget, but it didn't seem to make any sense to me.

There were others along the string of names that were constantly on the washing-line of conversation. Someone in America – that far-away country of which I knew nothing except that they made films and brought us Tom Mix and his cowboys, Rin Tin Tin, Charlie Chaplin and Al Jolson – Harding, Coolidge, Hoover and that fellow who flew the Atlantic, Colonel Lindbergh. Why, I used to ask myself, aren't they on the films with Charlie Chaplin? Can't be important if they're not with Charlie. No one answered my question.

And there was another name that used to emerge from the conversation of another member of our extended family – the family Communist who had strayed off to London but came to visit us sometimes: David Zerember. David was sometimes called another name because he had a huge black moustache and thick, black shiny hair. He was strong, swarthy and had huge hands. People said he resembled someone called Joe Stalin – so they nicknamed him 'Joe'. It became his family name. Funny name that, I thought, so I asked Grandma Rebecca who Stalin was. 'Where's Russia, Grandma, the country you came from?' For once she looked uncertain about her reply: 'Long way from here, *mein kind*, a long way ...' refusing to add anything to that. 'And who's David talking about, Grandma, who is this man Stalin?' She looked at me darkly. 'Don't ask. Go away and *spiel fussball* ...' Still, I'm glad I asked.

*   *   *

Our school in Stockport was completely without significance except, perhaps, for its name. Somehow it had acquired the title of 'The British School'. There seemed no evident reason for this other than the commonly known fact that it had been one of the early National Schools run by the church before the full development of state elementary education at the turn of the twentieth century. The school stood bleakly on its own on the main road south from the town centre. One side faced the huge, white-stone wedding-cake edifice of the Town Hall while the other wing of the school stood opposite a church to which it was once no doubt attached. The front of the school looked out upon the Stockport War Memorial building – yes, indeed, no mere obelisk or statuesque phallic-like monument, but a white marbled building designed like a temple in Greek style standing magnificently on the corner of this considerable cross-road junction. It matched the grandeur of the Town Hall. The two buildings were regarded as the focal points of the town's architectural achievements though, to my mind, the really outstanding construction was – and remains – the marvellous Victorian railway viaduct that loops over the Mersey, carrying the main line between London and Manchester. Its 22 arches, over 100 feet high, span the valley below, a true monument to the birth of the railways and the town when it was a notable centre of cotton spinning. It is still the finest viaduct in Europe.

At any rate the four cornerstones on that cross-roads by my school were the fixed firmaments of our little world – the Town Hall, imperious, remote; the War Memorial, towering with majesty; the school; and then, of all places the Infirmary. This blackened stone eyesore, the Stockport Infirmary, was a relic of the Poor Law from which its very name, Infirmary, still carried a particular connotation. The great hospital, sprawling alongside the main road opposite the Town Hall, seemed still to be under the spell of Florence Nightingale and the Crimean War. It was regarded with awe and fear because nobody we knew had ever emerged alive from its gaunt interior. Whenever we heard of some poor soul being admitted to 'the Infirmary' it came as the sound of impending doom.

So when my father was admitted into its maw to have (or so they told me) an operation to his nose, I was convinced that he was about to die from some incurable disease and that the story of a nose operation was merely a device dreamed up to fool me. When eventually he emerged alive from the hospital, apparently repaired, I found it hard to believe that this could be so. Indeed, I remained quite unconvinced that the Infirmary was anything more than a morgue. At any rate there seemed something symbolic about the cornerstones, hovering around the school: War and Peace, Life and Death. All the frontiers of relevance appeared to cluster round that junction.

Beyond these frontiers lay some pleasures like the football ground and the local cricket club. Stockport County FC was lovable, hopeless, a music hall joke at that time forever bound within what was then the Third Division, North. I listened to tales of the club's long-past greatness and glory at the bottom of the old Second Division into which they had once been promoted in the early 1920s. Even so, standing behind the goal at Edgeley Park was a joyous way of spending three old pennies. But the great attraction, to me, was the glory of going to Maine Road, Manchester to watch City – since nobody, then, gave two thoughts to the lowly neighbouring club of Manchester United. It was City with Matt Busby playing right half, Freddie Tilson at centre forward, Frank Swift in goal: that was real grown-ups' football.

And to Old Trafford to watch the greats of Lancashire cricket. One of Leonard Cookson's other attributes was a love of cricket, and it was his initiative that periodically took a group of us from school to watch county matches at Old Trafford. He organised the day out as part of our wider education (though it was clear that Tommy Humbles never approved) and provided the tea and sandwiches from his own pocket. One thing led to another; 'Cookie' coached the school cricket team and found time to have me coached as a fast bowler. He then arranged for me to have a trial at old Trafford where I was eventually offered a job on the ground staff. I fancied that – especially the idea of cleaning the boots of men like Eddie Paynter and George Duckworth. But it was not to be. My parents rebelled at the thought of my becoming a professional cricketer. What I needed, they declared, was a good steady and secure job – maybe in the Town Hall. I listened to this with silent horror; yet I never did sign on with the Lancashire County Cricket Club.

*   *   *

In one respect, I believe, I was probably more fortunate than most of my classmates at school. Being Jewish meant that I had to go to Jewish classes – Chaida school – in the evening, each weekday except Friday. The classes were held in a building at the rear of the Stockport Synagogue – which later became a bingo hall and then a builder's office. The journey from my grandparents' home to the Chaida involved a precarious walk through one of the toughest areas of the town, where gangs of marauding lads would lie in waiting to pounce on the Jew-boys who dared to cross their, mostly Catholic, territory. Our journey each night skirted a piece of waste land on the crest of a hill where the ground – which was really a tip for rubbish – rose and fell in mounds of scrap iron, tin cans, dog-shit and mud-ponds. Today no one would hesitate to describe, and condemn, it as an environmental hazard. But the hilltop was a natural battlefield, and it was there, around this miniature juvenile Somme, that the Jew-boys fought and frequently lost to the marauding anti-semitic fists. It was my first violent encounter with anti-semitism.

The skirmishing usually occurred on our way home – around 7.30 pm – in streets barely lit by gas-mantle lamps and hardly traversed by any sane citizen or, come to that, local Bobby. Sometimes there was fist-to-fist individual fighting or it could be stone-throwing, with a barrage opened up from 'the enemy' camp concealed in the bunkers behind the rubbish tips. It was not unusual for one of our lot to get a stone in the head and torn clothes in the scrapping. Then the choice would be either to stand and fight against the odds or run away, depending on our numbers. It was never easy to cope with this violence. We were scared as well as tired and drained after a day at school and an evening studying Hebrew history and language. It was a kind of early commando course in life's problems.

These raiding tactics became such a problem that a group of us decided to take up boxing training on Sunday afternoons following a morning at Chaida classes. The Berger family was a kind of sporting institution in the local Jewish community. There were six sons of Mr and Mrs Sol Berger, who ran a dry cleaning shop up the road. All six were expert in one or more sporting activity. Two of the Berger boys, Joe and Hymie, were very good part-professional boxers and my own closest pal, Colin, was the youngest of the six Berger brothers. Colin was a young toughie who became a brave wartime bomber pilot. At that time his chief distinguishing mark was a habit of wiping an ever-present drop of snot from his nose with a quick flick of his shirt cuff. It always fascinated me. Yet, try as I did, I could never emulate his speed and style. Nor was I as good a boxer as Colin. But the Berger family were my route into self-defence.

Joe and Hymie organised a group of the Chaida boys into a regular Sunday afternoon training course in boxing. They took us to a local boxing hall where they were involved in regular professional bouts, and we used the ring and the equipment there to learn how to become young Jack Dempseys. It certainly helped. In those days young street thugs did not carry knives or other lethal weapons. There were no drugs to excite malevolent passions. Apart from stone-throwing the battles of the day were conducted more or less according to Lonsdale rules, with fists at close quarters. Gradually we began to give 'the enemy' a bloody nose and force them to recognise us as a force to be reckoned with. In fact, we developed our boxing skills to a fairly sophisticated standard.

No doubt this was true of other Jewish communities, too, and helps to explain why so many promising young boxers in the 1920s and 1930s were Jews from poor backgrounds. Some of them, notably in London's East End, became world famous, of course – boxers such as Jack 'Kid' Berg who went on to gain a world championship. Wherever there was a Jewish community, in Leeds, Glasgow, Manchester, Birmingham, it was possible to find boxing skills of considerable promise. Of course, it was not only a useful skill to have against the anti-semitic bully boys of those days but, still more, an escape route from poverty for the more talented and tougher of the Jewish boys who had no wish, assuming they possessed the ability, to become doctors or lawyers. There are modern parallels, in Britain and in the United States, among the more talented young athletes from the black communities.

*   *   *

If I now return to the Stockport War Memorial it is not because of any wish to dwell on its architecture or its military history: the fact is that it provided me with my first experience of schoolboy courting and sex. I had taken a strong fancy to one of my female class-mates. All our classes were mixed, girls on one side of a dividing gangway splitting the classroom in half. My mind would frequently wander in a kind of silent reverie, moving easily across the gangway divide to focus on a slender slip of a girl with a gap at the upper middle front of her teeth. I found her irresistible and hypnotic, especially when I caught sight of her navy blue knickers at the top of those spindly legs of alabaster whiteness. This combination of a tooth gap and navy blue knickers, her smilingly pale open face, those wide innocent eyes – well, it was very difficult to concentrate on whatever was being offered in front of the blackboard.

I guess I was only about 10 or 11 and knew little about girls except that they were different. Her name was Maureen Tongue and she lived near the County football ground, which, I rapidly calculated, was really beyond my normal journey home from school. So if I were to divert her from her homeward routine I somehow had to devise a distraction. My solution was – the War Memorial.

I invited Miss Tongue to accompany me for a tour of the War Memorial on the grounds that it was a place we ought to honour. I had already reconnoitred the territory and knew that there were hardly any people inside the temple of remembrance at the time school finished for the afternoon. Moreover the interior of the building was always veiled in a kind of twilight, which added to the melancholic lustre of the memorial flame that glowed perpetually from a sunken seating in the centre of the main hall beneath the lofted dome. The side alcoves were usually smothered in poppies, throughout the year, great branches of them propped against the sides of the darkened inlets. Each alcove carried a list of the town's dead in the Great War, engraved on the slabs of marble wall.

I knew this would be an ideal setting for a kiss and cuddle with Miss Tongue – and so it proved. Having overcome her doubts about a visit to the noble tomb she readily agreed to what followed; maybe she had nurtured similar thoughts, though I was never sure about that. At any rate the young Maureen and the hopelessly novice Geoffrey hugged our immature bodies into a wrestle of infant passion amid the poppies and the names of our town's war heroes. Somehow it all seemed appropriate: life and at least the spirit of procreation triumphant was our way of saluting the memory of the dead.

Maureen and I were to develop this mildly illicit relationship to the point of some facile genital exploration as we groped our excited fingers over new territory. It was, of course, all quite inanely innocent stuff, never penetrating beyond the finger tip. And always surrounded by an immense sense of fear, shame and amateurishness amid the excited adventurism. Sure, it was sexual exploration at its most primitive, natural, though unfulfilling – yet highly enjoyable at the time. I often wonder what happened to Mo Tongue and whether she reflects on her earliest (as I am sure it was) sexual encounters amid the memorabilia of 'the war to end wars'.

*   *   *

My paternal grandparents, the Goodmans, lived in Manchester where father was born and went to school. The journey to their house in Elizabeth Street, Cheetham – then the Jewish 'ghetto' of North Manchester – was always an adventure because although it was only about seven miles the tram ride took two hours with two changes of trams. Wonderful clattering tram rides, which took me to strange foreign parts that seemed like another world – Levenshulme, Belle Vue, Ardwick, and the great square of Manchester's Piccadilly. Changing trams at Cross Street on a pedestrian island opposite the old *Manchester Guardian*. My mother regarded the whole operation as a major enterprise, not least because she had to remember to save enough money for the tram fares. A return trip for the two of us – my father rarely came with us – was about one shilling and fourpence (16 old pennies) and that was a tidy sum. To spend 1s 4d out of my father's unemployment pay of 22s 9d a week was a huge slice. It was equivalent then to two quarter-pound packets of Lyons Green Label tea – which was why my mother used to call our trips to Elizabeth Street, Manchester 'a half-pound of tea' journey. Which meant that the adventure journey by tram was not a frequent occurrence. Indeed, mother would always carry a look of expectancy when she arrived at my other grandparents' home – hoping, and indeed expecting, some kind of compensation from my grandparents to cover the cost of the journey. More likely that would come from my father's older sister, Fanny, who was blessed not only with a wonderful spirit of generosity but was one of the few members of the family with a regular job – she worked in the relatively prosperous raincoat trade of Manchester.

Fanny's job was of great importance to everyone in the family. She was the eldest of the family of three brothers, two sisters. Father, the eldest brother, was always close to her and she had 'adopted' me as her surrogate child (she never married) and was constantly buying me clothes that my parents could never afford. That Cheetham Hill 'ghetto' was a warm, closed, protective stockade that equated with my Stockport base but was very different in ambience. Grandfather Moses (Mark as he was Anglicised and usually called) was also a tailor. But he did not run his own back-room shop like Grandfather Davidovitch. Moses Goodman was not a man of enterprise. He was kindly, slow moving, meticulous in his personal relationships and business dealings and a devout Jew who, with Grandmother Katie, kept a strictly kosher household.

Michael, my father, resembled Moses in many ways. He was never a forceful character though always an honest seeker. His younger brothers, Leslie and Jack, were keener, sharper and altogether more enterprising. Father tramped his way through the First World War as an infantryman with the Royal Sussex Regiment – though he was never sure how he had ended up with the Royal Sussex lot since he had enlisted in Manchester to join the Lancashire Fuseliers. He didn't complain. Just put on his khaki and off he went to the trenches. He finished the war shortly before the 1918 armistice (he joined in 1914) with severe trench feet, blistered legs, shrapnel wounds etc. and was invalided home to a hospital in Edinburgh where he decided to marry my mother, Edythe Bowman.

Before the war father had started work as a clerk with the Manchester Ship Canal Company. But when he was finally discharged from hospital and demobbed there were no jobs for the likes of him with the Ship Canal Company. He began his postwar life looking for work – like thousands of others disembarking into that land 'fit for heroes'. In many ways he was luckier than most because a cousin of his was manager of a cotton mill in Oldham, and the plant was looking for men to work in its cardboard box factory. Cardboard box making was a big deal at the time because they were needed for cotton reels. On the fruits of that job in Oldham – which meant quite a bit of difficult travel – father married and eventually found a house on a new council estate in Chorlton, south Manchester, which was just being developed as a major local authority community.

I have not the slightest recall about living in that house – I was a baby when we moved in and four when we left. But I do know, because my mother never ceased to remind me, that we were a short walk from Maine Road football ground, which was then being built to house the team that later was to become my idol. One of my modest boasts still is to be able to recite the Manchester City teams of 1933 and 1934, the first one beaten by Dixie Dean's Everton in the 1933 Cup Final, the second, which beat Portsmouth 2–1 in the succeeding 1934 Final – that epic final after which a young (I think he was 19) goalkeeper, Frank Swift, fainted in the City goalmouth as the referee blew the final whistle. All rather symbolic of an age in which depression had settled everywhere – outside the football grounds.

* * *

Father, very much the Mancunian Jew, was schooled in an elementary Victorian building in Derby Street, Cheetham, whose fame developed from the very constituency into which it had been pitched. It was the local 'Jews' school' because it was the nearest to the Cheetham Hill concentration of Jewish families. Which meant that the young Michael Goodman happened to be in the same classrooms as members of the Marks family (of Marks & Spencer); of the Laskis (Harold, Nathan, Neville etc.); of the parents of the Lever family, and of countless other groups of Manchester Jewry whose first steps to fame and wealth were taken in that Derby Street school.

Alas, the young Michael Goodman was not in that category. He was intelligent enough but lacked the drive and self-confidence of his more celebrated class-mates. His close friends included members of the Marks family and in later years when, staggering from unemployment queue to short-term jobs and back into the queue, he might have benefited by their help he was always too proud, or perhaps fearful, to approach them. He did once try to overcome this inner resistance. One day in the 1930s when we had moved to London father, in some desperation, actually plucked up the courage to walk into the M&S headquarters in Baker Street to ask if he could see and talk with his old chum, Ephraim Marks. His account, to me, was that he couldn't get beyond an unsympathetic commissionaire. He never tried again.

His sisters, Fanny and Raechel, often urged him to get in touch with his old school chums, especially the Marks family. He would wince and nod in embarrassed silence. I knew he would never take up their advice; nor, to the best of my knowledge, did he ever tell them of his Baker Street experience. Fanny and Raechel were remarkable women and as different as Sappho and Clio. Rae, clearly, was Sappho – a strenuous mix of nymphomaniac along with a deep devotion to her father Moses and her home. She devoted the latter part of her life to looking after her father who was dying of Parkinson's disease. Her sexual appetite which, as I subsequently discovered, was pretty inexhaustible, brought her immense suffering and personal tragedy. She was exceptionally attractive and, as I recall even from my childhood, endowed with a remarkably youthful and graceful figure. But it was her downfall. She had three children from different fathers – though, paradoxically, none from her legal husband. All three children – boys – died before they reached puberty, all stricken with rickets. The one I knew best, a handsome boy named Leslie, was confined to a steel frame and bed-ridden for as long as I can remember. Raechel's magical attractions turned to a bitter frustration within a climate of living defeat. She withered and perished in the end like a collapsing rose, petal by petal, shrivelling into the ground.

Fanny, the Clio of the two, remained unmarried and possibly celibate to her dying day. She, who did so much to ease my way as a child and whose care and attention bridged so many of the practical needs of my early life, had all the honour and reputation of her Greek parable with an even greater depth of unhappiness.

Jack, the youngest of the family, fled to Ireland in 1914 to escape the draft, married a non-Jewish nurse and remained an outcast of the family until after the death of his parents. On the rare occasions I met him, as a child, I always held him in great esteem not least because he seemed altogether more interesting and exciting than the others – and, most important of all, because he bought me my first, most memorable, toy motor car.

Leslie was the middle brother, who went to war shortly after my father enlisted and joined the Royal Corps of Signals because he was fascinated by the invention of radio and drawn to the name of Marconi. In 1917, somewhere near the lines at Ypres, he was fixing a communication link when a shell dropped and took off his left leg. His life remained on a thread for quite a long time. Somehow he survived and recovered in a French and then a Manchester hospital, where he was fitted out with an artificial limb. Leslie was then found a job as a civil servant under a scheme that provided wounded war veterans with priority work. He began work in the old Ministry of Labour and Pensions Office opposite Strangeways Prison in Manchester and later moved up the ladder to a senior post in Bury. He ended up having the best-paid and most secure job of any member of the Goodman family – thanks to having only one leg.

In fact, Leslie was the most jovial, convivial and gregarious of the Goodman pack. He was forever joking about his 'dolly' leg – his description of the contraption that he daily strapped to the remaining stump of his thigh. He and his wife Jean had no children so, again, I tended to be regarded as a surrogate son. In fact I was regarded as the only surviving son of the Goodman clan for though Jack and his wife, Dolly, had two sons they were never wholly accepted under the canopy of the family because they didn't have a Jewish mother. It was a matter of immense distaste to me that they were so regarded but there was no way of changing that perception.

When the cotton slump hit Lancashire in the 1920s father's job in cardboard box making ceased to exist. With thousands of others he was chucked out and back on the dole. We couldn't afford the rent of the council house in Chorlton so the three of us then moved in with my Stockport grandparents. Father trod the streets looking for work throughout the Manchester area and beyond; but it was hopeless. He managed an occasional part-time job as a door-to-door salesman trying to sell 'Kleeneze' brushes to middle-class housewives whose husbands were in work. It was backbreaking and generally futile. A 'good week' would bring him about thirty shillings – just a few bob above the unemployment benefit of the time – but he had to pay his travel expenses out of that. The time was shortly after the General Strike of 1926 and a few years before the Ramsay MacDonald Government of 1929; unemployment was rising steadily and the world tottered on the brink of a depression that was already evident. Most families we knew either scraped a bare living or were on some form of relief.

Of course I had no conception of the gravity of all this any more than I could recognise that my instincts, attitudes, future prejudices and political mores were all being shaped and moulded and set. It was all being planted in the soil of the age, the unconscious sowing of seeds in a developing mind; all of them ingredients that both liberate, and imprison, us for all time.

3 The 1930s: The Devil's Decade

It is not possible to improve on Auden's description of the 1930s as 'a low dishonest decade'. But there is another quotation that attracts: Hugh MacDiarmid's wonderfully sharp observation in his critique of fellow poets and writers with the lines:

> Auden, MacNeice, Day Lewis, I have read them all
> Hoping against hope to hear the authentic call
> And now the explanation I must pass on this:
> You cannot light a match on a crumbling wall.
> (Cunningham, 1988)

I am not sure I agree: matches were struck on that crumbling wall. Some ignited and even fired a message into the fetid air. But MacDiarmid's revolution did not erupt. That's what disappointed, certainly surprised, him and countless others. By any standard of political analysis it should have happened, even *ought* to have happened. It didn't; instead we had the war, by which time Auden had gone off to America and things would never be the same again.

More than matches were struck as the walls crumbled and collapsed. The prewar world came to an end with a bang rather than a whimper.

What still surprises me is the amount of detail I can still recall from that period when my impressions of life were really being formed and the inescapable die was cast. Much of the contour of that devil's decade remains clear.

One of my earliest political memories is of the events in 1929 when I was 8. The general election of that year was held on 30 May and I had been staying with my paternal grandparents at their Elizabeth Street house in Manchester – one of those many shuttle-journeys to which I have already referred. But on that occasion the normal routine of my mother taking me back on the tram ride to Stockport was broken. My father collected me and said he had a little surprise in store. He was taking me to the 'illuminations in Piccadilly'. I pressed him to explain: 'Illuminations, Dad,' I enquired, 'like Blackpool?' No, he replied, these would be different. 'These are special lights for Manchester,' he explained mysteriously. And so they were. The 'illuminations' turned out to be the inaugural display of

Manchester's new indicator panel flashing clipped newsy messages along the top rim of a large grey building standing on the south side of Piccadilly Square. New York's Times' Square had come to Manchester. And the big switch-on had been timed to coincide with election night results of 30 May 1929.

My father lifted me onto his shoulders so that I could see 'the lights' as they flashed their dotted political message. Around me, as I still recall, was a sea of heads, mostly men in caps; a few women but not many. As the results flickered across the strip of dotted electronics the crowd would cheer, or groan, with even the occasional muffled boo, a bit like the football crowds of those days.

Labour were winning seats in Lancashire. I thought my father looked rather pleased as he cocked his head upwards toward me enquiring: 'Are you alright?' It was a remarkable good-natured, friendly crowd around us, sober as far as I can remember and extremely orderly. There was no menace, hardly a Bobby in sight – although, no doubt they were hovering somewhere in the shadows. No one was provoking trouble, and I certainly heard no stories of arrests, though there must have been several thousand people in the Square that night.

It was very late when we returned to Elizabeth Street on a late-night tram. I can still recall the sense of rejoicing about the election results which, although incomplete, showed that a Labour government appeared to be on the way to victory and Stanley Baldwin's Tories were going down to defeat. Of course that is what transpired in the shape of a second Labour government under Ramsay MacDonald, which, although still a minority government, had emerged as the largest single party in Parliament for the first time in history. Baldwin's 'Safety First' election campaign – as it was labelled – misfired and Labour's attack on the unemployment crisis had scored a remarkable victory, especially in the north and even more significantly in Lancashire, then far from a Labour stronghold, because of the collapse of the cotton industry – the collapse which had put my father on the dole. Labour doubled the number of seats it held in Lancashire in 1929 compared with the 1924 election.

Of course, I was wholly unaware of any of this political stuff as I sat on my father's shoulders that warm evening in May 1929 marvelling at the 'illuminations': those stuttering, jerky symbols, those sparkling dots fluttering into the night sky with their message of new political hope. That was my introduction to politics, aged 8. That experience has always remained with me as a kind of reference point coupled with names like Ramsay MacDonald, Philip Snowden, who was Chancellor in that 1929 government, Jimmy Thomas, the former railwaymen's leader who later became disgraced for leaking Budget secrets from which he made a fortune, and of course Oswald Mosley, Chancellor of the Duchy of Lancaster and the author of that remarkable report that urged the MacDonald Government to adopt a socialist economic strategy to help cure mass unemployment. MacDonald rejected that, and Mosley broke with Labour to form his New Party, which eventually became the British Union of Fascists. It was an extraordinary period of political tumult: the Wall Street crash, the collapse of MacDonald's Government in 1931, the virtual break-up of the Labour Party after the 1931 election and the steady road to the Second World War. And there was I, a kid on my dad's shoulders, when all that was starting to roll.

*   *   *

Unemployment stalked our household throughout the whole of that period. My father found his quest for work, any job that was going, quite hopeless and soul-destroying. Everything around us seemed to be collapsing. His job in the cotton trade disappeared as the industry itself shrank. Indian and Far Eastern cotton imports completely undermined the Lancashire trade. Even by the early 1920s cotton exports had fallen to half their 1913 level and by the early 1930s had sunk into deep crisis. It was similar with coal. Coal exports dropped every year between the end of the First World War and 1930. So the impact of collapsing cotton, a shrinking coal industry, fewer and fewer orders for the shipyards and steel plants – this combined depression cut across the entire north of England, and even into the Midlands and southern England. But it was the north that had to bear the brunt of this collapse – especially the zone stretching from the Mersey to the Tyne as well is in Scotland and south Wales.

Those who had the energy and the will began to migrate south, heading toward London where the streets, they said, were 'paved with gold'. Alas, it wasn't gold so much as dust. Still, when it became difficult to find the rent, and pay for the food or buy meagre clothing the temptation to 'get out' of northern England became over-whelming to thousands of the unemployed. My father reasoned that London dust might be more hopeful than scratching around the sooted desolation of a jobless north-west. So he came south to look for work, and we moved into a couple of rooms in Camden Town – not least because it was close to Euston station where we had arrived.

Euston station in the early 1930s to me seemed like the centre of the universe. The time was 1935 – so I suppose it *was* the centre of the universe. Everything I clapped eyes on appeared like a New World. The people were better dressed than the ones I had grown up with. Maybe they didn't think they were all that well groomed but it was better than anything I had seen before. The red buses looked posh. Shops with windows full of goodies, albeit at prices we certainly couldn't afford. Even the hoardings with the Bisto kids sniffing the soup appeared to be bigger, brighter, sharper than 'oop North'. So are illusions etched on a young and simple mind.

But father found it no easier to get work in London than in Manchester. His skills were limited: a semi-skilled operative from a redundant cotton mill in Oldham with experience in making cardboard boxes for cotton reels was hardly regarded – in London as elsewhere – as a golden offering in a stricken labour market. Eventually he found a job as a casual door-to-door salesman working again for the Kleeneze brushes much as he had tried to do in the north-west. In a good week the exhausting job of lugging a case full of brushes around the suburban estates of London where a few housewives might be expected to offer sympathy, and buy one, brought in 30 shillings (£1.50). That was marginally better than the dole – by about seven shillings – which was quite a consideration since the rent of the two rooms in Camden Town was 12s 6d a week, inclusive of bugs and the piss-bucket on the landing.

I mention the bugs because in the summer especially they became a source of entertainment and even merriment. The two rooms in a house in what was then called Hamilton Street (long ago renamed) were on the first floor of a three-storey terraced house with a basement. There was no bathroom in the house and only one toilet, situated on the ground floor behind the stairs. We had a slop-bucket on the first-floor landing, rather like a gaol slop-bucket. For washing my mother devised a system where we used a large enamel basin in the 'living room' seated on a marble slab. Luxury it wasn't. Nor, come to think of it now, was it particularly in tune with most living conditions even for families of the poor in the mid-1930s. Most people unless in dire poverty had something a touch better than that. Still that was our introduction to London life.

That's why the bugs were so entertaining. It took one's mind off the slop-bucket. The bugs would emerge – I don't think there is another word to describe their antics, they simply 'emerged' – out of the wallpaper in warm weather to saunter along the pattern on the paper rather like friendly pets going for a walk. They generally came in threes: heaven knows why, perhaps a couple and their minder. We never found out. The game was to see how far they would move along a line of the patterned wallpaper before making a sharp right-hand turn – again it always seemed a right-hand turn – before retreating into a shadowed niche on the wall. My mother and I would make moneyless bets on the winner – before killing one of them, or more if we felt particularly venomous. The killing process was a telling feature because when you hit the victim there would be an audible cracking sound.

Counting them in and counting them out came back to mind some years later as we logged up the numbers of Luftwaffe aircraft shot down by Spitfires and Hurricanes in the Battle of Britain. And I could never rid my mind of the euphemism of 'the bug' when, in my RAF days later, a German 'plane cracked up. Funny parallels that life offers us.

*   *   *

My mother's sister and her family lived in Delancey Street, a short walk from our two-roomed mansion in Hamilton Street. I grew to know the linking street, Park Street, extremely well and, in particular, Tommy Meredith's dairy shop halfway up Park Street. Tommy and I became firm pals. His small shop had a reputation for good-quality food at low prices so both my mother and her sister favoured Tommy Meredith's dairy. And it was Tommy who started me talking about politics in an odd sort of way. He seemed exceptionally well informed – well, to me as an ignoramus, anybody who could spell the name 'Baldwin' would become an immediate genius – and Tommy would start off discussing the latest gossip about the Prince of Wales, soon to be king, Tommy assured me, who – claimed Tommy in these precise words – was 'busy fucking some American woman named Wallis Simpson'. The man in the dairy complained bitterly about the newspapers refusing to print any of this – 'even though most of us know what's going on'. Well I didn't, for one.

In my frequent trips to Tommy's shop to buy stuff for my mother, or even my Aunt Jeannie, he would discuss the current scene as he folded the bacon or put the eggs in a neat box. Baldwin had just become prime minister again after Ramsay MacDonald finally resigned, having slumped into a sad, lonely wreck. Tommy kept me educated about what was going on just in case I hadn't heard from other sources. 'Baldwin?' he asked, before answering his own question: 'Terrible lot, those Baldwin Tories'. He would then look at me for response. I just nodded. 'Me,' he continued, 'I'd give that bloke Mosley a chance. Seems alright to me,' Tommy claimed without passion. 'He'd be better for the likes of you and me.'

Mosley? But, hang on, Tommy, I queried, that's the fascist chap. 'Yeah, suppose he is: but he talks a lot of bloody sense ...' Tommy insisted. Gradually, as the penny began to drop we stopped going to Meredith's dairy. Pity because his stuff was good, cheaper and I liked old Tommy. And I am sure he wasn't alone in his fascist sympathies at the time. He was not untypical of the people from the lower middle class and the working class who were drawn to fascism all over Europe, and indeed especially in Germany and Italy. I often wonder what happened to Tommy and whether he ever realised that I was a Jew-boy.

At that time I spent a good deal of time at my aunt's home in Delancey Street not least because it was a pleasanter place to be. She kept a boarding house in which she housed all kinds of odd characters – I think they covered the rent – from all parts of the country but especially from Tyneside and Yorkshire. Mary Dodd from Tyneside was probably a prostitute but that didn't seem to matter; Mary was a wonderfully warm character full of fun and not without a seriously shrewd intelligence. She could clearly afford the rent of a room she had on the ground floor. I vividly remember Mary because I hardly ever saw her out of a dressing gown, which she wore rather loosely.

Then there was David Zerember whom I mentioned earlier – my mother's cousin who looked like Stalin. He was frequently at the Delancey Street house and often stayed there for days, probably weeks for all I knew. I have a feeling that Mary Dodd was one of the incentives. At any rate David, who supposedly lived with his supposed wife somewhere near Fitzroy Square, was usually at Delancey Street when I was there. What an astonishing character he was. His mother – my grandmother's sister – had come to England from Russia with my maternal grandparents. I was told that David had been born in Russia and was brought here as a tiny baby on that timber boat into Hull. I was never clear about that, though it may well have been true. At any rate his mother was a deeply religious Jew who took on the role of a female Rabbi when such things were simply not on the Talmudic agenda. She didn't worry about things like that since she was as much a revolutionary religious fanatic as her son David was to become a revolutionary and fanatical founder member of the British Communist Party. When I encountered David at my aunt's Delancey Street establishment he was already a veteran Communist whose God was Joe Stalin and whose physical appearance, quite plainly, he had determined to mirror. He succeeded.

On the occasions I stayed at Delancey Street I slept on a rough old camp bed in the basement. Along the opposite wall was David, snoring away on another camp bed. But before he started to snore he would regularly regale me with the wisdom of Marx, of Engels and Lenin; the corrupting character of the capitalist system and the nature of what socialism promised for the future. Into this web of dialectic he would weave Stalin – of whom he kept a photograph permanently in his pocket, albeit unsigned, and would take it out at the slightest pretext. David was to die years later in Brighton where, at I think the age of 90 something, he had become a local landmark of unusual eccentricity even for that resort as he shuffled along the promenade to the name, of course, of 'Joe'.

It has to be remembered that when I listened to David's camp bed ramblings the year was 1936. All Europe was in the throes of crisis and the rise of fascism. Mussolini was well established in Italy, and Hitler after three years in power held a firm and ruthless grip on Germany. The Spanish Civil War was about to break out; Austria would soon be annexed by Hitler in the Anschluss and Sir Oswald Mosley's blackshirts were stamping around London and other major cities of Britain with their uniforms and military characteristics styled on Mosley's principal mentor, Benito Mussolini, Il Duce. That is what had attracted Tommy Meredith; but, certainly, not only Tommy in his dairy – for although Mosley never succeeded in recruiting mass support he certainly won over a significant section of the British upper classes and a much smaller element among the middle and working classes.

There was a great deal more support for Mosley's fascists from the Establishment than has ever been admitted. National figures of great prominence helped to finance the fascist movement at that time – including the car magnate Lord Nuffield (William Morris). The Duke and Duchess of Windsor were among Mosley's 'secret' links. Lord Rothermere's *Daily Mail* was the only national newspaper to give brief public support to Mosley's fascists but there were other newspapers, regional as well as national, who regarded the fascist threat as a mere irritant and possibly even a useful tool with which to combat the left in general and not just the communists.

Viscount Rothermere himself had a signed feature article in the *Daily Mail* (15 January 1934) headlined, 'Hurrah for the Blackshirts', justified with this introduction:

> Because fascism comes from Italy shortsighted people in this country think they show a sturdy national spirit by deriding it. If their ancestors had been equally stupid, Britain would have had no banking system, no Roman law, nor even any football, since all these are Italian inventions.

Such was the climate in those mid-1930s, that extraordinary 'devil's decade'. But there were other elements, more heartening to the human spirit. Books, poetry, drama, music, even political dialogue to dramatise the epoch. There was a feeling, a mood in the land that became infectious and bold; there was a courage and an intrepid spirit abroad amid the sloth, the dross and collapsing pillars. It was, I still believe, impossible to be young at that moment and not feel at least something of these impulses. Not to feel bruised or inspired or both; intoxicated at times with the explosion of quite shattering events that were both heroic and desperate. The pulse of life actually seemed to quicken. As a youngster I had no doubt that I was being infected by the times I lived through; but so, too, were older people. It was difficult for anyone living through those times not to become politically aware, however mildly. It would have required an oddly wilful detachment to have achieved absolute neutrality. It was indeed the decade that both deformed as well as determined the shape of the rest of the century.

* * *

Reflecting back on that period, the really surprising aspect is why the British working classes, impoverished, workless, often hopeless, remained so comparatively passive when most of Europe was in turmoil. A great political and social storm was raging across the entire European continent. Hardly a country remained untouched by the rise of fascism, the sound of marching jackboots and shriek of bombs falling on Republican Spain. We had the unemployed marches and great protest rallies, while thunderous rhetoric from great radical voices echoed across the land. Yet on the whole it was a relatively peaceful scene in the streets except for the opposition to Mosley's fascist rallies.

It has often been suggested by more recent observers that Britain and the British seemed to go to sleep at that time. That wasn't quite true. Part of the explanation for what seems like indolence, apathy or complacency lies in the fact that the poor and indeed the working classes in general were isolated. It is hard now to imagine the degree of isolation that existed in those days. Communication was still at a primitive stage. There was no television; the telephone rarely existed in a working-class home; radio was still in its infancy and the press was firmly in the hands of the Establishment. Even the Labour-supporting and TUC-controlled *Daily Herald* – despite a then record-breaking circulation of two million plus, the first national daily paper to break the two million barrier – was more concerned with building up a big circulation among people *at work* rather than summoning a revolution. To be sure, all these impediments existed throughout Europe as well. But the difference there was that the revolution was being led by the right and with the support of a controlling elite. It was a very different scene in Britain, certainly in England.

The Communist Party was strong in the trade unions but weak and largely ineffective as an electoral force with the general public. There was only one Communist MP in the Commons, Willie Gallacher from Fife. The party paper, the *Daily Worker*, had a very low circulation of about 20,000 and depended heavily on street corner and factory sales by devoted party members. The general newspaper distributors weren't interested. Yet in spite of this narrow base as an electoral force the Communist Party had a wholly dispro-portionate influence, even power, in the trade unions and fringe groups around the Labour movement. They inspired and led such groups as the National Unemployed Workers' Movement, which sought to harness, galvanise and politicise the unemployed. The NUWM was disowned by the mainstream of the Labour Party, and even the unions treated it with a distant gaze because the unions had always resisted organising the unemployed in any official and formal capacity. In fact much of the radical space to the left of official Labour was vacated – leaving it fertile ground for the Communist Party to campaign against fascism, especially to fight Mosley in the streets, for intervention against General Franco in the Spanish Civil War and the organising of a British contingent for the International

Brigade – indeed anything that required spontaneous, or organised, radical response.

The Communist Party also set about organising a 'United Front' of the left to match Leon Blum's Popular Front in France. It had some success, especially when the Socialist League was formed at the initiative of Sir Stafford Cripps in 1937. Cripps persuaded the Communist Party and leaders of the Independent Labour Party, James Maxton and Fenner Brockway, to join together – quite a remarkable feat in itself considering their fierce rivalries. They all signed up to a 'Unity Manifesto' – including some of the most prominent figures in the Labour Party, Aneurin Bevan, George Strauss, Harold Laski and John Strachey as well as Cripps himself. They all joined hands with the Communist Party and ILP leaders in the fight against fascism.

But it was always an uneasy alliance, and when the Labour Party officialdom demanded the disbandment of the Socialist League and threatened expulsion if the Labour Party names refused, it began to wither. In fact some expulsions did take place – Aneurin Bevan, Cripps and Charles Trevelyan were expelled for refusing to toe the official line. It was a sad, often bitter sequel to what promised to become an inspirational joint campaign.

That was about the time I joined the Young Communists after becoming disgusted at the weakness of Labour's attitude and the pusillanimity of Labour's leadership. It was late in the day, of course, though I was still too young to go to Spain, which I wanted to do. Instead those of us who felt that way and were still too young to join the International Brigade were left with another potent, if slightly less dangerous, option – to fight Mosley's fascist troops in the streets of London.

*   *   *

The pinnacle of the street violence, I suppose, was Mosley's march into the East End on 4 October 1936, the notorious Battle of Cable Street, when the British Union of Fascists clashed in the streets of East London against a combined force of Jewish organisations, Communists and many Labour Party activists. It was by far the most dramatic of the 2,108 BUF meetings held in East London between August 1936 and December 1938, and it finally forced the government's hand. By the end of 1936 a Public Order Act was introduced to curb the activities of the street battles between the fascists and the combined forces of the left. In his meetings and marches in the Jewish areas of East London Mosley was in some respects ahead of Hitler whose main campaign against the Jews, the trade unions and the German left was just gathering pace in 1936. *Kristalnacht*, the Nazi's widespread street violence against the Jewish population in which synagogues were burned to the ground in an organised desecration of everything Jewish throughout the cities of the Reich, came to a head on 9/10 November 1938.

In Britain the scene was very different, apart from the violence surrounding Mosley's campaign. The hunger marches from Tyneside and South Wales were conducted like a well-disciplined military operation without any violence. The march organisers had their own stewards to police their demonstration, and the whole operation astonished everyone, especially the critics, with its dignity and self-control. Even to the climax of the events with tea at the Ritz in London, though with silence from the MacDonald–Baldwin Government.

It was a time of great radical literature and poetry – of Auden, Isherwood, Spender, Cecil Day Lewis; of J.B. Priestley, Shaw, Orwell. Glittering phrases flowed across the land. Some radicals became members of the Communist Party, others travelled along a similar and parallel path without a party card. Some went to Spain at the first opportunity – to begin a path to disillusion, like Orwell; others, like Priestley, travelled the country to write (in his *English Journey*, 1934) about a land of great paradox, hopelessness mingling with hope, despair with ambition and dreams, wealth and poverty. All rebelled against the hypocrisy and double standards that symbolised the age; the posturing and the cant of governments who relied on a mixture of ignorance and apathy to conceal what was really happening just beneath the crust of society. It was an evil, cowardly, weak and menacing epoch.

Yet it was an age that also had its heroes, including the unsung school teachers who reached out beyond this ambience, trying to focus young minds on something better. There were many of them, not unlike my own good fortune in having Leonard Cookson. Some of the heroes were even politicians, not only on the left but even among the back benches of the Tory Party as well as the Liberals, who tried to cry out against the lies and the hypocrisy. After all Winston Churchill himself was one of them in his undaunted, and often unrewarding, warnings against the growing menace of Nazism.

There was Victor Gollancz, that remarkable publisher who launched the Left Book Club as a landmark attempt to educate an adult population as well as the young in the philosophy of progress and hope. Those low-cost, crimson-coloured hardbacks (and soft covers) became one of the most influential forces for radical political education in my lifetime. The Left Book Club established branches throughout the country in a mass education process – not merely on politics, but on science, art, literature, economics, history and even astronomy. From January 1936, when Gollancz launched his remarkable scheme with John Strachey and Harold Laski, the LBC editions poured out their message and continued throughout the war circulating the books to the armed forces wherever they were. The process continued up till the early 1950s when it was finally wound up in the misguided belief that its job was completed.

Gollancz's book club anticipated the wartime system of adult education, ABCA – the Army Bureau of Current Affairs. If ABCA was the first serious national attempt at an Open University, which, in effect it was, then the Left Book Club provided the prototype for that and much else. Most of the active prewar left came together under the umbrella of Gollancz's club – Marxists with non-Marxist socialists, liberals, even Tory 'wets'. For a few shillings anyone could join, as I did, with Victor's revolutionary club house, and each month we received a crimson-backed book. The authors' list included some of the finest writers of the 1930s, the outstanding radical political figures, a vast range of socialist academics and, of course, George Orwell – although he and Gollancz never got on well. Within a year of its launch in 1936 the LBC had recruited 50,000 members – an astonishing achievement and far exceeding the then still infant Penguin Books started by Allen Lane in 1935, though it should be emphasised that Lane's Penguins also contributed enormously to the task of widening the horizons of an entire generation – my generation.

These were the tributaries that fed into the river of awareness as we approached the war. They were the vital ingredients that frequently made up for the gaps in our formal education; all contributing to the eventual bursting of the dam and developing the capacity to combat the apathy and political indolence that immobilised so many layers of that 1930s society, and most of all the working class of those days.

* * *

The real point about almost all the political and economic policies of the 1930s is that they were – consciously or otherwise – a prelude to the Second World War. That is why it is simply not possible to understand the 1939–45 war without coming to grips with what was happening in Britain, and the rest of Europe, in the decade 1929–39. I sometimes get the feeling, looking back on that period, that the entire history of the century was unfolding in those years; that everything was being squeezed into that decade. The Labour Party – the pre-Blair Labour Party, that is – was both destroyed and rebuilt in that epoch; the socialist idea, crucified again and again by what was happening in Soviet Russia, particularly during the Moscow trials of the old Bolsheviks and the expulsion of Trotsky from the Soviet Union, was resurrected by the war; Hitler rose from small-time thuggery in a Munich beer cellar to dominate most of Europe; Spain was torn to shreds in a civil war that left its mark on the whole of the half-century or so that followed – and indeed became the symbol of resistance to fascism throughout the world; Japan, arguing for 'Co-prosperity' throughout the Pacific, put its military machine into operation, first in China and then eventually across all South-East Asia.

The left was in perpetual debate trying to balance perfection on the eye of a needle, fragmented, engrossed with internal argument about how to resist fascism, whether to support rearmament or not, how to react to what was happening in the Soviet Union, whether the socialist idea could ever be implemented by peaceful, democratic, Parliamentary means – or to seek revolution. Nothing was ever resolved. Meanwhile the right courted with fascism, not least because it feared the spread of Stalin's Soviet communism.

So the war came one Sunday morning, just after breakfast. It filtered into the two rooms we had in our Hamilton Street abode. I still remember so clearly the warmth of that September morning in 1939 as the street came slowly to life; as the curtains were drawn back on a world that would never be the same again. The sun was warm and the sky streaked with a few slender shreds of ribbon cloud. The message that came through the radio speaker was chilling but hardly surprising. Neville Chamberlain's voice, thin with a reedy strain in the tone, informed the nation at a few seconds after 11 am that since Adolf Hitler had misbehaved we were now in a 'state of war with Germany'. He squeaked as he spoke. I felt no chill. We all knew it was going to happen at any time. The gas masks had been issued weeks before. Most people regarded Chamberlain as a silly old chump and hardly swerved from that view for months before 3 September 1939.

I was just 18 and felt a quite irrational impulse to go to war. I didn't attempt to explain that feeling to myself or anyone else. There were no rationalised thoughts about wanting to fight for 'a better world'. Nothing like that. I simply wanted to be amid the violence and to fight *against* something; perhaps to express a disgust at the kind of society that surrounded me, piss-bucket and all. In the three years we had lived in that bug-ridden runway, the bucket on the landing, the wash-basin alongside the breakfast dishes, the smell of rot and rubbish all around – in those three years I had listened to the sound of the footsteps of war drawing closer, audibly and for that matter visibly, as well.

I became increasingly conscious of the appalling burden on my father as he struggled to find, and retain, any job; of my mother's quiet anguish, which would, oft times, erupt into sudden uncontrollable spasms of tears and despair at our plight and her own weakening grip on life. She was ill and suffered greatly, albeit stoicly, as she tried to sustain her small family with the scrapings. One of my proudest achievements – and I count that as such to this day – was to rescue her engagement ring from the pawnbroker after a few weeks of pay from a local paper to which I had become attached as an apprentice reporter. Rescuing the ring cost £5 – which was a great deal of money at the time.

As I listened to Chamberlain that Sunday morning, and reflected on war and violence, possible, maybe even probable, death, it never occurred to me to be hesitant about becoming involved. Looking back, I suppose that subconsciously I must have seen it as a way out of the anguish that surrounded me and my parents. But that sort of sophisticated analysis was certainly not on the agenda at the time.

The bubbles of the 1930s still spring to life in my memory. I have the canvas of it all in that special little computer we all store somewhere at the back of our mind. Spain; the Rhineland; the Anschluss; Munich; Winston's speech to the House of Commons in October 1938 when he warned that the 'bitter cup' that Hitler had forced Chamberlain to drink from would be thrust in his face again and again; the fire at the Crystal Palace, which seemed to light up the land at a time of the Abdication like a bonfire of our fantasies as well as our vanities. The whispers, soon to materialise into startling headlines, about Edward VIII and Wallis Simpson – just as Tommy Meredith had said.

Outside Camden Town tube station on Friday and Saturday evenings Oswald Mosley's boys were selling their BUF weekly paper,

Action, while across the street, only a few punches away, the Communist Party paper, the *Daily Worker*, was on offer. There were scuffles, sometimes more violent fighting, before the police intervened. The BUF were especially renowned for their knuckle-dusters and thuggish methods. They were tough and dangerous and better trained than the Communists. Bravery was survival and, often enough, fast legs.

The 1930s: it floods back so easily. Manchester City beating Portsmouth in the 1934 Cup Final after being a goal down, and the exceptional performance of City's young right half-back, that Scots ex-miner, Matt Busby; of Harold Larwood, my boyhood hero, taking 5 for 27 for Notts against Lancashire – the club I almost played for – when I last saw him at Old Trafford; of Maureen Tongue and the Stockport War Memorial. It all closed down for the duration on that Sunday morning, 3 September 1939 when the world in which I had grown up paused to take death on board.

4 The War Years: My University of Life

If now I write about the war years in a somewhat sketchy way, no doubt more sketchily than might be justified, it is not because of modesty and certainly not a breakdown in memory, but mainly because I hold the view that enough has already been written by the participants about their own experiences – whether in the army, navy or, as in my case, the Royal Air Force. I want to try to avoid being drawn into a lengthy account of what it was like and all that. Maybe I won't entirely succeed in this; we shall see. The ego plays tricks and lays snares: in my mind I have put up the sign – 'beware'. Yet I realise only too well that when we start talking about battles, air battles, bombing, the whole ugly magnificence of war, the tendency is to romanticise and exaggerate. It comes with the rations. So beware.

The war years were traumatic for all those involved in whatever form. The horrors are, as always in war, self-evidently horrific. The business of killing is a skilled trade and it reaches its apotheosis in total war. The paradox is that though fear, terrifying fear, frequently grips the participants – and no one who has ever been involved in war can possibly deny that – there is also elation, a discovery that there has never been an experience which more fulfils the emotional frenzy of supeme thrill at the achievement of some appalling destruction. Without doubt it *is* madness; the summit of human contradiction. Yet it would be idle and dishonest to deny that this feeling exists; it certainly did in my own experience. And I have no pleasure or satisfaction in saying these things. It is simply necessary to confess to such feelings if I am to report honestly.

The other factor about discussing our war years is that distance lends an inescapable romanticism to any event that happened some sixty years ago. Yet I have to say that even at this distance I still regard my nearly six years in the RAF as my real University of Life. We all grew up quickly, too quickly, and let's admit it, somewhat brutally as well.

War is brutalising, cruel, corroding, maybe even futile. Yet it would be absurd to claim that it contained no justification or drama, no self-fulfilling emotion, no excitement, exhilaration and even a form of sexual thrill on a grand scale. It is a unique condition in the aggressiveness of human beings since war liberates as it kills and kills as it liberates. It contains all that is life, and therefore death, in rapid succession and at a speed and thrill unequalled by any other experience. It is there to be rightly condemned and deplored by all rational thought – and yet we know the irrational is always with us, available to be recruited and shaped into an emotional spasm. War contains every paradox and hardly any answers. It raises hope in every breast, excites dreams about the solution of problems and finally leaves its victors as well as its victims disappointed, dismayed, disillusioned. But war also offers its survivors in battle one supreme piece of imagery – the feeling of having been through the turmoil of fire and having lived to mourn one's comrades in arms. It is an experience unmatched in relationships within a non-violent corpus. This perhaps helps to explain its attraction and even its intoxicating lure to the warrior instinct in all of us, buried away as it is with the feeling of insecurity and fear in our subconsciousness.

This is certainly not an argument in justification of war but an attempt to try to understand the whole process. In his book *The Anatomy of Human Destructiveness* (1974) Erich Fromm offers this observation:

> War, to some extent, reverses all values. War encourages deep-seated human impulses, such as altruism and solidarity to be expressed – impulses that are stunted by the principles of egotism and competition that peacetime life engenders in modern man. Class differences, if not absent, disappear to a considerable extent. In war, man is man again, and has a chance to distinguish himself, regardless of privileges that his social status confers upon him as a citizen. To put it in a very accentuated form: war is an indirect rebellion against the injustice, inequality and boredom governing social life in peacetime ... the fact that war has these positive features is a sad comment on our civilization.

*   *   *

In my preface I claimed that this book is a kind of testimony to a generation; inescapably subjective. It is also about the generation that fought in the Second World War, and indeed those who were involved in so many ways without actually taking part in combat. They were all mainly children who grew up in the 1920s and 1930s, and mostly, like myself, inadequately educated, even if they went to 'good schools'. Children of the unemployed, the insecurely employed as well as those who clung to jobs they hated but dare not admit that even to themselves. All of them were suddenly pitched into a wartime cauldron of dramatic change, which eventually helped to transform almost everyone into quite different characters than would otherwise have been the case. War exploded class barriers, as Erich Fromm's book notes, even where it didn't destroy them. Its blood-flow made a mockery of separation by accent or even eating habits. An enduring community of spirit at all levels contained qualities that the vast majority of those of us in uniform had simply never before experienced. It took a long time to realise the changes taking place within ourselves. We resisted the inner confessionals. It might be taken as a sign of weakness, an unthinkable manifestation in time of war. But inside that shell, underneath the carapace, we all knew we were changing into different human material. That's why I describe the whole experience as the University of War. That indeed is what made 1945 so special, so different and probably unique.

I have already admitted that there are dangers in such romanticism – if that is how my description might be regarded. There is another interpretation: that such a transformation in people can only be achieved – certainly in that form – by war. That is not my claim, though there may well be some degree of psychological truth in it. Yet that bald, and indeed deeply depressing claim, would oversimplify the explanation of what happened to those of us who travelled through that momentous epoch. It was deeper than that, as I have tried to describe in the preceding chapters. All the experiences I have related came together in wartime, perhaps welded together in a form that was indeed unique; the war was a climax to those years of the 1920s and 1930s. And the whole combined operation was, I dare say, a form of commando course for the eventual social and political transformation that took place in the vote of July 1945.

As I have referred to earlier, as I joined the RAF the war had already enabled my father to find a permanent job after years of unemployment or insecure part-time work. He was recruited as a messenger in the civil service and shortly afterwards began work at the newly formed Ministry of Aircraft Production under Lord Beaverbrook, whom Churchill appointed to transform supplies to the beleaguered RAF (Beaverbrook became the minister on 14 May 1940). A messenger's job was dogsbody work – but it *was* a job. My father had been mostly unemployed for about eight years. The casual work he managed to get from time to time was purely 'survival' stuff. He was compelled to accept even the most menial part-time jobs in order to qualify for unemployment benefit. His hopes, if not his spirit, had already been drained away and the engine of purpose almost destroyed. Then, in 1940, another world war produced the great irony – work on the shoulders of organised destruction. What seemed unattainable in peacetime became essential to the national interest in war.

*   *   *

Life in the RAF began in the usual way – square-bashing, training in how to obey orders and disciplined instructions; commando courses to toughen us up – and even though we were aircrew recruits it was also necessary (we were assured) to know how to use a bayonet. So on a commando course on the east coast I learned how to pierce a sandbag with a bayonet. All this was before I began my flying training at an EFTS (Early Flying Training School) in Derbyshire, of all places. This seemed unfair to me since so many of my chums were sent off to Canada, South Africa, even the United States to do their flying training in rather better conditions than a Derbyshire village. But I drew the short straw. Still I did get to know, and like, Derbyshire.

Training for a pilot/navigator course at that time was a minimum of 12 months depending on operational requirements. And it was toward the end of 1941 before I completed my own training – tough, rigorous and highly disciplined as it was and had to be. The final stage of OTU (Operational Training Unit) was at Cranwell, the Sandhurst of the RAF, where we flew Wellington bombers. In 1942 I was transferred to Bomber Command to fly Wellingtons, Whitleys and eventually a brief spell on Lancasters before I was retrained for a role with Coastal Command in the special area of photographic reconnaissance. But not before I had grown to know the Lincolnshire airfields and countryside – and pubs – like a village roundabout. All those names still ring bells of nostalgia, as well as fear; Elsham Wolds, Metheringham, Coningsby, Dunholme Lodge, Waddington, Woodhall Spa – and the wonderful sight of the beautiful Lincoln Cathedral standing out like a home-warming beacon from its pinnacle on the hill in that special city of our recall.

In the two menacingly final years of 1944 and 1945 when I flew Mosquito planes for photo reconnaissance – unarmed, very fast and with a capability of flying at the then exceptional height of up to

42,000 feet (in the case of the PR Mark 32 from the end of 1944). Most operational heights were between 25,000 and 30,000 feet, for the Mosquito Mark XVI and an earlier Mark 32 with the Merlin engine 72/73 and 76/77.

My last squadron finished up guarding and feeding the northern flank of Montgomery's advance into northern Germany from airfields in France and as he moved up across the Rhine from old Luftwaffe airfields. We finished up on a pitch just north of Kiel at a place called Üttersen, not far from the Danish border.

It was at that point that I had my first real encounter with German civilians in the streets of the post-Hitler Reich. It was, of course, a traumatic experience. I would drive into Kiel and then on to Hamburg through what was a kind of lunar landscape of destruction. The mountains of rubble especially in nearby Kiel were haunting. I remember a Sunday afternoon walk through those shattered streets: looking, as if transfixed, at the great piled heaps of twisted metal, concrete, stone slabs and brick, and pondering what lay beneath these dunes of destruction. There was an eerie silence about them. Occasionally a German, an aged man or woman, shuffled by cloaked in black anonymity. Not a word was exchanged. Perhaps there was a furtive, expressionless glance in our direction – perhaps even a first sight of an 'enemy uniform'. We also exercised the furtive option.

Yet, oddly, I did not feel a shudder of conscience. Perhaps I should have done: but it wasn't there to offer. In any event the scale and magnitude of the carnage was too great to place into any rational process of thought. Maybe if I had seen bodies torn and tossed and crushed and mutilated as the bombs fell – maybe, then, I would have felt some terrible twist of conscience. But not now. Nor indeed when I had been flying above all this. Now I was actually walking through the valley of death for some of which, it is possible, my comrades and myself had been responsible.

The sight of mutilated bodies does have the capacity to remind even the least sensitive of us that death and destruction can reduce us all to savages. To stare and to contemplate the quiet isolation of unidentified death in such circumstances is, I suppose, to understand a little more about the minuteness and transitory nature of everything. Here and there were strewn the trinkets of life. Sad, insignificant objects soon to be swept away by wind and rain and to disintegrate like the rest of the tapestry. Holes in the ground in which distorted sinews of what was once a living space remained to remind of an earlier moment. A chair leg, broken mirror; a dog's paw clutched behind a broken brick. Winter was coming. A snowflake fluttered. Soon there would be a thin white sheeting to cover this frozen picture. My feelings? Very hard now to recapture the thoughts travelling through my mind. Regret? Not really. A terrible admission of the brutalising affect of war? Probably. I had no nightmares about this scene of desolation.

As I moved about in those first few months of post-Hitler Germany, to Hamburg, Dusseldorf, Hanover, Berlin, Cologne, Bremen it was a never-varying picture of rubble; of British soldiers and airmen swapping cigarettes, soap, chocolate for the bed of a fraulein – once the ban on fraternisation had been formally removed, though informal, illicit sex between the occupying forces and German women was already well established; it was all part of an unreal world in waiting for whatever the postwar Jerusalem had to offer. What that was going to be was always a question on the agenda.

What kind of new world would arise from all these ashes? Of course, we believed in some 'certainties' – that the prize of conquering the evil empire of the Nazis would herald a rebirth of decency, fairness, greater equality, a society in which the egalitarianism of war would be transferred painlessly into civvy street. The entire experience of war and wartime life was a kind of reinforcement to collective hope and, to be sure, wishful thinking. We had little idea of what was happening to political life back home. Hardly at all of the intricacies of Westminster. The newspapers were available in the mess; they were often piled up, unread, in the canteen atmosphere of the NAAFI and the Salvation Army 'hotels' of the main German cities. We saw the headlines. Churchill, Roosevelt, Stalin, Charles de Gaulle and the goings on around them. It was all part of the backcloth in our unreal world.

Of course, not everyone saw the postwar vision in the same light. Some regarded the war as an interlude – a break away from the boredom of a comfortable albeit uneventful life in prewar England. Some of them looked with a mere idle casualness on a return to the status quo of their prewar lives. Their conversation was always a revelation to those of us, the majority, who saw things differently. Especially when they discussed, with a distinct air of indifference, a return to their prewar wives. They were a minority yet a not unimportant few. Yes, of course, they were mainly the products of secure and even prosperous prewar homes who saw no fundamental reason why they shouldn't return to a similar uninspiring security. The older ones among them, those who had reached a voting age in the 1930s, had probably voted Conservative and did so again in 1945; possibly Liberal. But the majority, the vast majority, looked out on to a future that they believed – no, not simply believed; they were convinced – would have to be better than what they had known before 1939.

I was on an airfield near the Rhine when voting took place for the July 1945 election. We held our own mock election, organised by the officers and men of our Mosquito squadron. By an overwhelming majority we elected a 'Labour MP'. The Liberal candidate came second, though well down the running order, and a Communist candidate came close up on the Liberal. Way down among the stragglers was the Conservative candidate. He laughed it off and drank his beer. All over the RAF and army bases something similar was happening – with similar results. So it was certainly no surprise at all when the results of the real election came through from home – there *had been* a Labour landslide. No one I knew expected anything else. And when, later, I read that some of Attlee's colleagues – like Herbert Morrison and even Ernest Bevin – had feared a different outcome I was astonished that they could have been so out of touch with the reality of opinion in the armed forces. The Labour Party, with its 1945 design for a 'New World' was pushing at an open door.

In recent years some writers have started to demote the influence of the Second World War as a major factor in producing the political changes of 1945. Their argument has two main components: first, that widespread social and economic change would have come in any event, war or not, because of the scientific and technological advances that were already emerging before 1939. These developments, the argument continues, would have forced changes in conditions, style, structure and would have obliged any government to act accordingly.

The second point they make is to question the breaking down of social barriers during wartime. The counter-claim of the sceptics is that these barriers were not fundamentally broken down and there was only a superficial and temporary transformation in the class nature of British society. Old traditions and old customs, old prejudices and habits, they have argued, remained firm even if they were dented by wartime experience. Class divisions remained almost impervious and certainly strongly resistant to lasting changes in attitudes while the ownership of property and wealth was scarcely affected at all. Parliament, the press, industrial and commercial management, even the trade unions, remained largely unaffected as institutions, deeply rooted in their past traditions and practices and only marginally changed by the war years.

That is the substance of some of the more recent analysis about what really happened to social change between 1939 and 1945. There is, of course, some truth in all of this. But the case against this benign conclusion is strong. There is every evidence that scientific and technological innovation was propelled to a geometric degree by the pressures and demands of war. It is a hypothetical calculation at best but the increasingly accepted view is that it might well have taken another thirty or forty years of peacetime development to match what was achieved in the six years of war. Indeed, something like two-thirds of all scientific and technological innovation of all time emerged in the decade after 1945 – most notably in the field of space exploration, which was a direct derivative of the wartime work on rocketry, jet propulsion and nuclear energy.

Maybe the case arguing for a more cautious approach to the social changes brought about during wartime holds more water. Perhaps we were over optimistic in assuming that the class barriers collapsed so substantially. No doubt the divisions were stronger and more resilient than we believed at the time. Yet even from this distance in time I remain convinced that the experience of the wartime generation did profoundly change the postwar climate of class divisions. The scale and the nature of 'social mixing' during wartime was unique. It was an education in itself, assisted greatly by the seminal experiments in adult education for the armed forces conducted by ABCA (Army Bureau of Current Affairs), which encouraged an explosion of reading and awareness among young people who, previously, had no real tradition or culture of books. It was all part of the matrix that went to constitute the University of Wartime.

*   *   *

For me the end of the war contained a special personal element that was to shape the rest of my life: my meeting with Margit Freudenbergova in Prague in the summer of 1945. She has been my wife for over fifty years.

While awaiting demobilisation the squadron did not have a great deal to do. There was a special assignment to Norway where we photographed and scanned the fjords, ostensibly in search of U-boats that may be harbouring some of Hitler's escapees – like Martin Bormann, Hitler's deputy and closest confidant as the Nazi regime was collapsing. It had been reported that Bormann committed suicide by taking prussic acid, though his body was not found (in 1972 a skeleton was unearthed during excavations in Berlin and identified as that of Martin Bormann; even so a mystery remains). In fact, in 1945 British intelligence were convinced that Bormann and others had escaped to Norway where U-boats were waiting to transport the surviving Nazi leaders to South America. My squadron was sent off to Norway to fly low-level reconnaissance over the fjords in an effort to check on this assumption. We did not find Bormann. But we did create a completely fresh map of the Norwegian coastline!

There was a lot of time to spare after that operation. So I organised myself a temporary billet in Hamburg to work on the army magazine *Soldier*, which was then being run by a former *Daily Mail* man, Jack Hallows, who was a captain in the army. In a bar near the Alster I discussed with Jack the possibility of him using his influence to arrange an unorthodox and, of course, temporary deal with the RAF for me to be transferred on a short-term lease to the Army Newspaper Unit in Hamburg. The reasonable justification was that I could pick up a few journalistic threads in preparation for my return to civvy street. To my astonishment the RAF group command agreed to this highly irregular arrangement, a piece of unofficial cutting of red-tape for which I am ever grateful to those non-bureaucrats of RAF Command centre, North-west Germany. So I joined *Soldier* magazine as a reporter and feature writer. It was, in effect, the beginning of my re-entry into journalism, albeit a highly tentative foot in the water.

I did various assignments for Jack Hallows' magazine – rather a good production it was, too, printed on presses that later produced *Die Welt* and *Die Zeit*. I covered the departure of the Canadian troops from Holland; interviewed Kurt Schumacher, the German Social Democrat leader who had just emerged from a concentration camp; I wrote profiles of devastated German cities, such as Kiel and Hamburg; and I did all this in RAF uniform – which, I must admit, helped considerably.

Then there followed a key assignment – to go across Europe with a train load of horses specially imported from Ireland to help rehabilitate some of the farmlands of central Europe. It was organised by UNRRA (United Nations Relief and Rehabilitation Administration), whose role was to help rebuild the devastated lands and their peoples. The retreating German armies had stripped the farmlands of all livestock and machinery. Horses were needed to pull the ploughs – back to primitive systems – until sufficient mechanised agricultural equipment became available again. My job as a reporter was to join the horses' train that would leave Hamburg for Prague to journey across Europe. No, there would be no need to interview the horses unless I particularly fancied that task. But it would help if I become fully acquainted with the Czech army chaps – fresh from battle – who were to accompany and guard the train to Prague and to make sure the gee-gees were fed and watered at every stop. I became very chummy with the Czech army.

As we travelled across Germany I also became adept in knowing how horses should be fed and watered; moreover, with a photographer, an old pal called Charlie Jacobson, we virtually slept with the horses. Well, no, that's a slight exaggeration. We had a truck to ourselves with straw on the deck – fresh straw, of course – to sleep on and Czech army rations to feed on. Well, yes, we did stop off at the odd tavern for a German beer. Someone always had to keep guard over the horse-train just in case a stray German fellow thought it worthwhile pinching one of our horses. We didn't lose a steed.

Arriving in Prague with a good story and even better pictures we decided that the priority was – sleep. So Charlie and I found a small hotel near the city centre where we shared a room – and slept for a day. After about five days in that train with the horses we were as fatigued as I can ever recall. We both needed that day of sleep. Then we met up with our Czech army friends and went on the town. Prague, circa summer 1945, was just coming back to life after liberation. And to be in the city at that time wearing an RAF uniform was to be feted like a King of Prague Castle.

One evening, after I had phoned Jack Hallows in Hamburg to check out on deadlines, Charlie and I strolled into a bar at the Hotel Atlantic. We had a few drinks and felt hungry. I looked at the menu, which, hardly surprisingly, was in Czech. Charlie was no expert in that language any more than I was. So we looked around for help. Sitting at a table in the restaurant were two girls both of whom broke into occasional English. We approached them for translation help and they guided us round the menu, had us sit at a neighbouring table and were quite at ease with a couple of RAF chaps who had, oddly, descended on the hotel. Margit Freudenbergova was one of the girls. That's how we met.

She had not long since returned to her native country from – of all places – Britain, where she had spent the war years. Her story was grim but far from unusual in Europe 1945. It was the story of the Holocaust.

Margit's father, Julius, and her brother Paul were taken away by the Gestapo from their Pilzen home when the Nazis moved through the Sudetenland into Bohemia on 14 March 1939. The Freudenberg family then moved to Pilzen from their home and wholesale food business in Marianske Lazne (Marienbad) when their business was seized by the Germans in the wake of the Munich agreement of October 1938.

Her mother, Irma, and Margit waited in Pilzen in the hope that her father and brother would be released. They weren't. Then Irma took her daughter to Prague, already occupied by the Nazis from 16 March; but there was no solace there. The city was firmly in the grip of the Gestapo. So in July 1939 Irma succeeded in arranging for her 17-year-old daughter to join the *Kindertransport* operation. That was a terrible moment of parting. Margit was deeply resistant to moving from her mother. But it was already clear that there was little option if she wanted to survive arrest under the anti-Jewish laws.

So on one of the last trains out of Prague in July 1939 she waved goodbye to her mother – whom she never saw again. Her parents perished in Auschwitz. Her brother Paul somehow survived the concentration camps of Buchenwald and Auschwitz and was liberated by the Soviet army in 1945. Margit was in Britain throughout the war, mainly working as a nurse in Glasgow where she had been 'adopted' by Emmy and Georg Sachs, cousins of the family who had managed to flee from their Vienna home after the Anschluss of 13 March 1938. Emmy and Georg became her surrogate parents.

In 1945 Margit returned to Marianske Lazne to try to pick up the pieces. Her brother Paul had survived – albeit grievously damaged by his experience. An uncle, Edmund Pisinger – Irma's brother – had also managed to escape in 1939 and spent the war years in England. Together they returned to Marianske Lazne and began the exhausting, frustrating and deeply melancholic process of rebuilding something. Margit took a job in Prague as a translator for a Czech toy manufacturer. She had friends who had also returned from exile in England. They were the two girls Charlie Jacobson and I met in the Atlantic Hotel that evening as we recovered from transporting horses halfway across Europe.

Margit returned to England in December 1946 and we married on 9 January 1947. I took a day off from writing leaders for the *Liverpool Daily Post*.

I supposed the war was over, though I was never quite sure. I had not really rehabilitated myself. No doubt the rational thing to have done would have been to delay getting married until I had resettled back into ... but back into what? I had no automatic niche anywhere. My parents were still very poor even though father continued to be employed as a civil service messenger in the Whitehall machine. His wage was just about enough to keep them in rent, food and clothing – but little else. My demob money was now to be spent on getting married and trying to find a pad for the two of us. Work in Fleet Street of 1946/7 was tough and quite rough; those journalists who had been in the war were returning to an utterly different world, hoping, dreaming, believing – but insecure within themselves as they tried to come to terms with an older generation of newspapermen who had not 'been away' and who inevitably resented the returning 'war heroes' even when such irritation, born of envy as well as hostility, didn't openly manifest itself.

It was a very strange, funny, old world for the new boys like myself.

5 Postwar World: Civvy Street, Fleet Street

The more I reflect the greater becomes the relevance of Karl von Clausewitz's famous dictum; *'Der Krieg ist nichts als eine Forsetzung der politschen Verkehrs mit Einmischung anderer Mittel'* (War is nothing but the continuation of politics with the admixture of other means). And by the same token it could be said of the relationship between peace and war: that peace is the continuation of war with the admixture of other means. It seemed a bit like that to me when I landed back in civvy street, or to be more precise, Fleet Street.

It was all very strange and, frankly, uneasy. I knew I had to make a swift decision: either return to basic local journalism, or go to the provinces to work on a local evening paper and then move back to Fleet Street by the usual circuitous provincial route. But that would be time-consuming and, in terms of my personal life, difficult to organise, especially if I now had marriage in my sights. I talked with a few chums who were in a similar spot, and they all agreed that it was worth the gamble of trying out the Fleet Street scene before abandoning the Great Wen for the 'outside world'. Then by a sheer fluke the great big lucky break came along in the shape of a wonderful Irishman – or ought I to say, Ulsterman? – called Patrick J. 'Paddy' Monkhouse.

Paddy, who had not long been demobbed from the Royal Ulster Rifles, was still in his retailored (and dyed) army officer's greatcoat when we first met in The Clachan, the pub at the rear of the old *Manchester Guardian* office above the Fleet Street Post Office. I had just completed a day's work writing a piece for the paper's prestigious London diary, which Paddy, as acting London editor of the paper, was masterminding. He said he liked the piece and ordered himself a Guinness. I had a bitter. We chatted – inevitably about the war. I was still in my demob suit so we shared a joke about demob clothing. ('So long as you get your arms into the jacket sleeves and your legs into the trousers, it fits' – standard demob suit joke.)

'Have you eaten?' Paddy asked me. The thought hadn't crossed my mind.

'No, not really' – the 'not really' being utterly redundant, as it frequently is.

'Ah,' he said. 'Like to try a Greek place I know in Charlotte Street? Not bad – considering it's still wartime round there.'

'Yes, OK; that would be very nice. Thanks for the idea.'

'Good; have another beer and we'll catch a bus up there ...'

I often thought about that remark – 'we'll catch a bus up there' – in later years when snapping up a taxi at the corner of Fetter Lane became a mere casual habit. Still, I dare say that *Manchester Guardian* expenses in those days, even as London editor, would hardly stretch to joyriding around in taxis. I realised that myself a short while afterwards when my weekly expenses as an *MG* reporter would hardly ever come to more than a couple of pounds.

At any rate Paddy and Goodman went off to Charlotte Street that night for a meal – the first one I ever had bought for me by a Fleet Street executive, and, needless to say, the most important. Paddy took to me and I to him. From the first mouthful of conversation we seemed to hit a rapport. He looked like Boris Pasternak, and that was before his hair turned a flintstone grey. He was kindly, generous, rather like an elder brother to me, sympathising with the problems facing any youngster coming back from the war. Paddy was about ten years my senior. In that Charlotte Street restaurant, that same night, Paddy hired me as a reporter on the NUJ minimum, which was then nine guineas a week (at that time salaries were mostly in 'guineas' for some odd reason); and so began a brief but wonderfully exhilarating (as well as often frustrating) spell with the *Manchester Guardian* – a newspaper I had been reared on from the days when Leonard Cookson read Cardus to us schoolkids. Somehow, I felt I had arrived; not sure *where* I had arrived, mind you. But I had a strong sense of having put a foot on some sort of ladder.

I stayed with the *MG* for quite a while after Paddy returned to Manchester, where he eventually became deputy editor to the editor, the formidable A.P. Wadsworth, and should really have taken over the paper when Wadsworth became terminally ill and retired in 1956. But Paddy did not succeed. The job went to Alastair Hetherington – a man without the experience of Paddy but who went on to become an outstanding editor of the paper. For Paddy Monkhouse it was a severe disappointment, which he hid beneath a carapace of characteristic Monkhouse quality – dignity, modesty and commitment to the newspaper. He was a second-generation *Guardian* man, immensely popular with all the journalists on the paper, a quintessential *Guardian* journalist. But it was not to be. Paddy soldiered on brilliantly as deputy editor until his retirement.

Of all the mentors along my journalistic road – and there have been quite a few – I have a special corner of affection and respect for Patrick J. Monkhouse, not merely because he gave me that first, crucial postwar break but no less because he set down standards of professional integrity that I would like to believe I have tried to maintain, however inadequately. As my friend John Cole has written (*Guardian*, 9 March 1993) Paddy was 'the greatest editor the *Guardian* never had'.

*   *   *

My own development from that point was considerably influenced by a decision to join the Communist Party shortly after I was demobilised. A good deal of subsequent life in Fleet Street was substantially affected, and certainly impeded, by that early decision. It may even have contributed to my premature departure from the *Manchester Guardian* in 1947 since A.P. Wadsworth was notably intolerant of having Communists on his staff. Political discrimination of any kind is always difficult to prove, and although there were several more 'political blips' along the road I doubt whether it fundamentally damaged my prospects of becoming editor of the *Guardian* or for that matter any other national daily. The odds were always stacked against that possibility. It certainly did not prevent my being offered another job with the *Guardian* in the 1960s, when the Odhams' empire was being taken over by the *Daily Mirror* group. Alastair Hetherington offered me a return ticket in a senior capacity with the *Guardian* (he gave me a choice of three senior editorial posts) and showed not the slightest sign of any concern with my having once been a member of the Communist Party – which, it must be said, I had by then long since left. I didn't accept Alastair's offer but instead chose to join Hugh Cudlipp's *Daily Mirror*.

My Communist past? Well, there is nothing surprising or dramatic about any of this story. Set it against the tapestry of my teenage years in prewar London, my parents' struggle against the odds, my Jewish background, that wilderness of the bug-ridden rooms in Hamilton Street, NW1 and the sheer physical as well as emotional demands of coping with life and its problems. I already had strong links with the Young Communist League from about 1937, and I have already explained how attractive the CP became to the young minds of the 1930s. Far more so than the Labour Party, which, apart from individuals like Cripps, Bevan, Lansbury, George Strauss, John

Strachey and Harold Laski – whose lectures at the London School of Economics I was starting to attend – seemed hardly capable of handling the threat coming from Mosley's fascists. There was little incentive to join the Labour Party. Moreover I had the message from David Zerember ringing in my harvesting mind.

There was enough drama, all around, to persuade an untutored receptive mind that the Communist Party and its fringe organisations had more clarity and vision than all the others put together. The poets echoed a similar sentiment; and Spain evoked passions unequalled by any other single issue. It was all of a piece with the powerful influences of virtually all the great radical writers of the day. I had no heart-searching in reaching my own decision. It all seemed so clear-cut, uncomplicated, natural.

*   *   *

But during the war it was a different matter. There was no question of membership of any political party. No point in it. No doubt there were many dedicated individuals from all the political parties who simply kept up their membership of the Conservative, Liberal or Labour parties and, probably, even the Communist Party. I saw no relevance in that kind of formalism. It seemed to have no place in the daily business of fighting the war, though it never prevented me getting involved in fiery debates over the beer. On the other hand, there was also a tight security vigilence on any member of H.M. Forces becoming involved in what might be construed as 'political activities'.

Even the most innocuous discussion groups courted trouble, as I discovered during my training spell at Cranwell. In that period I became involved with a discussion group, which met weekly, when convenient, in a room at the rear of the NAAFI building. I had no idea that this was 'against the rules', and I doubt whether the majority of the others did. The subjects we debated were – at least, so we thought – quite harmless: looking at the items now, it will seem absurd that such isues as postwar Independence for India could have caused the slightest tremor. But at the time we hadn't allowed for the fact that Nehru and other leaders of the Indian Congress Party were jailed in India for advocating the same thing. So it came as a nasty shock to discover that our modest little discussion group had been spied on by the RAF police and station security. Several of us were approached by the RAF police and accused of taking part in a 'political conspiracy', simply because we had met in 'clandestine assembly'. It was all absolutely absurd but such banalities were not unusual in wartime.

There then followed a chain of even more grotesque occurrences. The RAF district Provost Marshal at Lincoln took a hand and required our attendance for two days of cross-examination at Lincoln RAF police headquarters. We were closely questioned on every detail of that harmless discussion group. The interrogators – RAF officers of the Provost Marshal department – sought to discover whether there was a hidden hand of political conspiracy behind the whole thing. Innocent, and honest, responses such as 'We were a mere discussion group debating items of current affairs' met with a sour, cynical reaction. In the end we were 'released' – our interrogators reluctantly forced to accept our innocence even if they clearly believed otherwise. It was obvious that the RAF police were wholly unconvinced. I was also made aware that the record of our experience would not be expunged from personal files. Nor was it.

It did not, fortunately, prevent me from continuing to help win the war but I am quite certain that the stamp of 'Communist sympathiser' or 'Politically dubious character', or even 'troublemaker' or whatever, remained engraved on my personal record from that moment. I spent little time worrying about the incident, although from time to time there were odd experiences to remind me that my file had not been lost. It became apparent again when I was first recommended for an RAF commission. What could one do but simply shrug and hope that, eventually, some sense would dawn on the limited imagination of official bureaucracy.

My prewar reading and political studies led me inescapably to Marx. I began reading old Karl when my only readily available reading space was the back room of those two bug-ridden rooms in Camden Town. I started absorbing Marx via a Lawrence & Wishart edition of his selected works published in 1938. I would read for long hours under a flickering 60-Watt bulb attached to a wire that stretched from a socket in the next room. That was as far as our modern lighting facility allowed. My mother regarded my reading habits with a tolerant despair; she felt I would be much better off going to the local cinema or even mating with some young bird – though she never to my recall ever actually suggested that. But she was patiently non-interfering and certainly disinterested in the subject matter of my reading. 'You're always reading that political stuff,' she would protest without really inquiring further. So came my intellectual grounding in Marxism supplemented and made coherent by Laski's lectures at LSE, where I was attending as an external student.

After demobilisation it was an altogether different story. As a member of the St Pancras branch of the Communist Party I then began to rub shoulders, and arguments, with the like of Andrew Rothstein, Robin Page Arnot, Margot Heinemann, Betty England and Yvonne Kapp, all members of that extraordinary St Pancras branch. It was even more extraordinary than I realised at the time. Having tasted that ambience and political ferment I can, at this distance, imagine what it might have been like in the Smolny Institute in 1917! The strategic discussions on how the British Communist Party might assume power and begin to reshape the social order were the norm in that St Pancras epoch.

From this distance in time it all seems like tragi-comedy. But it was deadly serious stuff in those days. Later when my wife Margit also joined the party and we moved to the Hornsey branch it didn't contain such an array of Marxist stars, nor the ebullience of St Pancras in the 1940s, but perhaps made up for that by having that Archdeacon of the British Communists, Ranji Palme Dutt, in its ranks. Not that he regularly attended branch meetings; in fact, I think I recall him attending only one meeting in my presence. He was regarded as a kind of sacred figure, removed from day-to-day events of party activities and remote from the ordinary comrades. Perhaps it was as well since he was also renowned for his stiff, stern intellectual orthodoxy and a refusal to countenance anything that may have fringed on criticism of Soviet orthodoxy.

My first real brush with the party activists followed a visit to Czechoslovakia with Margit shortly after the death of Jan Masaryk. We were in Prague at the time of Tito's break with Moscow, and the Czech press naturally gave Tito's apostasy the full blast of Stalin's contempt. For myself I felt drawn to Tito's critique of Moscow, and on our return from Prague voiced my concern at a branch meeting in Hornsey. I coupled this with several other critical remarks about the behaviour of the political police in Czechoslovakia. It need hardly be said that this did not go down well with my party comrades in Hornsey. Then came another incident that did my popularity star no good at all. I had the audacity to criticise the aerial 'buzzing' of an RAF patrol over Berlin by a Soviet 'plane. That was *before* the blockade of Berlin – though clearly part of the preliminaries.

The problem was that I had begun to have my doubts about the purity of the Soviet line and the incorruptibility of various aspects of party policy. The reluctance to discuss these aspects even in private, let alone in public debate, was profoundly disturbing to me. Our close friends in the Hornsey party were generous with their sympathy and understanding but careful not to commit themselves to my implied heresies. It was becoming clear that I was not regarded as a 'sound' party member. My basic case was pretty clear and straightforward. I was arguing for greater openness and honesty about what was happening in Eastern Europe. I suggested, to their consternation, that we should be quite open in admitting that the development of socialism required the use of social discipline and even some force to protect the frontiers of socialism. It was rough and tough but that was the brutal truth of Cold War politics. I argued that the socialist countries clearly felt compelled to use unpleasant, unattractive measures to protect their political development against the intrigues of powerful anti-socialist forces promoted, without doubt, principally by the United States. In short, why shouldn't we, as political adults, discuss and debate the realities rather than hide behind clichés and slogans?

But, alas, all this was seen either as political naivete or, still worse, deliberately courting political explosions. I found very few party members who were prepared to put their heads above the parapet, even though some of my friends privately admitted the validity of many of my points. Moreover when I argued that even allowing for the obvious provocations from the United States, the launching of the Cold War and the depth of anti-Soviet propaganda throughout the western camp – allowing for all this, surely there was strength in recognising the need to criticise our 'own side' where we believed such criticism was justified. The response usually was a flat rejection on the grounds that any criticism of Soviet policy by British Communists would simply strengthen the proponents of the Cold War, weaken the Soviets and do no good at all. I refused to accept this, though I did recognise the force of their argument.

My personal political crisis came to a head shortly before Stalin's death in 1953. The Kremlin produced the notorious allegation that Stalin's life had been put in jeopardy by a 'Jewish doctors' plot'. It sounded like nonsense to me. Something very odd was clearly happening in Moscow, and I knew that a moment of terrible decision had arrived. I discussed it with Margit and told her that I could not accept the story about the Jewish doctors. I was aware that Professor Hyman Levy, one of the outstanding minds in the British party, had been to Moscow with Johnny Campbell, the editor of the *Daily*

Worker, someone I knew and greatly admired. They sought an explanation of what was going on, especially regarding treatment of the Jews in the Soviet Union, but had come away from Moscow with nothing. Indeed, it emerged later that they had been treated with contempt.

So I reached the climax in my break with the British Communist Party. It came with a meeting with Peter Kerrigan, then national membership organiser of the party, a member of the party executive and one of its half-dozen top figures. I knew and liked Peter very much. His huge, boxer-like frame carried an air of physical menace, yet it concealed a generous and caring nature, a wonderful humour and a devoted comradely spirit. Peter and I met by arrangement one evening in a Camden Town pub, the Mother Redcap (long ago renamed of course). His mission was to try to persuade me of my errors, to reassure me about the party and to quell the doubts. I explained my views and didn't dismiss any of the arguments as 'rubbish' or anything like that. He listened carefully to my own anxieties and frequently nodded agreement. I was surprised by his concurrence, indeed a bit puzzled.

Then Peter put his cards on the table. He said he agreed with a good deal of my criticisms but, in terms of *Realpolitik* they were beside the point. There was no way the British party could publicly criticise Soviet policy without undermining its own credibility as a political force in Britain. If the Communist Party were to take such an openly critical line then it would be seen as an independent force, outside the Soviet sphere, perhaps even agreeing with Tito; that would destroy its effectiveness as a force separate from the Labour Party. It would simply become another wing of the Labour Party and ultimately levered into an anti-Soviet position. Kerrigan regarded my arguments as wholly unrealistic. Moreover, Peter went on, 'if you leave the party you'll never find another political movement that will satisfy you. And I will tell you something else ...' he continued, but without any menace in his tone, 'You will lose your political sheet anchor'.

Of course, he was correct. What he meant was that I would lose my sense of political certainty. Once out of the 'church' of absolute belief no other certainty would ever suffice as a substitute. That was his most telling and profound observation, and one I was unable to contest. Peter did not seek to contradict my criticisms of Soviet policy nor my premature doubts about Stalin's sanity. His answer was that the Soviet leadership 'probably have their reasons', though he was intelligent enough to know that this was an inadequate answer. But

Peter was the total loyalist. His allegiance to the party was absolute. He had fought in Spain alongside names that were, and remain, heroic in the hall of honour from that terrible civil war. Even so he was far too honest to brush aside my criticisms of Moscow. Indeed, in the final moments of our memorable dialogue that night, Peter admitted to me that he, too, frequently despaired of the Soviet line, and indeed the responses to that line from some of his comrades in the hierarchy of the British party. No names were ever mentioned. He left that to my own imagination.

Peter could see that I had made up my mind. We had another whisky. His huge shoulders lifted and fell with the resolve of sad resignation. 'Ach,' he offered as a kind of final appeal, 'we've got to accept the bad with the good. It's never going to be smooth or perfect. Nothing ever is, nowhere. Never has been. Never will be. Don't you think?' he looked at me with a final quizzical challenge. I stared back at big Peter and paused. His large expressive eyes, the shock of closely trimmed grey hair, the huge frame; it all seemed to come together in an appeal, rather than a demand, for my support. He needed that for himself more than for me. He had used the crucial argument about my needing the anchorage of the party. It was an ace card – but it had failed to trump my doubts. We parted with a handshake as firm as any I can ever remember. 'I'm always around if you need me for any help,' he offered as a parting condition of friendship if not future comradeship.

Peter was a fine man; as fine an example of the best in the human material of socialism as I ever had any dealings with. Like Johnny Campbell, I felt then, and in retrospect still feel, that it was people like them who made me feel justified in being a Communist. I felt deeply wounded inside my own mind and body at being unable to comply with Peter's persuasiveness. I knew I had lost something that I might never again possess – that certainty of knowing the solution to the problems facing all of us in the future; the comfort of belonging to that special Brotherhood of the Faith. It was like leaving the security of the big ocean liner and fumbling down the rope ladder into a small, individually navigated rowing boat. Peter, of course, knew his message would strike precisely that chord.

Many people who have left the Communist Party over the last fifty, sixty, seventy years tell a similar story. The isolation, political loneliness, spiritual void is as omnipresent as leaving the womb of the church. Perhaps that is one reason why so many former Communists then embrace the Roman Catholic Church. Or they will sometimes explode in a frenzy of *mea culpa* confessions. I was attracted to neither. Kerrigan knew the force of his argument about the 'sheet anchor'. Those who have never experienced the power of such commitment cannot really grasp the nature of the psychological problem.

But I knew I could no longer accept the blind allegiance required by membership of the Communist Party; the assumption that, despite all evidence to the contrary, the party had to remain above reproof, beyond doubt, and outside one's critical faculties. To remain a socialist, certainly a Marxist, demanded not blind allegiance but a constantly expanding ability and capacity to try to understand and certainly to criticise the astonishing changes taking place in our world. That, surely, was the essence of what Marx was saying and writing throughout his lifetime. How could anyone describing themselves as a socialist reach any other view?

That was, indeed remains, my position. Without that political life has no substance. It becomes slavery to blind belief and self-delusion. Which no doubt is why the party of ex-Communists must rank as one of the largest political groupings in the world! So my journey in journalism continued – in a kind of liberated condition, unclamped from the old iron code, released from a fixed star. I was a reporter at large, without a sheet anchor. Sometime later I joined the Labour Party.

* * *

Of course I had already been through various phases in Fleet Street when I broke with the Communist Party; after the *Manchester Guardian* came a brief period with the *Liverpool Daily Post* as a leader writer, followed by short spells with the *Daily Mirror*, the *Sunday Express* and the *Evening Standard* before getting the job I had long aimed for – a reporting role with the *News Chronicle*. I joined the *NC* early in 1949 just after Robin Cruickshank had taken over the editorship from the great Gerald Barry, who had been seconded by Herbert Morrison to take charge of preparing the 1951 Festival of Britain. It was a magical moment for me, despite being in such a minor position, to be joining a team of outstanding *News Chronicle* journalists, which constituted as fine a team of writers as ever assembled under one editorial roof in Fleet Street in the twentieth century.

And in my experience no national daily paper has ever matched the *News Chronicle* in being able to contain the qualities of a great national newspaper, which, despite all its failings and frailties, was able to offer its readers an exceptional range of oustanding reporting, brilliant feature writing and radical independent views. Of course, it lacked the financial resources of the Beaverbrook or Rothermere press; it often dithered and hesitated when it ought to have shot from the hip; it suffered all the disadvantages of being in the middle ground of politics and journalism – it stood to be kicked from both sides. But by the sheer quality of its journalism that newspaper managed to overcome most of those handicaps; most, that is, except one – it finally fell under the control of Laurence Cadbury, the last of the Cadbury dynasty to run the paper. Sadly, he simply didn't have the nerve or the commitment to continue the fight for its independent existence. He sold it off to – of all groups – the House of Rothermere, to be incorporated within the *Daily Mail* from October 1960. No national daily newspaper has ever filled the gap vacated by the death of the *News Chronicle*.

When I joined the *News Chronicle* the outgoing editor Gerald Barry (who was subsequently knighted) had established a remarkable reputation for the paper. When he took over the editorship in 1936 from Aylmer Vallance, Barry had already been features editor for two years. He was effectively in charge of the paper's direction and policy throughout the crucial years of the 1930s during which it was Barry who campaigned against the rise of fascism in Europe, and Britain, and took the paper famously against Franco in the Spanish Civil War when Arthur Koestler was one of the *News Chronicle*'s correspondents in Spain along with Willie Forrest and Geoffrey Cox. It was Barry who sent A.J. Cummings to the Reichstag trial in Leipzig where Dimitrov was under sentence of death by the Nazis, accused of plotting the fire, and to the astonishing Soviet trials of the 1930s. Cummings' reporting from that period remains among the examples of epic journalism of the 1930s. Gerald Barry conducted the paper throughout the war and into the 1945 election campaign. But the tensions between him and the paper's chairman, Walter Layton (later Lord Layton) became increasingly explosive. Layton, the Liberal, was frequently at odds with Barry's more left-wing radicalism. In 1947 the tensions erupted and Barry resigned because of Layton's persistent interference.

Barry's successor was Robin Cruickshank, whose real name was Robert James Cruickshank but who preferred to be known as 'Robin' to all his colleagues. Robin was a careful, cautious, gentle, highly sensitive journalist who made his reputation as the paper's correspondent in the United States in the mid-1930s during the rise of Roosevelt. He was a marvellously considerate editor to work under, but, as with Barry, hampered severely by the interference and penny-pinching of both Layton and subsequently Laurence Cadbury. Cruickshank didn't possess Barry's vigour and creative aggressive-ness, which meant he was an easier, if terribly pained, victim for Layton and Cadbury. By 1954 Cruickshank's health wilted under the stress and he resigned. It was not only a grievous loss to the newspaper but probably the end of the *News Chronicle* as an independent entity.

From that moment until October 1960, when it collapsed into the arms of the *Daily Mail*, there was an unending struggle to keep the paper alive and commercially viable. The Cadburys – at least in the shape of Laurence – simply refused to invest sufficiently and as the circulation dipped in the late 1950s a variety of editorial techniques were tried, along with new executives, only to produce an ambivalence in terms of content and policy. As a commercial operation the *News Chronicle* developed a severe limp. Yet, the paradox was that as a journalistic product it remained an outstanding paper full of brilliant reporting, features and columnists including names like Ian Mackay, Robert Lynd, Percy Cudlipp and still with Arthur John Cummings to cast his unmatched eye of experience across the globe. The names of James Cameron, Ritchie Calder, Willie Forrest and Geoffrey Cox have to be added to that cast list. And there was Vicky, after David Low probably the greatest satirical cartoonist of the century. I can only repeat: no newspaper I have ever worked on encapsulated, under one editorial canvas, so much ability and quality at any one moment.

When I joined the paper at the end of the Barry regime this was the orchestral symphony of journalistic excellence that played on my mind. It was also an exciting time to be involved in domestic journalism. Much was happening abroad, to be sure, and I was tempted to make a bee-line for a job in Germany or somewhere in Europe to report on events. But at home the scene was still more exciting – or so it seemed to me. It was a period when the Attlee Government was still in its learning curve; when the foundations for the 'New' postwar Britain (note: the word 'New' is one of the oldest in the book) were being laid down. The great industries were being taken into public ownership – coal, railways, electricity, gas. The Bank of England had been 'nationalised' – whatever that may have meant; the National Health Service was set up by Nye Bevan in 1948; the National Insurance Act created the nerve centre for the Welfare State; roads, schools, houses, hospitals, even New Towns were being built. The country was buzzing with movement and political argument. The Conservative Party, still led by the postwar version of Winston Churchill – a somewhat different figure compared with his wartime grandeur – were desperately trying to find a new platform of protest.

This was the ambience of the period and I was drawn to reporting that scene. Or perhaps I should describe it as a drift toward that focus. Drift is the selected phrase because though I began at the *News Chronicle* as a general news reporter I quickly found myself reporting strikes and various social disputes. There were a lot of them at the time. I worked briefly in the lobby as a young assistant political reporter to Geoffrey Cox, who was the paper's chief political correspondent (they didn't refer to them as 'Lobby' correspondents then, and certainly not as 'Political Editors'). I went to my first Labour Party conference as Cox's assistant in 1949 and tried to report Ernest Bevin, then still Foreign Secretary. But my shorthand couldn't cope with Bevin's sentences, which went on like a Wagnerian opera without pause, without punctuation and with his gravelly Bristolian dialect defying my then quite useful shorthand. I reported Nehru's visit to London; I often reported on Winston growling away. Almost by chance I was acquiring a reputation as a political reporter. Then came a switch to industrial reporting alongside Ian Mackay and Margaret Stewart, the principal industrial correspondents of the paper. Mackay had more or less relinquished the role to Maggie Stewart to allow him to concentrate on his twice-weekly columns, which had already established him as the oustanding essayist of Fleet Street.

Again it was all by chance. I was asked to cover one of the big dock strikes in 1949 and did rather well. Robin Cruickshank sent me little handwritten notes of congratulation on my reporting. No doubt he saw it as reasonable encouragement for a young reporter. For me it was a tremendous accolade. And since there were numerous dock strikes around that time – one particularly bloody and brutal one concerned Canadian seamen on a strike-bound ship in London – I began to establish myself as an 'expert' on the industrial scene in dockland. Cruickshank did nothing to discourage this; quite the contrary, since he would have me brief him personally on the various social intricacies of life in London's dockland. In fact he wanted me to occupy more space in the paper than was feasible. It did my ego no damage at all.

So it was an especially sad day for me when Robin's early retirement was announced. His place was taken by Michael Curtis, an able young man who had been chief leader writer and who, clearly, had been selected by Laurence Cadbury for his malleability. Michael was a man of principle – but not of an aggressive, radical nature. He was a kind of younger version of Robin albeit without the experience and sagacity. Yet he did have some remarkably bold and unorthodox views – such as refusing to have first editions of the other morning papers brought into the office at midnight in case they weakened the resolve of the 'back bench' (the main production centre of a newspaper) about the selection of stories for the *News Chronicle*'s front page. That required a great deal of courage; but Curtis persisted with his policy for some time until gradually it broke down under the sheer weight of circumstances – by which I mean internal argument when the paper missed out on some big stories, an inescapable price one pays for that kind of independence. But he was right to try the experiment and many years later it was attempted again by the newly launched *Independent* – though I have the feeling that their experiment was even shorter-lived than Curtis's move.

The struggle to keep the *News Chronicle* independent and commercially afloat in the end proved too much for Michael Curtis as well, and two years before the paper finally folded into the maw of the *Daily Mail* Curtis departed to become the adviser to the Aga Khan's various enterprises including a newspaper in Kenya. His place was filled by Norman Cursley, a veteran *News Chronicle* man who had started in the Manchester office of the paper prewar and who became an assistant editor in London in 1951. He was another kindly, generous spirit – but quite incapable of preventing the ultimate fate. His brief span as the paper's last editor was a melancholic experience for him and for all the journalists still clinging to the sinking ship.

I left shortly after Cursley became editor to join the *Daily Herald* as industrial editor, and my main reason for doing so was a private conversation I had with Michael Curtis before he departed. When Curtis heard that I had been offered a job with the *Herald* he privately advised me to 'snap it up' and in great confidence told me what, in his opinion, was certain to happen at the *Chronicle*. 'Don't hang around,' he advised, 'there's no future here – which is why I am going. I don't know what Laurence Cadbury is up to but I suspect the worst.' He had no need to spell it out further.

But chance had again come to my assistance. As Gore Vidal observes in his *Palimpsest* autobiography, 'Before the cards that one is dealt by life are the cards that fate has dealt.' How true.

I hated leaving the *News Chronicle*, and I was certainly not over-enthused by the prospect of joing the *Daily Herald* despite its rejuvenation and increasing independence from the chains of the TUC, which had so limited its development as a national paper trying to compete with the big guns like the *Daily Express*, *Mirror*, or even the dear old *News Chronicle*. The ideal solution for the *Herald* and *News Chronicle* would have been a merger – which was actually discussed at one stage in the 1950s but came to nothing largely because of objections from Lord Layton and Laurence Cadbury. Still, the offer from the *Herald* coupled with Curtis's warnings made the opportunity something I could not turn down. I joined the paper in time to cover the 1959 General Election with the special assignment of accompanying Aneurin Bevan on his nationwide election tour. It was an experience I shall never forget and eclipsed any regrets I may earlier have harboured about joining the *Daily Herald*.

6 Aneurin Bevan: From NHS to The Bomb

I first met Aneurin Bevan in my early days as a *News Chronicle* reporter. It was shortly after his launch of the National Health Service. The scene was the St Pancras Town Hall, improbable maybe but a place of some esteem and distinction even in the late 1940s. And indeed why not? After all George Bernard Shaw was once a St Pancras Vestryman, as he reminded me on one of his famous pink postcards, which I was privileged to receive from his acerbic hand on one occasion.

Bevan was addressing a conference of doctors many of whom retained strong doubts, and resentments, about his NHS. The opposition to the concept of universal free medicine was deeply ingrained in the medical profession regardless of the encourgement they had received from the British Medical Association. The Minister of Health – the secretary of state logo had not then been fashioned – did not like journalists. We knew that. I was all too well aware of the risks involved in reporting Aneurin Bevan. His distrust of newspapermen – we are still talking of the pre-television era – was borne out of the fury unleashed on him by most of the Conservative press – which meant the majority of national and regional daily papers, and even by some of the otherwise pro-Labour press like the *Daily Herald, Daily Mirror* and a few lesser lights.

The pro-Labour newspapers were not averse to sniping at Bevan because of his radicalism and what they regarded as his intemperate language. Yet there was no sense of a beleaguered Health Minister standing on that platform in the conference hall of St Pancras. He was flushed with pride and achievement at what was already perceived as a revolution in the nation's health services. Nor was he aggressive. He charmed the doctors as, previously, he had charmed the consultants whose arrogance Bevan subdued by sheer competence in the handling of their problems, assumed or real.

Of course he derided his critics in Parliament and the press. To Bevan the National Health Service was a sacred symbol of something even larger than the concept itself; it was his idea of socialism in daily practice. Bevan never minimised the problems that would arise in the future. That would have been out of character. He was never a politician to gloss over the realities or the difficulties whatever the subject. But for him the NHS was the fulfilment of an ambition he first conceived as a young councillor in his native South Wales town of Tredegar.

He had no illusions about the countless problems ahead. He told the doctors on that occasion: 'We are on the footpath to the future ... and that future lies very much in your hands, not mine.' His vision of that future was a Health Service at the core of a caring, civilised, compassionate society. He spread out his ideas for the design of hospitals, of how wards should be regulated and surgery facilities improved; he urged a new relationship between doctors and their patients and reminded patients that they, too, had responsibilities to help make the system succeed; he spoke of the nature, and problems, of funding and the role of government; the need to enhance the status of nurses; to harness modern science and technology to help cure lethal diseases like cancer. It was a remarkable tour de force, especially as we are referring to a speech nearly a half-century ago. I can still picture Bevan on that St Pancras stage – flicking back the slick of hair that fell, persistently, across his brow; pausing, standing silent for a fragment and then gently bending forward toward the microphone as if to caress it with his soft, high-pitched words, a faint smile lighting up his face as he ridiculed a chosen critic.

Bevan left that meeting at St Pancras Town Hall by a side door. I spotted this and moved to waylay him as he left to a waiting car. He was wearing a Basque beret, a favourite and familiar headgear of his at the time, as I stepped in front.

'Mr. Bevan,' I began hesitantly, 'can I ask you a few questions?'

He looked at me askance. I sensed a message going through his mind – 'Who the hell is this? Another of those bloody young vulturous reporters'.

'Come on then,' he demanded impatiently. 'Who're you from?'

'*News Chronicle*, Minister.'

'Ah, well boy, it's not a bad paper as bad papers go ... what do you want to know?'

He had softened. It was far from an unfriendly encounter. There began a long association, which developed into a warm friendship.

No journalist, it is rightly said, should ever become too closely friendly with his subject; that can be seriously corrupting if it is genuine. So be it. I made the error once or twice and have had no reason to regret it. In the case of Aneurin Bevan I still regard 'the error' as a privilege. If, in the course of time, it made me a lesser journalist then that is a price I have no regrets in having paid.

*   *   *

The St Pancras 'incident' was the starting point to an extending range of contacts I had with Bevan, helped on, without doubt, by my friendship with Michael Foot, who at the time was editing *Tribune*, the left-wing weekly that Bevan helped to launch in 1937. At the time I was writing anonymously in *Tribune* while working for the *News Chronicle*, and my contact with Michael was fairly regular. We would meet in The George tavern opposite the law courts and close by *Tribune*'s old office at 222, The Strand, famous for once housing Bevan, Orwell, Foot, Jennie Lee *et al.* all under one roof, talking at the same time.

At one of those meetings, in The George, Michael came in looking rather crestfallen and uncharacteristically morose. He had just had the first of what was to become a catalogue of terrible conflicts with Nye Bevan over nuclear disarmament. Michael trooped into the pub where I was with Ian Aitken, then on Beaverbrook's *Daily Express*. Michael confided to both of us that there had been a hell of a bust-up at the *Tribune* editorial board meeting over The Bomb. He gave us a blow-by-blow account, and both Ian and myself published the story in our respective newspapers; both the *Express* and the *Chronicle* ran it big on page one.

Bevan and Jennie Lee were outraged. Michael came under even greater pressure from them – most of all because he admitted 'leaking' the story to Ian and myself. Nor did he try to pass on any of the responsibility to us. Michael defended our right, as journalists, to report what he had told us. It was an act of exceptional courage and loyalty to one set of his friends against his devotion to another set. Both Ian Aitken and I felt deeply guilty at having landed Michael Foot in such a predicament and we sought to apologise. But Michael, being the extraordinary fellow he is and always has been, simply waved aside our guilt. He took the full blast and the blame.

Oddly enough, the incident, which might easily have wrecked any prospect of a trusting friendship with Nye and Jennie – especially Jennie – did no such thing. It was never referred to again by any of the people involved, which, I suppose, says everything for the kind of bond that existed between that group of remarkable *Tribune* people.

Before I left the *News Chronicle* for the *Daily Herald* there was one further experience with Michael and Nye that should be recounted. It was in the mid-1950s when Bevan was – again – almost expelled from the Labour Party during his battle with Gaitskell, and in particular his campaign to oppose the rearming of West Germany. Bevan and his supporters organised a campaign to win support from rank and file trade unionists, and especially his own union, the National Union of Mineworkers. It started with a mass rally in Manchester, which received powerful press coverage. I went up to Manchester to report the rally – and travelled with Bevan and Michael Foot, at Michael's invitation. The three of us were uninterrupted for nearly four hours – the time it then took from London to Manchester (and often still does) – as we discussed the entire political agenda.

To describe that journey as an epic experience in political education would be to understate the occasion. But I think it enabled me to enter the mind of Bevan in a unique way. It always remained as a kind of dramatic backcloth to all my subsequent dealings with Nye. It certainly enabled me better to understand and come to grips with the long fight he had waged inside the Labour Party and the power of intrigue webbed around those who opposed him, hated his views and most of all were deeply envious of his extraordinary gift as an orator and political thinker.

*   *   *

It is frankly impossible to go further in this saga without involving the great issue of The Bomb. For the latter five years of Bevan's life, years in which I became closer to him, the question that overshadowed every other was nuclear disarmament. It impinged on all other issues, in domestic as well as foreign policy. The Suez debacle and the Soviet invasion of Hungary combined to sharpen everything on the international agenda. Macmillan followed Eden into Downing Street; the United States' defence budget escalated and the American finger twitched nervously on the trigger as even President Eisenhower worried about the 'military–industrial' complex running the United States. Khrushchev banged the drum, or rather the rostrum dais, with his shoe and bellowed defiance in irreverant Russian. The atmosphere was not a happy one.

I had become engaged in the Campaign for Nuclear Disarmament at a fairly early point. A number of journalists on the *News Chronicle* were involved from the inception – notably Ritchie Calder, the paper's science editor; Vicky, the outstanding cartoonist, and, of course, James Cameron. They were all Aldermaston marchers. Ritchie was indeed a pioneer and very much a leading light behind the original meeting that launched CND in the study of the Dean of St Pauls, Canon John Collins. Ritchie (later Lord Calder) had been alerting audiences to the dangers of nuclear arms from the early 1950s. He used his articles in the paper consistently to draw attention to the growing menace of what he regarded as an uncontrollable threat to mankind. He was not a pacifist but he was among the first in Britain to recognise the threat to the future of all life on the planet.

The *News Chronicle* under Robin Cruickshank never committed itself to nuclear disarmament, but the paper gave space to Calder, and Cruickshank himself was considerably influenced by Calder's argument. It was one factor behind the growing bond between the paper and people outside like Michael Foot at *Tribune*. Foot was then temporarily out of the House of Commons, having lost his Plymouth Devonport seat in the 1955 General Election and was not yet the MP for Ebbw Vale.

Calder had an interesting background record in his experiences with the atom. As a young reporter in the 1930s, in fact then working for the prewar *Daily Herald*, he had interviewed Rutherford at Cambridge when the great man split the atom. That experience turned the young reporter from Dundee into a science addict. It also fortified his conviction that humanitarian values must take precedence over the use of scientific discovery. That was always the emphasis he put on his contributions at public meetings – such as the one I organised for him in the mid-1950s in Southgate, North London which packed to the doors a hall in that middle-class traditional Tory constituency.

Came the 1957 Labour Party conference at Brighton. I was there as the *News Chronicle*'s industrial correspondent. The tradition then was for industrial reporters to take precedence over political cor-respondents at the Labour conference – as distinct from the Liberal and Conservative conferences – because of the influence of the trade unions and their block votes. The lobbying of pre-conference party executive meetings – the executive was then a very powerful body with the trade union members holding the key positions – was the domain of the industrial reporters. So we knew about the extra-ordinary battles going on inside the executive about nuclear disarmament; we knew that the left-wing members were demanding a commitment from Nye Bevan, then Foreign Affairs spokesman, to support CND. He refused to give that pledge and indeed shocked his friends and allies on the executive by moderating his opposition to The Bomb. The weekend newspapers were full of sensational stories about Labour's 'split'. The entire left wing of the party was in disarray. The great debate on The Bomb was scheduled for Wednesday.

Bevan and Jennie Lee had just returned from a visit to the Soviet Union where they had been holiday guests of Khrushchev. Bevan had returned convinced that it would be a grave error of judgement for any Labour Foreign Secretary – as he anticipated he could well be within two years – to commit himself to unilateral nuclear disarmament.

Twenty-four hours before the Brighton conference was scheduled to debate The Bomb, I was strolling outside the conference hall and saw Nye. He beckoned me and suggested a walk on the promenade. For about forty minutes we walked and talked – one to one – about his visit to the Soviet Union. I still have the notes I made afterwards. Bevan emphasised how impressed he had been with Khrushchev's grasp of world affairs and especially his understanding of the British Labour Party position. Bevan told me that he was convinced that the Soviet Union was in a state of slow but relentless change. Remember, we are describing a situation circa 1957. Bevan's prophecy was that the whole Soviet system would continue to change, perhaps even transform, for the next two decades before it settled down to some stability. He even predicted a turbulent period of great political unrest and a slow retreat, painfully, toward a more democratic outgoing society.

It was impossible, he went on, to be clear about how this might develop, and the turmoil it would almost certainly create not only within the Soviet system but also with the East European Communist satellite countries. In the meantime he was persuaded that the Soviet policy was not based on aggression. The truth is, he told me as we walked along Brighton front, that the Soviets were still fearful of the west, especially the United States. Khrushchev admitted to him that the country was still economically backward in many areas – though not in some spheres where, in Bevan's view, they were remarkably advanced (he meant in space technology etc.). It was all a great paradox.

So we got round to the Brighton conference debate on The Bomb. 'We cannot simply turn our back on the whole world scene,' he recited to me. 'That is what the support for unilateralism would mean, make no mistake.' He could not, would not, accept such a simplistic solution. Unilateral renunciation would be irresponsible, he went on. And he stressed that this was his view not because he happened to be Shadow Foreign Secretary – 'that might be transitory in any case', he reflected – but because he was convinced from his discussions with Khrushchev that such a renunciation would leave an incoming Labour government 'impotent to influence events'. Bevan's great anxiety was that he needed negotiating strength to deal with the Americans – not the Russians.

That is why the issue of The Bomb was never, for him, a purely moral question. It all hinged on the practicalities of power. For that reason it was quite wrong to assume that 'negotiating from strength' was necessarily focused *against* the Russians; it was vital for Britain to have a strength, however marginal, to negotiate with the Americans. One phrase that Nye did *not* rehearse as we walked that afternoon – and clearly it was a rehearsal, something he often practised on his friends and intimates before a major speech – was his famous maxim about not sending him 'naked into the conference chamber'. I suspect that phrase was still lurking in his mind, no doubt having been planted as a seed during the previous weekend (some claim by Sam Watson, the shrewd, influential, right-wing Durham miners' leader with whom Nye had a long-standing friendship reaching back to Watson's left-wing days in the 1930s).

Possibly. Yet more likely that Bevan himself toyed with the phrase after picking up the basic message, perhaps from Watson. Whatever the truth, the fact remains that this phrase has echoed down the corridors of time as one of Bevan's most notable, if maybe perplexing, contributions in his catalogue of oratory.

After his Brighton speech against unilateralism his followers were overwhelmed by depression. Vicky, I recall that evening, was in tears and beyond words as he reached for his sketch pad. Jimmy Cameron stared into the middle distance with a vacant puzzlement. Michael Foot tried to escape notice and suffer in a silent corner as if bereaved. Some years later Cameron reviewing Foot's biography of Aneurin Bevan for the London *Evening Standard* (1973), wrote about that moment in Brighton sixteen years earlier:

> It seemed at that moment the most awful of betrayals and Michael Foot knows it. Nye Bevan believed he had been cruelly misunder-stood even traduced. Vicky's cartoon that week was simply a drawing of Gandhi: 'I went naked into the Conference Chamber.

Many friendships were broken in those days ... but that is long ago and far away'.

But not too far away to indulge in some further reflection. The truth is that Bevan was right. He was certainly not being opportunist as so many of his critics, and even some friends, thought at the time. He always disdained the moral purist in politics. 'If you want to behave like a monk, then go live in a monastery', as he was fond of pointing out. He could no more have dodged the challenge thrown down in that 1957 conference than to have ducked out a fight with Hugh Gaitskell over prescription charges in 1951 – the issue on which he resigned from the Attlee Government. His chemistry could not have allowed that. He was the least calculating of all the major Labour leaders – otherwise he would have led the party and no doubt become Prime Minister. But by the same token he was the most impatient, intolerant, pugnacious. Defects that cost him a popularity that might in different circumstances have made him unchallengeable as a political leader.

But Bevan recognised the futility of an emotional posture that lacked a foundation of political realism. Of course he was attracted to the moral glow of unilateralism that swept the country in the later 1950s. He could sense its force because his own deep emotional impulses were drawn from similar sources – a reaction against the forces of evil. But he had the courage as well as the wisdom at that moment to understand that it would have been politically naive for Britain, in a one-off symbolic gesture, to cry 'Stop'. It may well have been the case that at some point in the 1950s, perhaps even as late as 1960, that a declaration of unilateral intent might have provided a powerful influence in persuading the Super-powers to limit the development of nuclear armouries – but that had to await Reagan and Gorbachev.

There are moments in history when it becomes politically feasible to act upon ideas that have been under discussion and debate for decades. But what is not possible is to impose the future on the present. Bevan saw that. In retrospect what might possibly have been achieved in that period was to have influenced secondary powers against becoming involved in the nuclear arms race. Today it is perfectly possible for any country – or indeed any group of terrorists – to manufacture nuclear weapons. Proliferation lives with us as a permanent menace, now virtually impossible to tame, let alone eradicate.

The unilateral argument appeared to be a powerfully persuasive one forty years ago to people like myself – not least because we believed, however naively, that Britain was still capable of offering a moral lead to the world; a moral and political lead combined against the spread of the nuclear demon. As a matter of fact there was one small contribution at the time to a greater sanity: it prompted the Prime Minister, Harold Macmillan, seriously to move toward a nuclear test ban. Macmillan confessed as much in his own memoirs. He admitted that the CND campaign swayed him in that direction and, paradoxically, it was a speech by Nye Bevan (June 1957) that Macmillan found particularly influencing as he sought to bring the Americans and Soviets to a test-ban treaty. Such are the paradoxes of history.

*   *   *

In that glorious Indian summer of 1959's autumn I had just moved across to the *Daily Herald* to participate in the paper's new image of 'independence' from its old policy masters, the TUC. This was a further attempt by the *Herald* management, Odhams Press, to shore up a falling circulation as well as a declining political attraction. The committed party-political daily newspaper was no longer a commercial success and the TUC, along with the Labour Party, recognised that as a serious handicap to the future of the newspaper. The competitive market was hotting up and a new circulation war had broken out, stimulated largely by the emergence of commercial television, which started to change the entire media agenda from 1956.

So it was decided that the *Daily Herald* should break free from its committed chains and more openly reflect changing times. There remained a still substantial TUC link with an agreement that the paper's editorial policy should 'reflect', rather than genuflect to, TUC policy. The theory was that this would enable the paper's journalists to write with a far greater freedom and, perhaps far more to the point, allow the paper's editorial line to be free to criticise both the Labour Party and the TUC. That was the theory. The practice was more complex.

When the new editor, Douglas Machray, an experienced and fine journalist, decided to support the CND campaign all hell broke out. He was quickly summoned to see Hugh Gaitskell and an assorted group of Labour and TUC leaders to explain his conduct. Machray was given 'Star Chamber' treatment and even accused of being a pacifist. He turned to Gaitskell, pulled from his pocket a bar of war medals and chucked them on the table in front of the Labour leader.

'Pacifist, did you say, Hugh? Now show me your medals.' The meeting broke up shortly after in some disarray. Machray held on to his job – but not for long. He was replaced eventually by John Beavan (the late Lord Ardwick) who was a strong supporter of Gaitskell. Great newspapers have always depended on the courage as well as the creative brilliance of editors rather than proprietors – of the left or the right.

Still, the *Daily Herald* I joined in 1959 stood a better chance of survival than some of its rivals – such as the declining *News Chronicle* whose circulation had by then slipped below one and a quarter million, well below the *Herald*. Fleet Street was a hard war zone then as now, albeit in a different form. The *Daily Mirror* was market leader with a circulation nearing 5 million (which it subsequently exceeded) and was by far the biggest media influence on the Labour vote. Hugh Cudlipp's *Mirror* had already established itself as one of the great daily newspapers in the world, not just in the UK. Lord Beaverbrook's *Daily Express*, the previous market leader and still a great newspaper, selling over 4 million copies a day, was the *Mirror's* great rival; Rupert Murdoch had not yet appeared on the London scene. In fact the Beaverbrook *Express* had the distinction of being read by the widest cross-section in the political spectrum of any national newspaper. No other national morning newspaper has ever been able to match that achievement.

*   *   *

The 1959 General Election was upon us almost as soon as I joined the *Daily Herald*, and it came as no great surprise when Douglas Machray asked me to spend the election with Labour's Shadow Foreign Secretary, and deputy leader, Aneurin Bevan. I invited Nye to lunch at Brown's Hotel to discuss his election programme, which was pretty arduous. I sensed at once that he lacked enthusiasm for the tour; he was uneasy about specific items on the programme but, more telling, he seemed to lack the political energy to fight the campaign. He admitted it to me. 'Oh, but I suppose it'll be OK once we get on the road,' he consoled himself. But he was already showing resentment at the way Gaitskell proposed to contest the campaign. He found it difficult to throw off a sense of defeatism. More significantly, he felt isolated among the party leadership; a lone figure fighting to hold aloft a belief in socialist values and a terrible fear that the cornerstones on which his philosophy was based were being eroded.

We looked through the election schedule. There was a heavy load of London constituencies prepared for his appearance. He hated the London political atmosphere and immediately grumbled about the number of meetings listed for him. 'I shall ask them [Labour election headquarters] to cut down the London list.'

He glanced through the rest: the Midlands, including a visit to Jennie's seat at Cannock; the north-west, parts of the west country, the north, Scotland, and of course, Wales, north and south. He grimaced and finished his whisky.

'OK, boy,' as he usually called me without affectation, 'let's meet next week to finish planning the tour if that's alright with you.'

The great election trek was on. Yet even as we began I had already begun to put a question in my mind about Nye's health. Something seemed wrong. Yet there was no other outward evidence of the illness that was to strike him down a few months later.

The only other sign was mid-way through the campaign when he caught a chill – or at least that is what we assumed. We had just visited Jennie's constituency, where he spoke to a packed meeting with an overflow into an adjoining hall – all his meetings were like that in the 1959 election.

That night, under pressure from Jennie, he agreed that we would return to his home at Ashridge farm. I drove him there in his own car, an ancient Rover, as I had been doing throughout most of the travel. He was not well. He went to bed as soon as we reached the farm, and the next morning when I went to his room he was clearly ill. His temperature was over 100°F and he said he felt weak and exhausted. We called the doctor, who diagnosed 'flu and said he must rest for a few days. This meant changing the schedule and, in particular, cancelling a meeting in Plymouth Devonport where he was due to speak for Michael Foot, who was trying to reclaim his old base. Bevan dreaded letting Michael down. He asked me for advice: should he go to Plymouth regardless? My advice was swift and firm; certainly not. I drafted a note for a telegram to Michael explaining the situation. I then wrote a piece for the *Daily Herald* about Bevan's brief pause in his campaign. As I wrote that piece I remember reflecting: is he really worse than any of us suspect? The omens seemed disturbing.

* * *

I had already spent several evenings talking with Nye about the future of mankind. After the scheduled meetings – often three each evening, or one at midday such as a factory gate visit followed by two in the evening, a punishing round even for a fit person – we would settle down for the night in a local hotel and have a few whiskies. It was then that he would unburden himself. He spoke of his fear that the election would be lost largely because the nation was not being told the truth about the problems nor being offered honest solutions. Yet, paradoxically, he also felt deeply anxious about the problems he might face if Labour were to win the election with Bevan as Foreign Secretary. 'How can I work with Gaitskell?' he repeatedly asked me, though in fact he was asking himself that question. Bevan was contemptuous of the way the Conservatives were fighting the election campaign and what he saw as Macmillan's posturing. But he was also hardly less contemptuous of Labour's election strategy.

His speeches divided into two categories: first was foreign affairs, in which he castigated Conservative Government policy in the Middle East, Cyprus, Africa (especially in Kenya and the then Nyasaland and the Hola camp incident). He ridiculed the Tories' lack of vision, imagination and their inability to recognise that the world of the old British Empire had gone for ever.

His second line of attack was on the UK economy and the need to use the public sector as an instrument of control and influence if full employment was to be preserved and live alongside a policy of anti-inflation. Yet he was always judicious in avoiding any overstatement of his socialism – not least because he knew that would cause as many problems in his relations with Gaitskell as it would tempt the Conservative press to exploit the 'Labour split' syndrome. These pressures were never absent from his mind.

I recall one night in particular after he had spoken at two meetings in Coventry. We were relaxing over a drink in a Coventry hotel, and I asked how he felt the campaign was moving. It touched a raw nerve and he exploded in anger using me as the butt. He was in a strange mood. Tired, quite fatigued by the whole business. His eyes were a curious green/blue and ablaze with a kind of half strange madness that seemed to sear through you in anguished contempt. He behaved like a caged tiger. I had not before seen him in such a mood as he spoke with immense irritation about almost everything. The nightly meetings were plainly a serious burden. That night more than any other occasion provided me with an insight into the raw side of his character; the profile that evoked so much enmity, opposition, serious dislike – as well as devotion. The tiger was wounded, tired, perhaps self-pitying at that moment of absolute stress. It was not an attractive picture. But as psychologists will always explain, it was a far from unusual condition in men of great power or, to put it the other way round, in powerful men of great sensitivity.

In any event, in retrospect it is impossible not to reach the conclusion that Nye already had an instinctive feeling that the end was near. The frustration that was gloomily manifest was not just political frustration; it was a subconscious upheaval against the limits that life itself was now putting on a vivid dream.

Similarly one evening in Llangollen, deep inside his native Wales. A parallel scene after a night of three meetings with a final tour de force at the nearby town of Corwen. We sat sipping the whisky long into the early hours of the morning. The window was open and the autumn air was warm. Outside one could hear the splashing cascade of the river falling over the stones. Nye was in full spate. Again he spoke of his dread at the prospect of going to the Foreign Office and working within the ambience of a Gaitskell-led government. The task facing an incoming Labour government would be enormous. He began to express serious doubts about whether he could stand the stress and strain of fighting the Foreign Office Establishment. His radicalism might prove too much – unless he had the backing of Gaitskell – and that would be questionable. Bevan wanted to reorganise the whole diplomatic service and refocus British foreign policy away from its past agenda on to the future in a dramatically changing world.

His ideas on this were indeed reflected in a tremendous piece of oratorical flourish at the Corwen meeting earlier that evening. It was an audience predominantly of Welsh-speakers – but Nye could speak only a few words of his native language. This did not prevent him producing a brilliant speech about his socialist values and the ethics of his political religion. He spoke about Britain living in a shrinking world; of technology and the rapid march of instant communications; of the complexities facing all politicians trying to work in a political and social climate of ever-widening cycles of change. His mind was literally alive with imagination about a future that, today, is transparently with us. Forty years ago it required his kind of mind to create the imagery. And the phrase – still scribbled in my notebook – with which he summed it up: 'We are moving into a world in which smaller and smaller men are strutting across narrower and narrower stages.'

He was wholly convinced that the world was near the edge of vast changes but that only a very few of the world's leaders had yet grasped the magnitude of that potential – and danger. His own list of favourites was a small one – Nehru, Tito, Mendez-France; a limited number filtered into Bevan's window on the future. The window looking out on a political landscape that he knew was being transformed with each hour. Time itself was collapsing on its own measurements.

*   *   *

One of my lasting final impressions was being with him on election night 1959. I went with him around his Ebbw Vale constituency, a tour of his native heath where he was idolised albeit not entirely without his critics. He knew that and never discounted the sceptics. 'They think I've left them because I now live and work in London; some of them think I've forgotten them. You have to live with that sort of thing ...' His voice trailed off into a shrug.

On the night of 7 October 1959, eve of poll, we sat in the home of his favourite sister, Arienwen, where he lodged when in Tredegar. She recognised that he was unwell and admitted so to me. He seemed feverish again. Together we watched Harold Macmillan's eve of poll performance on TV. The old actor–Prime Minister played with a large globe placed beside him for the cameras to focus on. He twirled it like a giant football, nodding toward this or that country as the world passed beneath his drooping gaze. It was Macmillan at his best – or most hammy acting. The Prime Minister strove to give the nation the impression that he, his party and his government could handle the increasingly complex global scene – and that it would be dangerous for the country to hand such a responsibility to those 'wild socialists'.

To my astonishment Bevan nodded toward the television and dismissed my critique of Macmillan. He defended him – not so much the man, whom he despised, but the politician, the party leader; the manner of his presentation may be 'hammy', he agreed, but he makes his point for his own party and his own class. That impressed Bevan. In turn he was angry with and critical of his own leader, Gaitskell, who, in an eve of poll speech in his Leeds constituency, had promised that a Labour government would be able to cut taxes *and* retain, perhaps even expand, the Welfare State. Bevan's response to that was instant. He turned to me and said: 'He's lost us the election – he should never say things like that. Every voter knows that this kind of talk is rubbish ...'

It was clear to me that Bevan had more sympathy with, and more understanding of, Macmillan than Gaitskell. But, more significant, it was yet another manifestation that Bevan was convinced that the chances of victory had been diminished.

It is easy enough now to analyse all this as the instinctive rattling of Bevan in the throes of death. Perhaps he did know he was entering his last few months of life; perhaps that was linked in the recesses of his mind with the long battle that lay ahead if his socialist ideas were ever to be fulfilled. Tiredness had taken over. His last public appearance came shortly after the election and Macmillan's triumphant one hundred majority over Labour. The Labour Party called a special weekend conference at Blackpool at which Bevan produced probably the most inspired speech of his life – which, of course, is a huge claim. It stands in the records as one of the finest pieces of oratory in Labour's long history. It was, as in retrospect I now realise, his last will and testament to his codex of socialist beliefs. The end, indeed, was nye.

7   The 1960s:
Postwar Interregnum

For my generation, the postwar world can be divided into two – before and after the 1960s. Sometime around 1960 and up till 1965 the postwar world, as we perceived it, changed into something different. It remains unclear to me precisely where the dividing line occurred. Only one thing is quite certain – it *did* change. Perhaps it is pointless even to seek a simple, clear-cut line to separate the two epochs. Better to leave it that there was a kind of blur of time as the ground shifted under our feet.

Not much of the 'old world' remained steadfastly in place by the time the 1960s expired. Whatever it was that suddenly created this transformation lay hidden, or at best emasculated, behind a kind of new language of the age. New words were born; fashions changed; attitudes shifted, at first uneasily, then relaxed into a new normality. Words themselves appeared to be searching for a new landscape of communication and form of expression. Our children, products of a notable postwar 'baby boom', were growing up into precipitately maturing teenagers swinging with the Beatles and the Carnaby Street culture. They transmitted the message of change to parents largely incapable of quite grasping what the hell was going on. How could we? The world of drugs, the Pill, the tone of exaggerated self-indulgence, the façade of glitterati and the celebrity culture – all these elements were taken in their stride by the products of 'the change' as they marched obliviously toward ... well, toward what? I mostly feel we are still trying to find out.

It made it hard for parents to understand their own children and especially for the children of the wartime generation to penetrate the eccentricities of parental mannerisms, addictions and attitudes. In retrospect it must be admitted that it made it almost impossible to have a rational system of education – even in the expensive privilege of the private sector. Teachers struggled mightily to try to understand how the sands were shifting under their feet – but they mostly failed. Little wonder that the system developed a chaotic virus; or that when Harold Wilson tried to preside over the galloping

1960s he was never quite sure exactly what kind of society his governments were trying to deal with.

Looking back on that period with the wonderful advantage of hindsight, it does in fact seem that the foothills of Thatcherism were already being approached, unconsciously, and without any overt political direction at the time, yet with a kind of anarchic rebelliousness against authority regardless of the direction the instructions were coming from – be it government, employers, trade unions, teachers, local authorities, priests or even doctors. The church in all denominations simply didn't get a look in. The clergy were even more baffled than the politicians.

All these voices and opinions of 'authority' were viewed not merely with suspicion by the kids growing up – they were ridiculed, they had to be opposed, challenged, sometimes automatically ruled out of consideration. The 'Me Society' had not yet matured into a coherent ideology as advanced by Margaret Thatcher, but the buds were there, beginning to sprout a few shoots. It was as if there had been a kind of sudden mutation in the behaviour pattern of the species which, like the biological parallel, defies any precise scientific explanation. One might be tempted, sniffily from the standpoint of my generation, to sneer at the whole business and describe the 1960s as 'The empty years'. That would be crass. If anything it was the decade of the postwar interregnum.

*   *   *

It was also the period when the media bubble burst into celebrity journalism via the television screen. Television came of age and grabbed society by the hormones rather than the mind, which was hardly surprising. Gradually we were being prepared for the Age of Murdoch and the Murdoch *Sun*. That, of course, was still some way off – November 1969. But Rupert Murdoch was already in Britain, having absorbed the *News of the World* as his bridgehead in London.

Let's be clear about this: Rupert Murdoch sensed the changing scene rather more shrewdly than the rest of us. He was one of the few media tycoons, in fact the only one in Britain, with the intuition to sniff what was happening just below the surface of British society and maybe a lot of other societies as well. Whatever else may be said of Murdoch, it is futile to deny that achievement. Of course, his product in the end was to scrape the bottom of the barrel. He perceived that this was an untapped lucrative market. The great days of *Daily Mirror* under Hugh Cudlipp had succeeded in producing a mass circulation tabloid daily paper selling 5 million copies – then a world record if we leave aside the old *Pravda* of the USSR *et al.* – and it did so while at the same time injecting into that huge readership a quality of serious journalism that was unique. But, as Murdoch observed, Cudlipp had lifted his reader's eyes above the navel, and Rupert reckoned that the future market lay in exploring the erogenous zone below the navel. He was indeed more in tune with the music of the age than the rest of us.

The Murdoch *Sun* was an astonishing success from the moment he acquired the title from the old Odhams' *Sun*, which my dear old friend Hugh Cudlipp sold to him for peanuts. That sale remained an albatross round Cudlipp's shoulders for the rest of his life. He was ever sensitive to the subject. He knew it was his aberration. For the tabloid genius of all our times to have sold off the title that established Murdoch and helped substantially to change the face of British journalism was a terrible shadow to live with. Yet Cudlipp always maintained that there was no tenable option because he wasn't prepared to stand by and see the jobs of hundreds of journalists and printers go down the drain if the old *Sun* had simply been left to die and fold up. Moreover, the truth is that Hugh Cudlipp did not believe Murdoch would succeed in turning the *Sun* into the extraordinary successful animal it became.

At the *Daily Mirror*, where I landed after the demise of the Odhams' *Sun*, we simply didn't realise what had hit us. Cudlipp began by laughing off the Murdoch challenge and deriding the Australian interloper as a 'belly and tits man', and most of us agreed with that judgement. Hugh always referred to Murdoch as the 'Dirty Digger', and few of us around him saw any reason to question that derision. But he was wrong, and so were we. Or at least if we were not wrong in the sense that we were discussing the character of the man we certainly misjudged the mood of the changing world we then inhabited and wrote for. Rupert did not make that misjudgement.

In fact those of us at the *Mirror*, had we but realised it, were an integral part of that 1960s divide – alas, on the 'wrong side' of the dividing line. The old *Daily Mirror* was still trying to keep faith with a postwar generation, the generation of readers that had built up the paper into the largest-selling daily tabloid in the world. That Cudlipp *Mirror* was the most seriously important tabloid we have ever had. It contained writing and reporting of the highest calibre, able to compete with the 'authority' of any of the so-called 'heavies' (the quality broadsheets). Yet the truth is that none of us, in that complaisant environment, sufficiently realised the nature of the change we were living through. We were in a sense writing for a disappearing age.

An emotional, even an intellectual, blindness kept us rooted to the belief that the values that had carried us through the war, through the 1950s and beyond Harold Macmillan's period, were of such enduring substance, perhaps even permanency, that they were impervious to a fundamental challenge. We were convinced that anything that attacked those convictions would eventually be beaten off. I would still defend the basis of our naivete and the ethos on which it was built, but it would be idle to deny our lack of intuition about what was really going on below that protected surface. Of such delusions the age of Thatcherism was born.

Naturally the full impact of the virus took time to penetrate the veins in our set of old attitudes. It was to be another ten years between Murdoch taking over the *Sun* and Margaret Thatcher landing in Downing Street; yet the signs were there, now only too clear to those of us with professorships in hindsight. To be fair to objective reporting, numerous other factors were injected into the picture. There was the astonishing about-turn by the Heath Government (circa 1970) after only a couple of years in office in which after trying to manacle the trade unions with an absurdly over-weighted and over-ambitious Industrial Relations Act Ted Heath went on to establish an extraordinary rapport with the TUC leaders, especially with Jack Jones, whom he had first met during the Spanish Civil War. That was something for which Margaret Thatcher never forgave Heath. Then in the summer of 1973 came the quadrupling in the price of Middle East oil, a political crisis in the eastern Mediterranean that triggered a rebellion by the British miners who saw it as a golden opportunity to put the pressure on the Heath Government – all of which led to the overwhelming political crisis of January and February 1974, the fall of the Heath Government and Harold Wilson's third, and subsequently, fourth, Government.

The trauma of the 1970s continues to haunt the British political scene not least because it was such a continuation of the tumult and convulsions of the 1960s. What is now clear is that neither Wilson nor Heath – nor for that matter Jim Callaghan – really understood what was happening. That is not meant as a reflection on their political gullibility but merely a statement of the obvious. They didn't understand what was happening any more than the rest of us in that generational bracket. To some extent, toward the end of his brief period in Downing Street, Callaghan developed a shrewder insight than the others. He sensed that the postwar dream was ending, or had ended, and that something very different was in the air.

The warning lights were blinking at him. The 'golden age' of non-inflationary economic growth, which had lasted a remarkable twenty-five years from 1945, had effectively come to an end at the close of the 1960s. Callaghan knew that the curtain was coming down.

*　*　*

For some odd reason when I reflect on that period of extraordinary change my mind slips back to the end of the 1950s when everything seemed so different and the postwar certainties were still largely intact. That is not to say it was a particularly noble period. Yet the fact was that a great deal of postwar hope was still kicking around at that time. It brings to mind, particularly, a visit I paid to the South Wales coalfield, then a mighty slice of Britain's industrial wealth, to write a piece for the *News Chronicle*.

You have to remember that the miners were still regarded as an heroic community, awkward, difficult, strike-prone but nonetheless struggling with nature in a manner no sensible person with a degree of choice would envy. There were still about half a million of them throughout the British coalfields, stretching from the tiny Kent operation in the south-east of England up to the tough militant coalfield in Scotland. A fifth of the mining population were in the strongholds of South Wales, that great cauldron of revolutionary song and politics, of poetry and male voice choirs, of literary fanatics, self-taught bibliophiles, prodigious drinkers and mountain walkers; a land of socialists, communists, angels and villains. It all came together with Cwm Rhondda.

My piece on the miners and their dreams – oh, yes, they still had a few dreams left as they handed me a souvenir miners' lamp to guide me, as they claimed, through life – was completed and filed off by old-fashioned telephone (no mobiles, then) to a London that seemed a long way off. That evening, work done, I met up with my old friend Leo Abse, who had just been elected Labour MP for Pontypool (he was elected in November 1958). We met in Cardiff and he immediately told me that we were on our way to meet Dylan Thomas. Why, I enquired. 'Because I've been invited to a party being given in Dylan's honour by a friend of mine, and I said I would bring you along,' was Leo's response. That was the night I met the great Welsh bard.

It was at the home of the eminent economist Professor Brinley Thomas, who was no relation of Dylan's yet knew him sufficiently well to be prepared for a night of heavy, solid drinking in the back room of his Cardiff home. Not that the particular scene was of any concern to Dylan's drinking habits. Brinley sensibly took the precaution to send his wife, Cynthia, off to bed at an early stage, leaving the room in the captivity of an all-male audience in deference to Dylan's style of communication.

The conversation, if that is what we might call it for the sake of a description, began with the usual desultory gossip about the certainties of our time, the political and social interplay of power, until the talk gradually descended into reality. Dylan didn't take long to get fairly well plastered as he sat lounging in a large armchair by the fireside, still burning splendid Welsh coal. Blasphemous language collided with an increasingly fascinating dialogue as we discussed the future of mankind, and Dylan relentlessly took control of the exchanges. Frankly, I have forgotten how many of us remained in the room by midnight; it is of no importance. Suffice to say that there were probably about half a dozen, all having fallen under the spell of Dylan's magical weaving of his literary thread as he simply burbled away in poetry as well as whisky. He spoke in blank verse in that soft, pausing lilt of the west-Welsh. He composed as he drank and drank as he composed. It was uncanny to listen to him sliding slowly into a kind of poetic trance, his eyes fixed, insofar as they were fixed on anything, on some corner window frame at the far end of the room.

As he drifted further and further into a wonderland of musing hyperbole in which the rest of us had long ceased to play any role, he reclined deeper into the grasp of the fireside chair. Dylan had, at the outset, collected some point raised by one of us about the failure of mankind. He took it up, held it within his imagination, mused to himself sometimes with barely audible whispers, and spelled out the results in some kind of poetic form. He moved back in time – never forward. From man back to the monkeys and the apes and on to earlier carnivores. As he moved further and further back tracing, in reverse, the path of the species and mouthing his poetry of retreat he finally decided that the end had been reached. The protoplasmic form of life had come to a full stop.

'And then,' he offered us his final glimpse. From deep within his alcoholic amnesia he stuttered: 'It' (no other description was offered, but 'It') 'came to the ultimate precipice in time, tumbled over, and was gone ...' Silence. The room was full of an eerie quiet, a combination of alcoholic stupor and perplexity.

I have always felt that Dylan would have been quite capable of producing a somewhat identikit version of all that even if we had suggested talking about the future rather than the past. Somehow it all seemed to come together in his mind in a joined-up imperfection. Perhaps that's why the Cardiff night comes into my own mind when I reflect on the dividing lines of the 1960s. Or perhaps it is the link with coal since the 1960s was the decade in which we started not to have a coal industry. This island 'built on coal', as Aneurin Bevan so often pointed out, 'and surrounded by fish', he added, before bringing up a famous punch line ... 'and, by God, we've made a bloody mess of both industries'.

Perhaps this is the reason why Dylan floats across my mind from that time, from that night in Cardiff, with my miner's lamp to guide me – a lamp that I still keep to stare at me. I met Dylan only once again after that – in a pub (but where else?) near the BBC, where he had been in negotiation with producers about another version of 'Under Milk Wood' the outcome of which I never did discover.

*   *   *

At any rate if I am at all justified in drawing this line through the 1960s, even if somewhat arbitrarily, it might help at least partly to explain some of the extraordinary events of that decade when a substantial section of the media, no doubt reflecting the mood of the country, began to regard Britain as 'ungovernable' – or perhaps one should say when people decided they didn't want to be governed by the old rules. Of course, it became the favoured cliché of the 1970s, a manifestation no doubt of the confusion that was so widespread at the time as people tried to come to terms with their changing world. This was true not only of political life but of almost everything – the industrial climate, the cultural world, literary life, fashion, style, sex, personal relationships and crime. The break-up of family life was already perceived. Everything was in the melting pot of change – 'pot' being, perhaps, the operative word.

*   *   *

The period between the General Election of 1959, which Macmillan won with an overall majority of 102, and October 1964 was certainly one of the most traumatic in the whole of postwar British political life. In that time the Labour Party lost its two most prominent figures – the deputy leader Aneurin Bevan and the leader Hugh Gaitskell. The Tories 'lost' its most colourful and arguably most successful postwar Prime Minister – if we leave aside Margaret Thatcher as a special phenomenon – in Harold Macmillan: and by 1964 Macmillan's successor, the aristocrat-laird-turned-commoner Sir Alec Douglas-Home, had lost Downing Street to Harold Wilson, the grammar school boy from Huddersfield.

It all seemed to begin with Bevan's death in July 1960, a few months after the 1959 election the experience of which I have described in the previous chapter. The impact of Bevan's death was enormous – not merely within the Labour movement but across the entire spectrum of British politics. A mountain had been removed from the scene. And within two and half years of Bevan's death Hugh Gaitskell was also dead.

Both events stunned the political world. Gaitskell was only 56, six years younger than Bevan, and had been leader of the Labour Party for just over seven years. To add to the irony the two years or so between the two deaths had seen Gaitskell fighting for his political life over issues that might well have brought him support from the departed Bevan – unilateral nuclear disarmament and the issue of Britain's membership of the Common Market.

In the autumn of 1960, less than three months after Bevan's death, Gaitskell was defeated at the Labour Party conference by the nuclear disarmers led by Frank Cousins of the Transport & General Workers Union. It brought from Gaitskell his famous speech to 'fight, fight and fight again to save the Party we love'. And a year later at the 1961 Labour Party conference a profoundly relieved Gaitskell managed to reverse the Scarborough vote on The Bomb. But he was immediately plunged into an equally passionate controversy over Britain's membership of the European Common Market and, to the bewilderment and chagrin of his closest friends and allies, the Labour leader came out firmly against British membership.

It was in many respects even more crucifying to Gaitskell's emotional condition than the H-Bomb debate because on that issue Gaitskell's allies, on the right of the party, were solidly with him. The Common Market split cut across the whole spectrum of left and right. Almost all Gaitskell's closest friends – notably Roy Jenkins – were strongly pro-Common Market and on the right of the party. The split with his allies and personal confidants was immensely wounding to both sides and seemed beyond repair.

At the Labour conference of 1962 there were real tears in the eyes of life-long friends – not just 'political tears' – and blood on the carpets in the hotel bars. It was an extraordinary situation, with many on the left praising Gaitskell for the first time because of his repudiation of what they then regarded as the 'capitalist club' of Europe. It is now quite clear that this split over Europe had a far greater impact on Gaitskell's health and political balance than was recognised at the time.

Hugh Gaitskell was generally seen as a high intellectual, even as a 'desiccated calculating machine', in Bevan's immortal description. In fact he was a deeply emotional and sensitive man, often impulsive and, in affairs of the heart, even reckless. His affair with Ann Fleming was an astonishing challenge to the accepted conventions, even allowing for the fact that we then had a far more discreet media. Many journalists knew about Gaitskell's affair with Ann Fleming, wife of Ian Fleming: some newspapers even had photographs of them partying together. But none were ever published. Gaitskell's wife Dora was aware of the affair – but remained silent and constantly loyal to her husband. Very little of this was ever discussed even informally in political circles, and the Conservatives made no attempt to exploit the 'sex sensation' surrounding the Labour leader. The political and journalistsic code was very different at that time. It may seem incredible to contemporary mores that such a situation could exist without a major public scandal being aired in the newspapers – but that was the 1950s and early 1960s, not the 1990s.

Among his close friends there was at the time a strong feeling that Gaitskell's emotional condition and political conflicts left him vulnerable to the virus that eventually caused his death in January 1963. He had been under constant strain for at least three years, and the death of Bevan, his great ideological opponent, by a strange twist of irony had actually led to an increase in the pressures on him rather than the reverse. He fell ill shortly before Christmas 1962 with what was thought to be a heavy 'flu. Within days his condition deteriorated. He was admitted to Middlesex Hospital in the early days of January 1963 and died there.

The diagnosis was that he fell victim to a rare virus. This led to speculation, often repeated since, that he was assassinated by enemy agents using the technique of a poisoned dart. Hardly anyone now (or then) gives any credence to this wild theory – certainly not his family nor close friends who, long ago, dismissed the whole idea as fantasy and rubbish.

Gaitskell's death was a savage blow to the Labour Party, and it led to another round of internal conflict as three prominent names jostled for succession – Jim Callaghan, George Brown and Harold Wilson. My own relationship with Hugh Gaitskell had always been affected by my well-known close friendship with Nye Bevan. Yet Gaitskell was always honourable in our dealings, and I never had cause for any complaint about our professional relationship. Indeed he was capable of great acts of personal, private kindness from which I myself benefited. Let me offer a prime example.

On the eve of the nuclear disarmament debate at the Labour Party conference in Scarborough in 1960 my father died. I was in Scarborough reporting the conference for the *Daily Herald*. A colleague happened to mention this to Gaitskell on the Saturday before the conference opened. He immediately came to my hotel to tender his sympathy – along with the extremely generous offer of helping with transport to get me back to London quickly. I didn't take up that offer but it was characteristic of the man. Here he was on the eve of a debate that threatened the very basis of his leadership yet he found time to offer help to a journalist whom he knew to be one of his critics.

Some time after Gaitskell's death I was in private conversation with his widow Lady Dora Gaitskell. We were discussing the relative merits of political leaders and in particular of Nye Bevan. With extraordinary courage Dora Gaitskell told me that day: 'You know, I never believed that Hugh was the natural leader of the Labour Party – the really natural leader was Nye. He ought to have been leader, not Hugh: but Nye threw away his chance. It wasn't Hugh who should have led the party – it was Nye. But there it is ...' I can think of few more honest, courageous statements made by the widow of a fallen politician about his principal opponent.

The sequel to all this was, of course, the leadership and then premiership of Harold Wilson, and by one of those strange twists of chance and circumstance I happened to be present when the great skirmish to succeed Gaitskell began. It started one night in Burnley.

A team of Fleet Street journalists had travelled up to Lancashire and the north-west to report on a tour of the unemployment areas by two of Gaitskell's senior Shadow Cabinet members, Douglas Jay and George Brown. They occupied different areas of the economic policy departments of the Labour Opposition – Jay specialising on trade and Brown on broader areas of industrial and economic policy. Brown was also deputy leader of the Labour Party. Yet the truth was that the two politicians were as far apart in their personal relations as it is possible to imagine. Not because they were ideologically opposed – indeed, on that score they were both well to the right of the party. They simply loathed each other personally. Brown, the working-class boy from London's East End had left school at 14 to fight his way up through the Transport & General Workers Union; Douglas Jay, Winchester and Oxford, was a brilliant economist from a highly privileged background. That was enough to spark Brown's envy; Jay's cool, detatched character did the rest.

Throughout the tour Jay and Brown hardly spoke to each other but watched, eagle-eyed, what each was saying to their journalist contacts. The tour was frankly pretty pointless except as an exercise in party propaganda. Everyone knew what the unemployment scene was like in the north-west – grim. Still, we landed one bleak evening in January 1963 in a Burnley hotel and filed dutiful pieces about what Brown and Jay had been up to. A group of us then settled in the bar.

Suddenly the figure of a white-faced George Brown pounded toward us and cried out: 'Don't any of you care? What the hell are you doing here when Hugh is dying in London?' It was the first we had heard about the gravity of Gaitskell's condition. 'I'm flying back to London tonight,' Brown shouted so that everyone in the hotel bar and beyond got the message. 'If any of you want to come with me you'd better pack now,' and then added as an afterthought – 'Mind you, you'll have to make your own arrangements because I have asked the RAF to fly me back from Manchester tonight.'

There was a flurry of activity as someone bought George Brown a large whisky to keep him under control and careful watch. Bags were packed, bills quickly paid, phone calls made to London. All the reporters made their plans to follow Brown to Manchester. No one seemed concerned about Douglas Jay, though he did catch up with events later. Three of us piled into a small car owned by the *Daily Mirror* man, Jimmy Beecroft. I was with Keith McDowall of the *Daily Mail*.

We began the drive just as a fierce blizzard started to sweep across the Lancashire moors. Brown's limousine was racing ahead, protected and guided by a convoy of police outriders. We could barely see them through the swirling snow-storm let alone keep abreast. In the end McDowall and I took over the driving from Beecroft who was nervous about this mad race across the moors in such conditions. Somehow, and I am not sure how, we managed to reach Manchester airport not too far behind Brown's escorted convoy and found him inside the terminal negotiating with an RAF crew. Douglas Jay was with him, but saying nothing.

While the RAF plane was being prepared I sat with George Brown in the airport bar discussing the succession to Gaitskell. By now it was clear that the Labour leader was dying. To McDowall and me Brown opened up his heart about his ambition to succeed – and make sure 'that little man' (Harold Wilson) did not. 'Yes, of course I want to lead the party and I must stop that little man,' he proclaimed in an uncharacteristic whisper. Is that why you're rushing back tonight? we asked George. 'Don't be so bloody stupid,' he snapped back, 'I am going because I want to be at Hugh's bedside before he dies.' It sounded less than convincing. Douglas Jay was ambling around the airport shops looking distracted. Anything to keep away from George Brown. The RAF crew beckoned the deputy leader: 'We're ready for departure, sir,' they said to the man who wanted to be leader. And he was off, followed by a frowning Jay, without a word being exchanged between them.

It did him no good. George Brown polled 88 to Wilson's 115 (and Callaghan's 41) on the first ballot and in a final run off was beaten by Wilson 144 to 103. He never forgave Wilson for winning. Nor did it do anything to improve his loathing for Douglas Jay whom he suspected of spying for Wilson – though there was little or no evidence for such suspicion since Jay was no more an admirer of Harold Wilson than Brown – though his objections were intellectual and less personally venomous. So began the age of H. Wilson; and in retrospect, that is how it mostly continued with the minimum of brotherly love between the majority of the Wilson Cabinet that was formed in October 1964. But we will come to that aspect shortly.

One final word about this extraordinary period. It was, of course, the end of Macmillanesque politics and the opening of Wilsonia. I had had some dealings with Harold Macmillan, and I confess to an affection for the old boy. He was very much the embodiment of the age that was closing: perhaps even the last of the Edwardians. He was also the last manifestation of the old Tory order of paternalism, the sense of a divine historic mission to be the caretaker of the 'National Spirit'; tradition, with all the hypocrisy and posturing that this so often demands, was part of the Macmillan *ouvrière*. Nor was the actor ever far from Harold Macmillan's repertoire, with a touch of Garrick or even Henry Irving occasionally showing beneath the drooping eyelids. All that was very much on display in the Prime Minister's eve of poll television performance as he twirled the large globe with his finger tips and I sat watching, with Nye Bevan, that night in Tredegar. Still, who can complain about political leaders playing at theatre? It's all in the same calling.

Macmillan himself was a remarkable mix. He was a deeply sensitive man, powerfully influenced and unquestionably emotionally damaged by his experiences on the Somme in the First World War, where he witnessed some of his closest friends die in appalling circumstances and where he himself was severely wounded. He never was able to cast off that shadow. Nor was he a natural Conservative – indeed he confessed privately, and sometimes even publicly, to a strong dislike of the Tory Party. At one point in the early 1930s he flirted with the notion of joining the Labour Party, but the break with his social ambience was too painful – especially against the background of his discovery that Dorothy Macmillan, his wife, was deeply in love with an old political friend, Bob Boothby, with whom she was having a torrid affair. Macmillan's personal life was ravaged by that and the uncertainty about the fatherhood of one of his children. Macmillan's capacity to put that in the margin and rise in the political hierarchy of the Tory Party was due entirely to his private courage and the ability to act a role that would have impressed Garrick.

In one of our meetings, shortly after he left Downing Street, we talked privately in his room at the Macmillan publishing house just off the Strand. He reflected on his introduction to the Devonshire household, Dorothy's family, at Chatsworth and a younger brother of Dorothy advising him on how, as a member of the Devonshires, he might wish to dress. 'The young man studied my clothes,' Macmillan reported to me, 'and noticed that they were spotlessly clean. He glanced at the lapels of my jacket and scoffed – "ah" he said, "you must remember always to wear a visible stain on one of your lapels; shows an indifference to convention – important thing for us Devonshires"'. 'So,' Macmillan continued, 'I always carried a stain on my lapel thereafter ...' emphasising the point with a languid wave of his right arm. I simply couldn't help liking the old chap.

It summed up the period; but it was over. The new world had already been launched.

8 Harold Wilson: White Heat and the *Sun*

Harold Wilson's 'White Heat of New Technology' speech at the 1963 Labour Party conference was effectively the launch of what we might today describe as 'New Labour'. But that is a label Wilson would never have considered using. He was much too sensitively tuned to the prejudices, suspicions and mores of the Labour movement to have contemplated such a thing. Yet there is no doubt in my mind that this was the theme at the back of his mind. He had long recognised that the Labour Party was desperately in need of modernisation.

Several years before he became leader Wilson was involved in an internal Labour Party inquiry into how the party was administered. His report came up with a damning verdict about its hopelessly 'Penny-farthing' organisation. Nor would Wilson have 'done a Blair' by trying to scuttle Clause 4: that would have smacked of something Gaitskell did consider after losing the 1959 election – and then quickly rejected. Wilson was too shrewd not to realise that this kind of confrontation over the party's sacred totemism was both unnecessary and counter-productive. After all it was still in the pre-Thatcherite age. Yet there is no doubt that the election of Wilson as Labour leader was seen, across the political spectrum, as the symbol of a new-style Labour Party led by this brilliant former Oxford don – the young grammar school boy from Huddersfield, with a working-class background.

Wilson had already established a reputation as a formidable House of Commons debater against both the Macmillan and Douglas-Home Conservative Governments. He had also secured a platform based on a sharp awareness that the world was moving into a quite new phase, technologically, socially and politically. It was all very much Mr 'White Heat' Wilson in those early days of 1964. The fact that it was to turn out somewhat differently and that even Wilson's highly focused antennae would finally prove unable to pick up the true depth and vast spread of this changing society is far less a criticism of his premiership than a measure of the speed of these changes and the impact they were to have on the fabric of all societies, not just in Britain. The year 1964 began with great hopes, vivid aspirations and ambitions as the thirteenth year of unbroken Conservative rule was deemed to be coming to its end and Harold Wilson poised to collect the keys of No. 10 Downing Street. It was, of course, to prove less simple than the pundits predicted.

In September 1964 I had lately returned from three months in the United States, most of which was spent at Harvard in the privileged setting of Henry Kissinger's then famous international political seminar. Much of the time was given to discussing the implications of John F. Kennedy's assassination and what really did happen on that extraordinary day at Dallas in November 1963. The Warren Commission had just reported but failed to clear up the innumerable lingering doubts. The 'insiders' from the Kennedy White House who came up to Harvard to provide us with 'secret background' were mostly sceptical of the Warren Commission. But their dark hints that the whole business was far more complex than the simple explanation of the paranoid charged with the presidential murder, Lee Harvey Oswald, rarely went further than hints.

Kissinger, privately, also had his doubts but kept them close to his well-protected diplomatic chest. His role in those days, apart from Harvard professorship, was chief adviser to Nelson Rockefeller, who was seeking nomination as the Republican candidate to run against President Lyndon Johnson. Rockefeller, and Kissinger, failed in that bid. The short straw to face Johnson went to Barry Goldwater. Kissinger relapsed into his own Harvard intrigues and had to await the arrival in the White House of Richard Nixon before achieving the preferment he had been seeking and so much wanted from Rockefeller.

Getting to know Henry in those pre-Nixon days was illuminating. He used his Harvard seminar, and his academic standing, quite openly as a bridge to his scarcely concealed ambition to get as close to White House power as was possible for a German Jewish refugee. He would dearly have loved to have been given the right to stand for even higher office. But since he wasn't born in a shack somewhere inside the United States that was a hurdle he could never surmount. His Harvard status was both resented and envied by his academic contemporaries, among whom it would be an exaggeration to say he was liked. Even so no one could deny his intellectual force: and the liberals who despised his lack of radical spirit would hardly raise their heads above the parapet for fear of being branded 'lefties' – a dangerous label to carry around the American scene, not least in

Harvard Yard. McCarthyism was still very much alive and, in some quarters, quite well.

It was a fascinating time to be in the United States but I wanted to get back to London for the election and for the great change that was about to take place in my newspaper: the *Daily Herald* was about to change its name, its style and its whole journalistic approach – it was about to become the *Sun,* pre-Murdoch, still owned by the Mirror Group, and an experiment in the launch of what was virtually a new national daily newspaper.

*   *   *

The *Daily Herald* was like a piece old 1930s furniture: well crafted, built to last through its generation, no fancy trimmings, just plain, utilitarian, loyal, wholesome, unimaginative, solid. It had begun as a printers' strike sheet in 1911 and developed into a weekly newspaper during the First World War, campaigning for socialism, peace and a postwar social transformation. After the armistice the paper was in danger of collapsing. Two great figures of the early Labour movement, George Lansbury and Ben Tillett, asked a young trade union leader, Ernest Bevin, if he would like to take an interest in the struggling paper. Bevin was just forming the Transport & General Workers Union and taking up the role as architect of a new-style TUC General Council. He raised the money to keep the *Daily Herald* alive, and in 1922 led the TUC and the Labour Party's national executive into ownership of the paper. It became Bevin's 'baby'. But it didn't prosper. The advertisers shied away from a socialist paper; the potential readership – the whole of the British working class – were either indifferent, poverty stricken or too engaged in trying to find work and survive. It was tough going. Yet the *Herald* then had a team of writers and journalists that included George Bernard Shaw and H.G. Wells, H.M. Tomlinson, H.W. Nevinson, Hamilton Fyfe and William Mellor.

In 1929 Bevin came to a deal with Odhams Press – establishing a partnership with Julius Salter Elias, later Lord Southwood, the head of Odhams. Between them, by 1933, they had turned the paper into the first national daily newspaper in Britain with a circulation of two million plus. It was called the 'Miracle of Fleet Street', and it was. The trick was to engage in competitive circulation-building, which all the national dailies were in up to their necks. But the *Herald*'s particular trick was to harness its working-class potential and offer its readers free insurance, household goods including furniture, and books – classical literature with a list that embraced Shakespeare, Dickens, Shaw, Wells, the poets *et al*. It coincided with political moves to expand elementary education opportunities for the generation of working-class children of fathers who were either unemployed or in precarious employment.

The whole operation was a piece of brilliant newspaper-building far beyond even the enterprise of a modern-day Murdoch. I had first-hand experience of all this since my own parents bought the *Daily Herald* principally for its free insurance and household furniture (how well I remember the joy on my mother's face when the dining table arrived with four leather-seated chairs – it was the first time we had tasted such luxury). It was the same with the books. Working-class families throughout the country began to stock books in their homes for the first time – to kindle an awareness among their children of names like Shakespeare and Dickens and Wells and Shaw. The daily tokens taken from the paper – you cut them out from a spot just below the masthead – fuelled a kind of mini-social revolution, which eventually fed into the bloodstream of the political body. It was all about to change as I returned from the United States.

The *Herald* held its strength during the war and for a period in the late 1940s during the Attlee Government's creative period. Then the circulation slipped against the rise of the other nationals – *Daily Express*, *Daily Mirror*, *Daily Mail*, but especially the *Mirror*, which by the 1950s had captured an enormous working-class readership and by the early 1960s had overtaken the Beaverbrook *Express*, with a circulation of more than four and half million and still rising. The Mirror Group, headed by Cecil Harmsworth King and Hugh Cudlipp, bought out Odhams Press in the early 1960s. It was part of an expansion that turned the group into the most powerful media force in Europe.

Cecil King, nephew of Lord Northcliffe and part of the extraordinary Harmsworth dynasty, was then the most exalted mogul of them all. But he still wasn't satisfied. He was committed to sustaining the ailing *Daily Herald* but didn't like the inheritance which he publicly ridiculed as 'King's Cross' – to carry with a wince rather than a smile. In February 1964 King and Cudlipp persuaded the TUC and the Labour Party to agree a sell-off of the TUC's 49 per cent holding in the *Herald* (the Mirror Group, renamed International Publishing Corporation, already owned 51 per cent which they had scooped in with the purchase of Odhams). At that point the paper was still selling 1,348,000 daily – but even on that circulation it was losing £1 million a year because it couldn't get the lucrative 'new age' advertising. King and Cudlipp then called in the whizz-kids to draw up plans for a new launch. Dr Mark Abrams, who headed one of the leading Market Research operations, masterminded a plan to change the title of the paper, redesign it and relaunch it as 'A Paper Born of the Age we Live in'. It was, if one needed such confirmation, yet another example of the dividing line of change in the 1960s.

As Douglas-Home called a general election and Harold Wilson zipped up his sweater to face an exhausting nationwide tour and campaign, the *Daily Herald* (RIP) became the *Sun*. It was 15 September 1964, a date we all marked in our diaries; the day Fleet Street changed, the day that beckoned Ruper Murdoch and side-stepped (for a while, at any rate) Robert Maxwell; the day a new-born paper called the *Sun* was launched ironically to support Harold Wilson's White Heat.

Certainly the title sounded good. It was conceived one evening by Hugh Cudlipp. He was strolling along Longacre, Covent Garden, with his close pal and colleague, Sydney Jacobson (the late Lord Jacobson), who had edited the *Daily Herald* when the Mirror Group took over and was then editorial director of the new operation. They moved toward a Longacre pub where the overhanging sign was swaying gently in the evening breeze. Cudlipp looked up at the sign and swivelled round to Sydney: 'That's it, Sydney!' he cried out. 'We've got it. That's the title ...' The pub's name was THE SUN. What was it that Thomas Edison declared about genius? Answer: 'It's 1 per cent inspiration and 99 per cent perspiration.'

Five years later the pub-sign-newspaper was to become Rupert Murdoch's own. But at that moment he was still back in Australia securing his own foundations.

It was, one feels sure even from this distance, probably a good time to launch a new newspaper. Even the concept was good – to have a bright, left-of-centre, albeit uncommitted paper in the way the old *Herald* had suffered from over-commitment: to have fine journalists writing good journalism along with a touch of modern-style light-hearted coverage to add a touch of tinsel to authoritative reporting and feature writing etc. To have all that with a dash of style, humour, fun and seriousness – it all seemed a good bet at the time.

Then came the thunderous reality – the first week was disastrously handled. The paper was a mess. A mix of cheap gimmickry, stale stories, silly pictures and inadequate promotion. For the first few days after the launch the paper sold over 3 million copies. Three weeks later it was back to almost the level of the old *Daily Herald*. It might still have been saved but the tremendous enthusiasm and hype of the launch had been drained away. From that point it was never to rise again above one and three quarter million despite the fact that after a couple of years the Odhams *Sun* (as one still prefers to describe it against the Murdoch *Sun*) settled down into a very good middle-market newspaper with some outstanding journalism to its credit. It had, in fact, become a kind of latter-day *News Chronicle* and had found a niche. But it lacked effective financial support, which should have been directed to promotion and winning more advertising.

By 1968 the Mirror Group had simply lost interest and were already looking for a likely buyer. In the early months of 1969 the Mirror board actually announced that the title was to be sold to Rupert Murdoch – in six months' time. It was a stunning decision, quite without precedent. No paper had ever been given a six months' death sentence and allowed to struggle on in decline. By any reasonable reckoning the morale of the journalists should have collapsed. It didn't. Miraculously we all fought on during that six months' death sentence still determined to produce the best possible newspaper.

It was a tremendous tribute to the professionalism and commitment of a wonderful team of journalists and print workers who, somehow, sustained the paper at a circulation of over 800,000 – which was the paper's daily sale at the point when it was handed over to Murdoch in November 1969. It was the strangest, most weird experience I have had in newspapers. The title, if not the inheritance, was handed to Murdoch for peanuts (the TUC had originally sold off its title rights to the Mirror Group for an astonishingly small £75,000). What an ironic ending to the tale of a printers' strike sheet that became the 'Miracle of Fleet Street', only to change its name under the swinging attractions of a pub sign.

Perhaps the Odhams–Mirror Group *Sun* was doomed from the start. On the Saturday evening before the 15 September launch Cecil King and Hugh Cudlipp hosted a huge new-birth celebration at the Café Royal in Regent Street. It began with a presentation by the Mark Abrams' team whose role was to demonstrate the remarkable nature of this new newspaper. Everyone seemed to be present. The Mirror Group in force, the entire editorial staff of the old *Daily Herald*; the hoi-polloi of the advertising and publicity world and many of the numerous hangers-on to the tailpiece of Fleet Street that it was reasonable to muster. They all crowded into the Josephine Suite of the Café Royal where the new logo greeted them – 'The Paper Born of the Age we Live in', with a huge graphic-designed orange blob against a black background, the paper's logo and symbol.

Cudlipp opened the proceedings with a characteristic display of verbal fireworks to set the occasion alight. Then came the advertising men to talk about the 'new image' of the paper – aimed at 'an entirely new readership', whatever that was supposed to mean. Nothing about tradition, history and all that stuff. No mention of any postwar generation or commitment. The melody that bounced round the room was 'we are now living in a new world – a world of leisure – shorter working hours – consumer spending – liberation', etc. The clichés were in regiments marching onward. 'Young people, today, want a newspaper that's not biased, not dull and loaded with all those old abstract political ideas … let's talk success; no more failures.'

Those around me, Jimmy Cameron, Tom Baitsow, Joyce Chesterton, Harold Hutchinson … were wincing audibly. What the hell was happening to us? We asked each other. There were no answers. A huge screen in the far corner of the room blazed away with slides introducing us to the wonders and charm of this new world. Hugh Cudlipp then flipped through the dummy pages of the new paper, flashed onto the screen by a projectionist who kept getting the pages in the wrong order – a bit like the real paper, as it turned out. Roger Wood, ex-*Daily Express* and then one of the planners of the new paper, reminded everyone that 'We will be writing for a new age of people'. The statistics rolled off the screen – half the population were now under 35; women were now working in greater numbers than ever, one-in-three compared with one-in-ten in 1941. Yes, we who gathered there amid all this bonanza stood with an icy scepticism about this 'new age'. We thought we knew better – and we were wrong. It was indeed the new age.

Perhaps the end-piece of that evening of the *Sun* launch was the most symbolic of all. Cecil King rose to speak as we all settled into our chairs after the big celebratory dinner. He had already been dubbed the *Sun King*. His contribution to our enlightenment was unmemorable. He spoke briefly, without passion or even commitment, and then departed for his home in Chelsea to maintain his habit of retiring early to bed. Before he left King mentioned, as a kind of afterthought, that £350,000 had already been spent on sales promotion, which was big money in 1964. It amounted, he claimed, to the 'biggest effort made for thirty years to a launch a new daily paper'. Then he was gone. We had little or no connection with him after that until his sensational dismissal from chairmanship of the Mirror Group (IPC, that is) three and half years later.

The Café Royal launch concluded with Clement Freud – then part of the old *Herald* editorial team – playing the Court Clown. He kept the party alive by telling splendidly bawdy stories including the one about the size of the Porcupine's penis, a phallus of considerable distinction and clearly of the age in which we were being born. It was, to be sure, an appropriate finale to the great send-off, or perhaps send-up, at the birth of the *Sun*.

*   *   *

I had known Harold Wilson from the days of his appointment by Prime Minister Attlee as the youngest Cabinet Minister of the twentieth century – President of the Board of Trade, in October 1947. But it had been a casual, superficial acquaintanceship until he was elected to the Labour Party's national executive in the 1950s when he became an extremely valuable source of information to any political journalist bothering to pursue him with a Sunday morning 'phone call to his Hampstead Garden suburb home. From that point we built up what can best be described as 'an understanding'. He would confide interesting aspects of what was happening behind the scenes of the Labour hierarchy, and I would, sometimes, write them into pieces for the *News Chronicle*. Wilson was always shrewd in his selection of leakable places – both in terms of newspapers and individuals. He was, in fact, a very good news reporter and his selection of stories worth leaking to this or that newspaper almost always hit target.

So it was that we gradually built up a kind of friendship. His formidable memory was invaluable to any journalist. By the time he became leader of the Labour Party in 1963 after Gaitskell's death we had developed a mutually useful – though not personally close – link. It was no great surprise to either of us when the editor of the new *Sun*, Sydney Jacobson, asked me to cover the 1964 General Election campaign with Wilson. I was to stay with him throughout the tour and, as it was gently suggested: 'not leave him out of my sight'. It was quite an assignment.

To this day I am still amazed at the way Wilson stood up to the rigours of that campaign. For the journalists covering the 1964 Wilson election tour – touching pretty well every corner of the country – it was utterly exhausting, crazy, requiring a novel tract to provide anything like a worthwhile description and absolutely riveting. It happened to be also the first British general election campaign covered by television from the word 'go', which, of course, placed a new and severe test on the tempers, nervous condition and patience of newspapermen who, at that stage had not yet become accustomed to the arrogant assumptions of television crews.

It also presented serious technical challenges. The timing of key sections of speeches made at evening meetings were geared to coincide with the evening TV news bulletins – commonplace stuff now, but pioneering scheduling in 1964. It meant that newspaper reporters had to work against new, and different, schedules, which affected long-established newsroom deadlines. And since none of the political party machines were then tuned to these new requirements it meant that we were literally organising things on the hoof with each new day of the campaign.

It was a considerable daily headache – except for Harold Wilson, who quickly adapted himself and his entourage to the new requirements and was well ahead of game plan in his handling of this new monster of intrusiveness, television. His speeches were timed to perfection. He knew precisely when, and how, to pitch his crowning remarks to achieve maximum impact on the TV screen. He never seemed to tire, though he was clearly under enormous pressure; he was always even-tempered in public and when mingling with journalists sparing his few emotional outbursts for the privacy of his hotel room when only Marcia Williams (Lady Falkender) – and, odd times, perhaps Mary Wilson – was present. The pipe was always at the ready, not yet having reached the stage where it frequently set light to his jacket pocket. He was very much in control and at his peak.

Only once during the campaign did his guard drop. Toward the end of the tour we had reached Birmingham for a major speech in the old Bull Ring. In the middle of Wilson's speech to a huge audience news of a searing attack on Wilson by Lord Hailsham reached those of us at the press table. Hailsham, in a counter-offensive against Labour's attacks on the private morality of certain Conservatives, referred to Wilson's own behaviour and implied that he was not blameless. A veiled reference was made to Marcia Williams, with the innuendo that her status might well be somewhat more than a political secretary. A note about the Hailsham speech was passed to the platform and shuffled along to Wilson. In mid-flow he glanced at it and pushed it aside. There was no pause or falter. But later back in his hotel room there were scenes of panic and even hysteria. Mrs Williams was in tears. Wilson sat in a corner of his room, silent. Mary Wilson was white-faced. News of all this was brought to me, waiting downstairs, by an old friend and former colleague, Alfred Richman, who was part of the Wilson entourage.

Meanwhile my editor was on the 'phone wanting to know if Wilson was going to respond. I had no idea at that point. I asked him what the paper planned to publish about the Hailsham outburst. 'We're carrying the speech without comment,' Sydney Jacobson replied. I asked him what the *Daily Mirror* was going to publish. 'I've spoken with Hugh [Cudlipp] and they are doing the same – but putting it on the front of the paper.' There was an air of real nervousness in that Birmingham hotel, and Wilson, meanwhile, was asking both the *Mirror* and the *Sun* not to publish anything because he was considering legal action against Hailsham. By the early hours the pot had stopped boiling, though only just. Wilson went to bed, calmed by Mary whose presence and demeanour that night was a source of great strength to her husband and, without doubt, a crucial factor in a night of crisis.

So, too, was the professionalism of Alf Richman. The whole event could have exploded, quite quickly, into a major crisis threatening to Wilson. Richman played the role of intermediary between Wilson's room of panic and the journalists waiting below. He had been a *Daily Herald* journalist for a number of years and had a wide and intimate connection with the Labour Party. After becoming leader Wilson asked if he could 'borrow' Richman from the paper to handle his personal press affairs. In fact Alf was treated as an adviser, personal aide and general dogsbody, always utterly loyal to Harold Wilson. He was devoted to his charge and, alas, rather undervalued in later years by the Prime Minister – an unusually rare example of Wilson behaving badly in his appreciation of personal loyalty.

There was another example of the Wilson–Richman relationship at the very end of the campaign, which illustrates even more clearly the dependence of Wilson on this mostly uncharted relationship. On the morning of Friday 16 October 1964, when it was already clear that Harold Wilson was to be the new prime minister – albeit with that uneasy wafer-thin majority of 4 – I travelled back from Liverpool with him and his team on the early morning train from Lime Street station. It was around midday when we reached Labour Party headquarters, then at Transport House in London. My editor had already asked me to do a 'first exclusive interview' with the new

Prime Minister, which I arranged to do once Wilson arrived back at Labour headquarters. We sat together in a first-floor room of Transport House chatting about the long weeks of campaigning and exchanging jokey yarns. Alf Richman came into the room just as I had begun my interview and stayed throughout the process. Harold Wilson had already begun to change from his travelling clothes into formal morning dress in readiness for his trip to Buckingham Palace to collect the seals of office from the Queen.

Richman stood beside the new Prime Minister as he stripped down to his underpants, put on a clean white shirt and pulled up his trousers to slip inside his braces. Richman stood back and looked at him, butler-like, in an admiring stance. He fingered a red carnation and moved forward to fasten it to the Prime Minister's jacket buttonhole. Then he noticed Harold Wilson's braces – red, holding up the pin-striped trousers.

He paused. 'Harold, you can't wear *them*,' pointing to the red braces. 'It's not the thing.'

'Why not?' Wilson replied, 'they're perfectly good braces.'

'You simply can't do that,' Richman responded with a sweep of his hand. 'You must have proper black braces to go with the rest of the outfit.'

Richman stood back to take in the full perspective of his master, like a tailor considering his craftsmanship.

'You look fine except for the braces. Remember you're going to see the Queen,' he smiled, with an air of chiding. 'Those red braces are out of place.'

It was like a final verdict. Richman turned to me for support, which I gave with a firm nod.

The Prime Minister protested plaintively: 'But I haven't got another pair of braces. These are all I have – unless either of you two can lend me a pair.' We couldn't.

'Then these will have to do; she'll have to see me in red braces,' Wilson decided impatiently.

Richman looked at his watch and snapped: 'There's just time – I'm going out to buy you a decent pair of black braces.'

And he did. While Wilson continued his interview with me Richman went round to a local store to buy a pair of splendid black braces, which he then proceeded to fasten onto Wilson's black striped trousers. A quick glance at his watch again and then to Wilson: 'OK, Harold, you can go to the Palace now; you're perfectly respectable.'

I have no idea whether Alf Richman charged the braces to his expenses, but it was the moment I most remember as the new Prime Minister went off to meet his Queen and become sworn in as First Lord of the Treasury etc. Day One of the Wilson Government, circa October 1964.

*   *   *

The night before at the Adelphi Hotel in Liverpool the buzz was electrifying. The exhausting campaign was over but most of us realised that the big excitement was only now about to begin. Going around with Wilson for more than three weeks had left most journalists on the tour convinced that he was going to win with a substantial margin. That is always the problem of being close to the figurehead in a political campaign – it is impossible not to become infected with the immediate ambience. I remembered that it was the same with Aneurin Bevan in 1959, so I was dutifully cautious. Even so it did seem that Wilson would win over Alec Douglas-Home with a handsome majority. The press corps gathered in the Adelphi bar that night shared this view, I think, without exception. I joined a group of my fellow reporters for a meal before the long night of vigil began. A few tables behind us sat Harold and Mary Wilson and Marcia Williams.

Half way through the meal I was called to the 'phone – it was my London news desk with the information that:

(1) Nikita Khrushchev had been ousted from his post as party leader and head of the Soviet Government and,

(2) Communist China had exploded its first atomic bomb using a technique and a device that was new to nuclear explosions.

Both items were justifiably regarded as 'sensational' in their own right quite apart from coming on the cusp of a British general election. The paper, quite rightly, wanted Wilson's immediate reaction to both. I was therefore the first to inform him of Khrushchev's departure and China's bomb. He sat at the table reflecting and then produced a made-to-measure quote about what a Labour Government would need to do immediately it took office. He said he would seek immediate talks with the new Soviet leader – Khrushchev's successor had not yet been identified. China's bomb was a more difficult issue: he was less sanguine about that, pointing out that in the absence – then – of a non-proliferation treaty between the major world powers it was inevitable that other nations, certainly one as important as China, would produce, and therefore test, nuclear weapons. Wilson was not a unilateral nuclear disarmer and never had been, but he was one of the earliest advocates of a non-proliferation treaty. So Wilson's reaction, which I managed to get into the later editions of the paper, was recorded, though too late, of course, to have had any influence on the way people voted that day.

Around midnight we were back in the Adelphi after a rapid tour of Wilson's Huyton constituency. In the early hours it did look like a reasonable Labour victory – or, as we calculated, at least a majority of around twenty. In his first-floor suite the Labour leader began jotting down names for his first Cabinet. I sat in the lounge bar with Frank Cousins, then general secretary of the Transport & General Workers Union (and about to be appointed to Wilson's first Cabinet) and John Bourne, the political correspondent of the *Financial Times* and an old friend. We were all making a list of our Cabinet bets.

At about 1.30 am Cousins was summoned to Wilson's suite (Number 100). Bourne and I speculated, of course. But we were wrong. My guess was that Cousins would be offered the Ministry of Transport; Bourne suggested another department. In fact he became Britain's first Minister of Technology. He returned to us an hour later to tell us, in confidence of course, that he had been offered a choice of three posts – Transport, Labour, and Technology, and had informed Wilson that he would prefer the latter.

At around 4 am the party broke up for some sleep – a couple of hours – before we caught the early morning train back to London with the final result of the election still very much in the balance. We were all astonished at how well the Conservatives had rallied, not only in the rural areas but with some unexpected successes in the south of England. Moreover the Labour Party suffered several extraordinary shocks: Patrick Gordon Walker, whom Wilson had jotted down for Foreign Secretary, lost his 'safe' seat at Smethwick, in the Midlands – defeated by a Tory who had exploited local racial tensions.

It was a far more nervous, tense journey back to Euston than Harold Wilson had envisaged. He refused to be interviewed on the train despite the relentless efforts by television crews. Even at Euston, when it seemed certain that he had won, albeit by a slender margin, Wilson would say nothing. He insisted on going straight back to Transport House for consultations – and a change of braces, of course.

*   *   *

Labour won the 1964 election by a whisker. Most observers were surprised, and even the Tories had not expected to run so close. An overall majority of 4 emerged from Labour's 317 seats (on a total poll of 12,205,576, which was 44.1 per cent) against the Conservatives 304 seats (polling 12,002,407, which was 43.4 per cent). The Liberals took 9 seats on a poll of 3,093,316, which was 11.2 per cent. Labour won 59 seats and the Tories lost 61, the Liberals picked up 3 extra seats. In fact the overall Labour poll was actually less than in 1959, which Macmillan won by a majority of nearly 100. It was another example of electoral eccentricity – and it disappointed Harold Wilson.

Despite all the ridicule he had heaped on Alec Douglas-Home, the man who did his economics with 'matchsticks', as Wilson described him, the Tory aristocrat who had seemed to lack any flair or charisma, came tantalisingly close to keeping the Tories in power after their 'thirteen years of misrule' – Labour's election cliché. Everyone, including the new Prime Minister, recognised that there would have to be another election before long. So Wilson began with a serious disadvantage, if not a precarious hold on power. The question on everybody's lips was: what sort of a Labour Government is this going to be? What sort of a socialist is Wilson?

Harold Wilson was never very strong on socialist theories. He always dismissed Marx and Marxism, and made a well-publicised virtue of never having got beyond the first page of *Das Kapital*. In his earliest days at Oxford he had toyed with the Liberals. At one point he was tempted to remain in Oxford as a don, and in 1938 Beveridge, with whom Wilson worked and who was a powerful influence on the brilliant young academic (Wilson graduated with an outstanding first-class degree with alphas on every paper) appointed him a Research Fellow at University College. But the power and influence of Beveridge was to prove less politically strong as that of G.D.H. Cole – the man who brought Wilson into the Oxford Labour Club and in effect set him on course for Downing Street.

Even so Wilson was no philospher or political poet in the genre of a Bevan. There was none of the revolutionary romantic in the Wilson bloodstream. What he did eventually develop was a tremendous instinct to understand what the Labour Party was all about: social justice rather than revolution. He saw the Labour Party as the instrument to correct social injustice and in that sense economic inequality. That remained the essence of Wilsonian socialism to the end.

Denis Healey, who had known Wilson as an Oxford contemporary in the 1930s, has advanced a severe verdict on his former Prime Minister. In his memoirs, *The Time of My Life* (1989), Healey condemned Wilson as a man who 'had no sense of direction and rarely looked more than twelve months ahead'. It was a cruel judgement. Yet in one respect Healey got it right: Wilson was not a political leader of great vision. He possessed an unusually high level of intuition, which went along with an exceptional memory. These were huge assets. But he always measured risk-taking very carefully and never liked to gamble on issues where he suspected that the problem could run beyond his control. He would go to great lengths to avoid unpleasant confrontations. All of this inevitably led to the growth of his reputation as 'an intriguer' and 'a fixer'. Numerous members of his Cabinets were always wary of 'Harold's intrigues'.

Yet in defence of Wilson there was all too often a strong justification for his supicions about his colleagues plotting against him. He frequently, and usually wrongly, suspected Jim Callaghan of being behind these intrigues. In fact it was more often Roy Jenkins, or at least the Jenkins entourage, who were always contemplating ways and means of undermining Wilson's authority. Too frequently Wilson relied on the Whitehall gossip, which was relentlessly picked up and siphoned into his ears by George Wigg or, more significantly, Marcia Williams.

Yet there is no doubt at all in my mind that much of what Mrs Williams then picked up was very close to the truth. Her political antennae were remarkable, and her sources without parallel in that world of intrigue which is, let us admit, the perpetual condition of all centres of power and influence. If the Court of Harold Wilson resembled the ambience of a feudal dynasty then it was no different, except in time and circumstance, from any other centre of power in the history of politics. And, in general, rather better motivated.

9 In Place of Courage: Journalism in Decline

Toward the end of the 1960s – as the *Sun*, literally, was setting on the Odhams' empire of Covent Garden and the local pubs were planning their own reformation into quick-food bars to cater for the Yuppie factor that had already begun to seep into the veins of 'the Garden' – I was on the move to Holborn Circus over which the old *Daily Mirror* building still dominated, alas, like so much else, no longer. It is now Sainsbury's emporium.

It was November 1969 and another parting of the ways. Just prior to the great upheaval I experienced my first real taste of Captain Robert Maxwell, MC. It was all connected with the future, if any, of the *Sun* for which Bob Maxwell had serious plans. He wanted to forestall Murdoch's bid for the paper with an ingenious scheme to finance yet another relaunch of the title as an independent daily paper of the left, without any formal links with the Labour Party, but to have its resources guaranteed by bringing the printing and publishing of all trade union journals under one production umbrella. It was an inspired concept. Whether it would have worked in practice is another matter but the idea, at least in theory, was a stroke of genius typical of Maxwell's thought processes. At the time Maxwell was still struggling to recover from the mauling he received from the Board of Trade inquiry into his dealings with the Pergamon Press – the report that declared him unfit to run a public company. His ambition remained, as ever, to own and run a daily newspaper. The fading *Sun* appealed as an ideal base from which to rebuild his empire and his gravely damaged reputation.

Maxwell made the first tentative moves to take it over from the Mirror Group early in the summer of 1968, sometime before Murdoch clinched his deal with Cudlipp. Maxwell actually appointed an editor, Mike Randall, to run the new paper. Randall was a gifted journalist with a long record of outstanding work in Fleet Street and had been editor of the *Daily Mail* before running into a personality clash with Lord Rothermere, grandfather of the current title holder of the Harmsworth–Rothermere dynasty. Randall edited the old broadsheet *Daily Mail* during one of its finest periods as a quality middle-market paper. Maxwell wanted him to edit his vision of a great new daily paper of what would now be described as the 'centre-left'. Maxwell then invited me to be Randall's No. 2 – deputy editor of the new paper. The whole idea eventually fell through and Murdoch gazumped him to acquire the *Sun*. But not before I had discovered an astonishing story about Cap'n Bob.

We met one evening in the early summer of 1968 in Maxwell's top-floor suite of his Pergamon office in Fitzroy Square. Compared with his later furnishings of grandeur and ostentatious opulence the Pergamon office was modest. Even his private top-floor suite was routine compared with his Citizen Kane style at the Mirror Group in later years. The two of us sat on either side of a low glass-topped coffee table on which stood a bottle of whisky. We talked briefly about the job he was offering, even the salary as deputy editor and I said I would reflect on it. He wanted an immediate answer, but I stalled. That irritated him. Bob Maxwell was a man who liked instant decisions, good or bad – usually bad.

We sparred like a couple of mismatched boxers and swapped wartime stories, having discovered that we were both in Berlin in 1945. He was only mildly interested in my views of Berlin circa 1945, the devastation and human degradation; the appalling inheritance after the fall of Hitler's Reich, my role in the RAF at the time. 'And what were you doing in Berlin, Bob?' I asked, knowing that he would be much more interested in talking about himself than in listening to my story. 'I was engaged in intelligence work,' he replied (his *Who's Who* entry listed him as Head of Press Section, Berlin 1945–7). 'Yes, sure, but what were you actually doing?' I pressed him as the whisky flowed. It was then that he told me the extraordinary story about Marshal Zhukov's safe.

Zhukov, commander of the Soviet army that liberated Berlin from the Nazis, had his headquarters in the Eastern sector of the city. Maxwell, who spoke Russian reasonably well – along with six other languages – was chosen to mastermind a plan to break into Zhukov's office, with an accomplice who was a senior officer in the Red Army. He worked on Zhukov's personal staff and knew the combination to the safe in which the Soviet Marshal kept his top secret papers. British intelligence, Maxwell told me that night as we sat in his Fitzroy Square office, knew that those papers contained details of Moscow's plan to strip Eastern Germany (the Soviet zone of occupation) of most of its valuable industrial plant and remove it to the Soviet Union. British, and American, intelligence wanted to know what those documents contained, and Maxwell plus his Red Army accomplice were given the job of breaking into Zhukov's iron-guarded lair.

Maxwell saw disbelief written all over my face.

'You don't believe me?' he demanded.

'I find it hard to accept, Bob,' was my tepid reply.

'I give you my word, that this is absolutely a true story.' He seemed anxious that I shouldn't doubt him.

'What happened to your Red Army colonel?' I asked.

'We got him out after he had taken the documents, photographed them and replaced them in the safe. We couldn't take any chances so we brought him over to the West.'

Years later there was an extraordinary sequel to this story. On the eve of Maxwell's takeover of Mirror Group, in July 1984, I retold this story to the editor of the *Daily Mirror*, Mike Molloy, and his deputy Peter Thompson as we sat in Molloy's office contemplating our fate. Thompson subsequently put the story in a book on Maxwell he wrote with another *Mirror* colleague, Tony Delano. Their book quoted me as declaring that I simply did not believe the Maxwell story, circa 1968. When their book was about to be published Maxwell's lawyers succeeded in obtaining an injunction to stop the book because of its inaccuracies – among which my refusal to believe his Berlin story was a prime example. I had departed from the paper by then but that didn't deter Bob Maxwell calling me and asking if I would come to see him to discuss 'those bastards, Thomspon and Delano and their book'. To what purpose, I asked Maxwell. 'Because I want to talk to you again about the Berlin story,' he shouted, as he heaped more abuse on the book's authors. I agreed to see him.

Maxwell was then involved in a series of attempts to prevent the publication of several books about himself – notably one by Tom Bower. He was so enraged about them that he had commissioned an in-house biography by Joe Haines to either forestall all other books or at least make sure that his side of the story was told according to his wishes and preferences. The Thompson–Delano book was especially infuriating to him because both authors had been senior journalists on his staff. Maxwell wanted to know whether I would be prepared to disown the Thompson–Delano account of my Berlin story and, if necessary, go into court to say so under oath. We met in spring 1988, twenty years after he had first revealed his Berlin story to me, in his luxury suite on the tenth floor of the W.H. Smith building, tucked immediately behind the Mirror block in Fetter Lane.

It was a breathtaking scene, eminently suitable to a Citizen Kane rerun. The darkened green décor, with shaded discreet lighting, did not conceal the magnificence of the furnishings. The salon had all the appearance of a mysterious grotto with the Wizard's Imperial throne set commandingly at camera-centre point. Xanadu, London EC4. Very different from the scene twenty years earlier in Fitzroy Square when the Berlin story first emerged. This time there was no whisky, but a bottle of expensive white wine on a low glass table. Maxwell sat in a huge throne-like chair and I was offered the one opposite – so huge that my legs dangled rather than touching the floor.

Cap'n Bob welcomed me warmly, poured the wine and immediately opened the batting: 'So,' he began a little sadly, 'you don't believe the Berlin story?'

'Well, Bob, put it this way,' I stalled carefully, 'I find it hard to believe.'

'Would you believe me if I were now to show you copies of the documents we took from Zhukov's safe? You read German, I know, so you can look at them ...'

I was, I admit, stunned at this. He clapped his hands, rang a bell, shouted for flunkeys. Several appeared and he demanded: 'Pass me the stuff.'

A range of photocopies of documents were spread across the table between us. 'Have a look at them,' Bob invited with a wave of his huge mitt.

The papers were – or appeared to be – listings of factories and equipment from various parts of Eastern Germany. The names of the factories and their identity were all marked. Dates, contents, specifications were all there. It all seemed authentic.

When I had finished reading them Maxwell injected his key question: 'Well, are you prepared to believe me now?'

I nodded. 'Assuming these are genuine, Bob, I haven't much option, have I?' was my weakened response.

And to assure me that they were genuine he asked me to speak with his lawyers – a top-flight legal firm who were fighting to pulp the Thompson–Delano book.

I did so and asked them what I regarded as the crucial question: 'OK, if I were to go to court and say that I now believed Bob Maxwell's Berlin story, what proof have I that these are copies of genuine documents?'

They replied: 'We give you that assurance and will declare so on oath in court.'

I will return to the story in a later chapter on Maxwell, but at this point it is important to make one further reflection. I remain puzzled to this day why Maxwell felt it so important that I should accept his word. He knew, even without my support, that he had enough evidence to have the book pulped. Yet he was adamant in pursuit of my approval. He purred like a great Persian cat as I left, as if satisfied that his honour had been vindicated even if by someone with whom he had no further connection, certainly no real interest, nor was in any way beholden to. It was an extraordinary episode in my altogether extraordinary relationship with Cap'n Bob. Of which more to follow ...

*   *   *

What left the strongest impression on me in the move from the old Odhams' *Sun* to the *Daily Mirror* in November 1969 was the comparative luxury of the facilities at Holborn Circus compared with the bare-bones resources at the old Odhams' 'factory'. I had never before worked in an atmosphere of such palpable success. The facilities, the staffing, the tone of the place was a spectacle in itself. Back along my road at the *News Chronicle*, *Daily Herald* and *Sun* (Odhams' version, of course) it had always been great fun amid the professional challenges, wonderful colleagues as well as nasty ones, good and poor editors, good and less adequate subs; Holborn Circus was a new world. All the other ingredients of life on a national daily newspaper were there, of course, the good and the bad, and the not so bad, but at the *Daily Mirror* at that time they all came with a touch of extra-theatre. It was obvious that the longer-term residents at the Holborn Circus Palace of Varieties had had it pretty good for a fair time. Not that they were flaunting their comfortable success; but there was a confidence and a self-belief that had been significantly lacking in some of my previous billets. It is undeniable that success carries its own powerful fuel of propulsion to further success – that is, of course, until complacency sets in, which it certainly did in later years at the *Mirror*.

Those early months at Holborn Circus were eye-opening as well as immensely stimulating under the inspirational force of Hugh Cudlipp, who was still very much the kingpin of popular journalism despite having let Murdoch slip in by the side gate. An example of this, in my own case, was when the Leicester Labour Party approached me to stand as their candidate in Leicester North-west – then a safe Labour seat about to be vacated by the late Barnett Janner (Lord Janner). Janner had been Labour MP in Leicester since 1945 and had decided to stand down at the 1970 General Election. The Leicester Labour Party wanted me to succeed him. But there was a difficult and embarrassing problem involved: the retiring member made it clear that he wanted his son Greville to succeed – while the local Labour Party were strongly in favour of a new broom. Whatever the qualities of Greville Janner, and they were numerous, the local party wanted someone else, and they made it clear to the regional Labour Party agent that their preference was for me. I had the support of several trade unions and had been short-listed for final selection at a meeting to be arranged. By then there was only one other name on the short list – Greville Janner. It was made pretty clear to me that I would get majority support.

That was the situation when I notified Hugh Cudlipp of what may be in the pipeline. His reaction was twofold: first was an explosion of contempt that I should even consider the idea of becoming a backbench MP as against staying with the *Daily Mirror* ('What the bloody hell would you do spending all your time on the backbenches while waiting to become a junior minister? What a waste of time and talent,' he thundered.) His second point was to offer me a regular weekly column in the paper in which I could write what I wanted, even if I disagreed with the *Mirror*'s editorial line. He would always guarantee my freedom to write what I wished. I would also remain the paper's industrial editor.

I took a few days to reflect on what was, I suppose, an offer that was nearly impossible to refuse. Even so it was agonising. Whichever way I turned I knew I would be guilty of letting someone down – the Leicester Labour Party or Cudlipp. Who knows whether such decisions are the right ones at any time? The fact that I chose to accept Cudlipp's seductive offer led to many years of privileged journalism on one of the great daily newspapers of our time. But if I had accepted the other option …? Well, no one can tell and it is fruitless to try. I knew that my decision to pull out of the Leicester contest would disappoint and anger many friends I had already made in the constituency. And it did. They were justifiably angry; they felt I had landed them with a choice they did not relish. I am still in debt to the Leicester Labour Party for their tolerance and for what, at the time, appeared to be an unfortunate piece of backsliding. But in

Greville Janner (now Lord Janner) they did get a very good MP who served the constituency in a style that I doubt I could have matched and, frankly, in a far less controversial manner than I would probably have managed.

*   *   *

I had already acquired a reputation for being highly critical of the Wilson Government's attempt to legislate against the trade unions when Barbara Castle produced her famous White Paper 'In Place of Strife', which followed the report, in 1968, of Lord Donovan's Royal Commission on the unions. Barbara, then Secretary of State for Employment and a leading member of the Wilson Cabinet, was set for confrontation with the unions. She knew full well the implications of that; so did Harold Wilson. What they did not fully appreciate was how deeply the White Paper would cut through the entire Labour movement, including the Parliamentary Labour Party. It was my own early instinctive belief that while the Wilson Government was right to challenge the trade unions and force them to recognise the needs of a new political and economic age, they were mishandling their approach work. This was the essence of my case in many of my columns in the old *Sun* during the late 1960s. Those were critical days for the Wilson Government. The government was fighting on a number of fronts and never seemed to be quite clear on its overall strategy. At the centre of the stage was its prices and incomes policy, which George Brown had started after the 1964 election by creating a Prices and Incomes Board under Aubrey Jones, a former Conservative MP. Brown had then gone on to produce a Declaration of Intent, which brought together government, employers and the TUC in support of a counter-inflation programme, greater industrial efficiency, higher productivity and all that. It was a major initiative in corporate enterprise and would not have been out of place in a Blair 'Third Way' agenda. But the mood of the country in those pre-Thatcher days was very different.

About that time I did a kind of J.B. Priestley tour of Britain for my paper. I travelled round the country interviewing employers, union officials, shopfloor workers, managers *et al.* to get their feelings on what was going wrong with Britain's industrial relations; indeed, I really went in search of an answer to the question – 'what is happening under the surface of British life?' I tried to reach below the superficial clichés and test the mood of those who were at the sharp end of industrial life. It was not encouraging. They all distrusted the government, albeit for different reasons. Whitehall was a long way from the shopfloor and neither side seemed capable of bridging the gulf.

George Brown's absurdly ambitious National Plan had already been written off and consigned to the shelves of history. It was a personal tragedy for Brown, who was then moved from the dying Department of Economic Affairs, which was very much his creation, to the Foreign Office. That too ended in farce and disaster for him, and he finally resigned from the Wilson Government in March 1968. Two years later he lost his seat in Belper (Derbyshire) in the 1970 General Election. He went to the House of Lords as Lord George Brown, finally quit the Labour Party and ended his life as a sad and sidelined figure. The working-class boy from Peabody buildings in the East End of London might have ended with a very different story but the forces of self-destruction within him were too strong. He was an extraordinary mix of brilliance and madness. The deep frustrations built into his psyche by his background exploded into a bitterness and anger at his university-qualified, upper-crust socialist colleagues: he despised them as he envied them their capacity to intellectualise themselves into and out of problems; his own drink problem was far less an addiction to alcohol than an escape mechanism through which he lost control of his inhibitions almost as if he was fully aware of a form of chosen weakness.

Yet above all this he had the mind of a political leader bordering on the exceptional. It was sometimes said of George that he came within a hair's-breadth of greatness – the trouble was that this hair's-breadth was stronger, thicker and more durable than any other kind of hair. His National Plan contained the nucleus of social and economic thought that remains relevant to this day. But it was ill-conceived at the time, hastily and inadequately pulled together and carried no real conviction. Much the same was true of the incomes policy, which George Brown more than any other member of that Wilson Cabinet fought so hard to steer into place. There was a powerful case for the essence of a fair incomes policy; but it was placed right in the centre of the Wilson Government's economic policy and simply couldn't carry that weight and responsibility. These were the issues I was writing about, and criticising, even before moving to the *Daily Mirror*. Then came the Donovan Commission, which referred to the two layers of industrial relations – the formal official scene at national level and the reality of life on the shopfloor, with all the unofficial strikes and the so-called 'British disease', which was strong currency at the time. Much of which I had myself already discovered in my tour of the country's industrial grass-roots.

In the months that followed the Donovan Commission Barbara Castle and her team of advisers at the Employment Ministry, which was then one of the most important departments of state, struggled to develop a strategy based on Donovan and indeed to take the commission's proposals a stage further. The Royal Commission proposed the setting up of an Industrial Relations Commission as a new institution to supervise a more rational system of industrial relations for the country. But both Wilson and Castle were more ambitious than this. They were convinced that new legislation was required to bring some discipline into trade union behaviour.

Barbara Castle's Permanent Secretary was Sir Denis Barnes, a brilliant civil servant whose career had started way back with Ernest Bevin in wartime. Barnes was by then single-minded in his view that new legislation was imperative. Denis was *not* anti-union; but after years of experience he had become exasperated at the narrow-mindedness and limited imagination of so much in trade union thinking. I knew Denis very well, and he confided to me at the time that he believed it possible to win over the TUC to the idea of new legislation that carried the Donovan proposals a step further. He told me that in private discussions with the TUC General Secretary, George Woodcock (who had been a member of the Donovan Commission), Woodcock surprised him by declaring his support if the government chose to take a tougher line. I was *not* surprised to hear this since in my many discussions with Woodcock, a man I greatly admired as the outstanding TUC general secretary of all the postwar TUC leaders, he had consistently declared in favour of the unions being given what he described as 'a real challenge by government'.

Woodcock had no illusions about the need for trade union modernisation – long before Thatcher and the Tory government took up the legislative cudgels. His case was that the unions had been reared and developed in the business of 'negative reaction' to events. That was because they had never been brought into the centre of decision-making. Their role was inescapably reactive. His frequent description of their historic condition was that they were 'rebels and outlaws'. Unions had been compelled to live and work 'outside the law' because of the uneven and class nature of society.

Woodcock, the first trade union leader to work his way from a 14-year-old factory worker to a brilliant Oxford degree, was the philosopher prince of trade unionism. Had he not been a practising believer and a Catholic he might well have been a passionate Marxist. His intellectual process had that cast and at times even that direction. He saw the inevitability of trade union change but he also argued that 'left to themselves they will do nothing – they must be challenged'. And he wanted the Wilson Government to produce that challenge. He did not underestimate the reaction he would receive from within the TUC General Council but nonetheless believed he could ride that storm – provided the government behaved sensibly. That was to prove a big 'if'.

Castle's team came up with 'In Place of Strife' shortly before Christmas 1968. The draft White Paper was scheduled to go to Cabinet at a special meeting called by Wilson for early New Year. On New Year's Eve at my home my wife and I gave a New Year party at which Barbara Castle and Jack Jones – then general secretary of the Transport & General Workers Union with over two million members – were among the guests. Around the midnight hour, I saw Barbara and Jack in a corner of the room engaged in a shouting match. I heard Jones cry out: 'You'll never get away with it, Barbara.' The Minister, shouting back, yelled at Jack: 'You watch me!'

I discovered later that Barbara had outlined her plans to Jones in advance of the Cabinet meeting. In fact I also knew that a draft document of the White Paper had already been shown to a few selected members of the TUC General Council on 30 December – and that Jones was among the selected few. So he was well aware of what was coming. The slanging match in the corner of our room on New Year's Eve was in fact a continuation of the explosion that took place when the TUC first had sight of the document.

It is worth recalling some of the points of that White Paper, now long forgotten and buried under the debris of all the Thatcher years of fighting the unions. The title itself, 'In Place of Strife', was provided by Barbara's husband, Ted, who was a first-class sub-editor with a ready headline. Ted picked up the idea – as he confessed to me years later – from Nye Bevan's book, *In Place of Fear*. It was a brilliant headline. The contents were less than brilliant.

The original White Paper contained 27 main items of which the most controversial was a proposal to establish a 28-day 'cooling-off' period, which the government would be empowered to impose on any dispute to allow conciliation to move in to try to find a settlement. There were also proposals for a ballot of members before a strike and legal sanctions to ensure that unions would be compelled to operate within the provisions of the new Act. The package contained sweeteners for the unions which guaranteed them status and recognition. But the essential feature of Barbara Castle's White Paper was to impose legal disciplines on trade union behaviour aimed, especially, at curbing unofficial strikes, which were so widespread at that time.

The package, of course, was dynamite. It was the first time any government in peacetime in the twentieth century had attempted such legal measures against trade union practices. And it split the Wilson Cabinet. Indeed, it came close to bringing down the Prime Minister, who had given his personal backing to Barbara Castle's proposals. A great deal has been written since then about the political drama inside the Wilson Cabinet – by almost every senior member of that Cabinet, Healey, Callaghan, Roy Jenkins, Dick Crossman, Barbara Castle herself and, of course, Harold Wilson.

Perhaps the most revealing and penetrating account comes in Jenkins's memoirs (*A Life at the Centre*, 1991) – particularly important because it was through a deal with Jenkins, then Chancellor, that both Wilson and Barbara Castle were able to find a compromise to a crisis that threatened both of them. The original White Paper was severely watered down and Chancellor Jenkins agreed to soften his Prices and Incomes legislation, which was due to be made even tougher in the following autumn. Jenkins makes it clear in his book that the Parliamentary Labour Party, as well as the unions, were so split over 'In Place of Strife' that it would have taken very little for him to have ignited an explosion that would have removed Wilson and replaced him as Prime Minister. But Jenkins had already agreed with Wilson and Castle to support modified legislation against the unions, and he writes (1991: 288): 'I was not tempted to renege on the bill in order to replace Wilson.'

Jenkins later regretted that absence of a killer instinct in his character; so, too, did many of his friends and allies of that period. Some never forgave Jenkins for showing such 'weakness'. Even so at the time it was a close-run thing. Moreover the whole affair, along with the ultimate retreat by the Cabinet with a fudged compromise that gave the TUC a fresh opportunity to introduce voluntary regulation of disputes, added to the growing discredit of the Labour Government. In my view, this was the crucial factor that led to Heath's election victory in June 1970.

The Conservative Party had long been working on its own version of trade union reform. Numerous drafts of planned new legislation to curb the unions had piled up on the shelves in Tory Central Office; some had been there for several years. Eventually they were rolled into the new Industrial Relations Act produced by the Heath Government after the 1970 election. But the groundwork had already been laid for the Tories by 'In Place of Strife', and it was the advanced awareness of Tory Party's plans that strengthened the hand of those in the Wilson Cabinet who were sworn to oppose Barbara Castle's proposals. Leading the rebellion against her was Jim Callaghan, who was then at the Home Office.

In Wilson's mind the Callaghan 'threat' was far greater than that posed by Roy Jenkins. Indeed, the main battle inside Cabinet, as well as the Parliamentary Labour Party, was the fight between the Prime Minister and his Home Secretary about the future of trade unionism. Jim Callaghan had the evidence from the Whips' Office that on a head count of the MPs he could beat the Wilson–Castle proposals. He was fortified by the personal and political support of Douglas Houghton (the late Lord Houghton), who was chairman of the PLP. Callaghan also had the full support of Victor Feather (the late Lord Feather), who had taken over as TUC general secretary from Woodcock, who had become chairman of a new Commission on Industrial Relations as proposed by the Donovan Royal Commission.

The interesting relationship, however, was that between Callaghan and Houghton – both former full-time officials of the old tax collectors' union, the IRSF (Inland Revenue Staff Federation). Houghton had been general secretary of the union before the war when Callaghan was a young official. Houghton had trained and encouraged the young Jim Callaghan – and now that his protégé was a rising Cabinet figure he had no intention of letting him down. Between them Callaghan, Houghton and Feather planned, and indeed plotted, the downfall of Castle's 'In Place of Strife', if not of Castle herself.

I have had access to Douglas Houghton's private papers, and there is no doubt that Harold Wilson was entirely justified in his conviction that there was a serious plot to remove him from Downing Street. Many of the secret meetings between Houghton, Callaghan and Feather took place in Houghton's Marsham Court flat, a few minutes' walk from the House of Commons. Feather was as contemptuous of Barbara Castle as the other two. My notes from that time record Feather telling me: 'Barbara's knowledge and understanding of how trade unions work and function is nil. What she is after is power. She is full of vanity.' And Feather was convinced that what she was doing was simply preparing the ground 'for future Tory legislation'. Nor did Feather have much more faith in Harold Wilson: 'Harold will have to climb down,' he told me. 'He has no alternative if he wants to remain Prime Minister. He knows he cannot get this legislation through the PLP.'

In fact there was a point when Wilson did consider resigning over 'In Place of Strife', and some cynics have suggested that it was only the appalling prospect that Callaghan would probably succeed him that persuaded Wilson to soldier on. Oddly enough, Wilson himself had already begun to have some doubts about Castle's proposals, and Barbara recognised this. But she would never have supported Callaghan as a replacement for Harold: they were old political enemies. Indeed, when Callaghan eventually became Prime Minister one of the first things he did was to sack Barbara Castle.

On 18 June 1969 Wilson backed down. An extraordinary series of meetings between Cabinet Ministers and the TUC leaders culminated in a face-saving deal – which in fact saved nobody's face. What became notoriously known as 'Solomon Binding', an Old Testament arbitrator, no doubt, appeared on the scene in the form of a 'solemn and binding' agreement between the Wilson Government and the TUC to reduce 'In Place of Strife' to a voluntary pact under which the TUC undertook to take responsibility for a voluntary system of discipline. This involved the TUC intervening in disputes – official as well as unofficial. It was a practice vigorously exercised by Victor Feather with some limited success for a short period. But the retreat from 'In Place of Strife' had unquestionably torn a great hole in the credibility of the Wilson Government.

On the evening of the great retreat and *after* I had written my story I spent an hour with Barbara Castle in a one-to-one at her department in St James's Square. The Secretary of State for Employment and Productivity looked crumpled and crushed by her experience – an unusual condition for the bubbling, sometimes frenetic, Barbara. She tried to pretend to me that the whole extraordinary exercise had been worthwhile. But it was transparent rubbish and she knew it. She had lost her great battle to bring some order into trade union affairs. She was even more scornful of the trade union leadership than of her malicious Cabinet colleagues. 'Bastards, that's what they are. Bastards.' She never forgot that moment: it was the lowest point in her colourful political career. Nor did she ever forgive those Cabinet colleagues whom – she was convinced – went to exceptional lengths to 'sabotage Harold and me'.

What was to follow in the 1970s and right up to Margaret Thatcher's premiership has frequently been put down, especially by trade union leaders, to Barbara Castle's 'In Place of Strife'. But the alternative argument is equally, if not more, valid. Had the Wilson Government shown the courage to take some, if not all, the legal powers they originally proposed and faced up to trade union opposition – indeed if the government had backed Woodcock – it is still arguable that the Thatcher programme of anti-union legislation may never have happened. Another of history's 'Ifs'.

Not long ago I discussed these things with Lord Callaghan. In the afterglow of his premiership and in his retirement Jim Callaghan is much more reflective about what happened in 1969 and the consequences. He now accepts that he 'probably' made an error of judgement in 1969 by under-estimating the need for some disciplining of the unions. Having gone through his own traumatic experience during the Winter of Discontent of 1978–9 he is much more prepared, with hindsight, to recognise that Wilson and Castle may well have been right – or at least not so badly wrong as he then assumed.

As it was the 1970 General Election turned Wilson's majority of nearly 100 into a Conservative majority of 30 and brought Ted Heath into Downing Street. The swing to the Tories in England was 5.1 per cent, in Wales 4.4 per cent and in Scotland 2.8 per cent. It was a low poll – 72 per cent – which reflected the fact that a large number of Labour voters had simply stayed at home. Labour polled a million fewer votes than the Conservatives. The result shocked Harold Wilson. But after spending almost the whole of that election campaign on the road I was certainly not surprised. I had spent one week with George Brown, a brief spell with Wilson and a few days travelling with Roy Jenkins in the west country. Nowhere was there any great enthusiasm for any party. The Conservative core vote was strong but they appeared to be attracting few of the 'undecided'. The Labour voters seemed apathetic, disinterested, detached. Gone was the flowing enthusiasm I recalled from 1964 and 1966. I remember talking with Marcia Williams (Lady Falkender) on my return from this latest round-Britain sojourn and advising her to inform the Prime Minister that I thought Labour were in trouble. But the Downing Street entourage simply wouldn't accept that view.

On polling night, 17 June 1970, the *Daily Mirror* threw its traditional election night party on the ninth floor of the Holborn Circus building. Hugh Cudlipp was host to a stream of the great, the good and not so good who dropped in for the smoked salmon, glazed turkey and champagne. A large blackboard was mounted in the reception area of the main hall and on the ninth floor to signal election results as they came through. After-midnight drinks were being served when the first results began to trickle in: a Conservative gain at Billericay, a weathervane constituency ... then came a flash – George Brown had been unseated at Belper. That was it. Wilson was out and everyone knew it. The American Ambassador, Walter H. Annenberg, a guest at the *Mirror's* party, didn't quite know whether to smile, grimace or simply go on sipping his champagne. Cudlipp growled and shuffled.

Jack Cohen, then unchallenged boss of Tesco – 'pile 'em high, sell 'em cheap' – was elated. 'I want the Tories to win,' he grinned at me. 'That'll stop all those people I employ robbing me ... robbing me, that's what they do, d'yer know that? They rob me ...' I never did quite get the point but I suppose he meant that his employees actually wanted to be paid for the pleasure of working for him. Great character, Jack Cohen of Tesco, like his daughter. But I never understood why Cudlipp invited him to the *Mirror* party that night.

It was the close of the first Wilson era, and there was little nobility in the political air that June evening. After 1964 there had been a courageous spell under pressure followed by a tremendous victory in the 1966 election, which ought to have set a foundation for a considerable government. It was then the largest majority Labour had secured apart from 1945. For a while even the staunch Conservative press gave Wilson a fair run. That quickly ran out after the economic crisis and the seamen's strike in the summer of 1966. The strike was badly handled by the government. The leadership of the National Union of Seamen, at that time, was corrupt and inept. The strike itself was led mostly by an unofficial group in which John Prescott was active. The men's grievances were extensive and largely genuine but their union leaders were incompetent and had long existed in a complaisant environment of closeness with the shipping employers. Of course there were seriously disruptive elements among the unofficial seamen's groups. But that is always inevitable in a situation of official incompetence. A tribunal of inquiry gave the seamen much of what they had originally claimed.

And when I wrote a piece critical of the government's handling of the whole dispute the Prime Minister asked his then press secretary, Trevor Lloyd-Hughes (now Sir Trevor), to call me up to explain the error of my ways and how my critical words had upset Harold Wilson.

I left him in no doubt what he should do with his – and the Prime Minister's – opinions. Interestingly enough, that sharp exchange did not affect my subsequent close association with Harold Wilson when he became Prime Minister again, which, I suppose, says something for H. Wilson.

It was indeed a most odd decade: full of absurdity and missed opportunity; rich in contradiction and quite unpredictable drama – such as Cecil King's dismissal from running Mirror Group Newspapers in the summer of 1968 after demanding Wilson's dismissal with his notorious *Mirror* front-page cry: 'Enough is Enough'. It was indeed *enough* for the Mirror's board, who then proceeded to sack the boss. It was the decade when almost everything changed and when British political life seemed to lose a sense of direction.

10 The Long March: Dropping in on China in the Cultural Revolution

Chairman Mao's China, circa 1971: Cultural Revolution and all that. It was indeed a dateline I had long sought. Then it suddenly happened, almost though not quite, out of the blue. A sequence of patience, self-discipline often hard to sustain, special lobbying and a considerable amount of homework came together to produce an extraordinary stroke of luck, which, of course, is always the essential ingredient in journalism as in most other things in life.

Dropping in on China in the middle of the Cultural Revolution sounds like a supremely old-fashioned newspaper scoop – which, in a way, it was. I had worked at the idea as a distant possibility for a long time. Throughout the 1960s, when I began a sort of desultory dialogue with the Chinese Legation in Portland Place, I had sought to persuade various members in the legation that it would be a splendid idea, from *their* point of view, to provide me with a visa to travel to China and report what was happening during the Cultural Revolution. My case was put quite simply – too simple, to be sure: that as someone who had always been fascinated by China and the whole epic struggle of Mao's Chinese Communists, kindled, I explained, long years before by a first reading of Edgar Snow's *Red Star Over China*, it seemed to me that I was well suited to report on events that were still perplexing the entire world outside China.

Over months, and even years, I established a rapport of sorts with the Chinese Legation. It was far from easy. There was a stiffness, a deep suspicion of and a rigidity of approach to everything. There were few concessions to the informal but I gradually built up a kind of distant trust. Occasionally it was possible even to bring the odd bit of laughter to a fixed gaze and the hint of an unplanned smile. For some time in the early and mid-1960s my principal contact at the Portland Place stronghold – it was still a long way off becoming a fully recognised embassy – was a senior diplomat whose status was First Secretary. His name was Li Wen-cheng. I grew to like him as I slowly penetrated the sheet-metal of his armour. Li was an army veteran from the revolutionary period when Mao's troops were fighting for their lives against Chiang Kai-shek's Kuomintang. He had joined up as a teenager to fight the Japanese and the Kuomintang together – which, of course, was Mao's great rallying cry to rouse millions of China's peasants against both the Japanese invaders and Chiang Kai-shek's collaborationist forces.

Li's story was probably typical of thousands of young men who rallied to Mao's Communist and, more important, liberationist banner. At any rate we built up an interesting rapport, often closeted together in a small, under-furnished room at the legation, sipping Maotai, a dynamite Chinese spirit that blows the top off any normal head. Behind Li's mask of convention and the obligatory catechism of Mao Tse-tung phrases I detected a suppressed eagerness to reach out. There was a warmth in Li's brown eyes, especially when he reflected back to his youth and his family's desperate fight to survive. He always held himself in disciplined control but there was a friendly strength in his handshake.

Throughout that tense and difficult period Li Wen-cheng and myself established a relationship of sorts: so much so that I actually succeeded in persuading him to come to my home for the occasional meal, something quite exceptional at the time. But when he came he always brought a junior colleague with him – a young man who was even more unrelaxed. If occasionally Li showed signs of social affinity the young companion grew solemn and troubled. I often felt that the older diplomat might be on the brink of waving aside some of the more grotesque masquerades of that period in China's image and admitting that maybe, perhaps, possibly, he didn't go along with everything that was happening in the Cultural Revolution. But Li never did that.

Film shows were regular events at the legation, and I was a sedulous attender. The front rooms of the ground floor at the legation were turned into a mini-film theatre for the ritualistic performances. The theme was daunting in its repetitive simplicity: 'The East is Red' came frequently – occasionally interspersed with some quite excellent technical productions of Chinese Opera and Ballet served up later with films about Chairman Mao rallying the masses. It was an arduous academy, and the apprenticeship in Chinese understanding required the stamina of a commando. Even so I always felt my grip on Anglo-Chinese friendship remained tenuous.

Yet I did – and do – admire the Chinese and their achievements. The arrogance that one sensed was always just below the surface was, I felt, part of their cultural uniqueness, and in some ways even the absurd posturing that surrounded the Communist Emperor himself was understandable given that this remarkable figure had led his people and their ancient civilisation out of centuries of obscurity and internal feuding back on to the world stage. Mao's leadership of the Chinese revolution was an apotheosis: it was brutal, as we now know far more clearly than we did at the time. Yet he also harnessed a spontaneous rededication and pride in nationhood. And what was equally amazing was the very concept of China struggling to cast off several thousand years of the Mandarin's yoke and the brutality of Warrior Emperors, and trying to replace all this with a socialist system, however primitive, that would be different from that in any other socialist country. It was too tempting to miss the opportunity to collect my visa to China when, eventually, it came through.

*   *   *

Foreign reporting has a special fascination for most journalists, and I had always nurtured a weakness for it. At every opportunity I had seized a chance to report from overseas during my years at the *News Chronicle.* And at the *Daily Herald* and the Odhams' *Sun* I could never resist the temptation to collect an assignment abroad. These had taken me throughout Europe, Scandinavia, into the United States, and in 1967 I covered the fiftieth anniversary of the Bolshevik revolution for the *Sun* on what was my third visit to the Soviet Union. Quite apart from the opportunity to break away from the routine of domestic reporting, of politics, industry or anything else, it was always evident that any newspaperman must be able to compare his own native territory with what was happening elsewhere. As I have confessed elsewhere, journalism is largely a career in self-education.

By the time the Heath Government was installed in June 1970 I had already shifted my Chinese Legation credentials to the *Daily Mirror* – a newspaper that no doubt puzzled my Chinese friends but did not appear to jeopardise my relationship. Quite the contrary, since the Chinese required me to explain to them the secret behind the *Mirror* phenomenon. Murdoch's *Sun* had only just launched, and the *Mirror* had not yet yielded its place as the largest-selling daily newspaper in the land. How is it, the Chinese enquired, that a paper like yours sells so many copies to the ordinary people of Britain? 'Because,' I explained as best I could, 'it understands the ordinary people of this country rather better than the other newspapers.' I doubt whether this explanation made the remotest sense to them as they nodded in a pretence of understanding. The legation still lacked ambassadorial status, which did not come until 1973 with Sung Chih-kuang, the first Ambassador to London from Communist China. By then I had been to China twice for the *Daily Mirror*.

*   *   *

I collected my visa from the legation one Saturday morning in the spring of 1971, to be informed that I was the first British journalist to be granted 'this privilege' by the London legation since the start of the Cultural Revolution. I was quite bemused by that thought. The *Mirror*'s editor at the time was Tony Miles, who acted with great speed and professionalism. Even though it was a Saturday and his normal day off he made immediate arrangements to get me on to a flight to Hong Kong the next day. On the Sunday morning before I departed Miles was in the office early to ensure that all arrangements were in place. He handed me a camera, a load of films and declared me a bona-fide photographer as well as reporter with a mission. Being pronounced a photographer was, of course, highly improper and against National Union of Journalist rules. I made no protest.

When I boarded Qantas flight No. 762 on Sunday 2 May I hadn't the foggiest notion of how long I would be away, how long the Chinese would permit me to stay or where I would be allowed to go. Nor did I have the faintest idea how I would get my stories back to London. It was very much a step into no-man's land. The only link that Tony Miles could provide was to arrange for the *Mirror*'s staff man in the Far East, Donald Wise, based in Singapore, to fly up to Hong Kong to meet me. He proved to be a saviour. Donald was one of the great war correspondents and foreign reporters of the postwar years. He had been most places where guns were being fired in anger and to kill. In Africa, especially in the Congo and in Kenya, he had miraculous escapes; in Cyprus and the Middle East he was rarely out of gunshot range; Vietnam came up with the rations, so to speak. He reported principally for the Beaverbrook *Daily Express* and then Cudlipp's *Daily Mirror*. He had been a prisoner of war under the Japanese after being wounded as a young officer in General Percival's army that surrendered to the Japanese in Singapore – where he then spent three and half years in Changi jail.

The best story I know about Donald echoed the theme of the film *Bridge on the River Kwai*. The Japanese in charge of Donald when he was captured tried everything to persuade – pressure is the preferred word – British officers to ignore the protection of the Geneva PoW convention and go to work alongside non-commissioned ranks. The Japanese, exasperated by what they regarded as the absurdities of western behaviour, cried out: 'Jesus Christ worked ... he was a carpenter.' To which Donald's immortal reply came: 'Jesus Christ was not a British officer.' Marvellous man, Mr Wise. He died on 20 May 1998 aged 80, and I miss him very much.

Donald's helping hand proved to be a crucial factor in my Chinese journey. He was at Kai Tak airport to meet me and took me to a small hotel, Ascot House, near the Hong Kong racecourse in Happy Valley. From that moment we began the detailed planning process for 'Operation China', to be code-named 'dodgem'. But first I had to obtain my official Chinese documentation from the China Travel Service in Kowloon. The CTS had assumed the role of an unofficial legation in Hong Kong representing the Beijing Government. They were required to approve and then rubber-stamp the visa I collected in London. A double check, of course. It took another 48 hours of tedious negotiations with the CTS before everything was completed. In the meantime Donald and an old Australian newspaperman chum, Richard 'Dick' Hughes, then reporting for the *Sunday Times* in Hong Kong, worked out with me a scheme to overcome any censorship hurdles I might encounter once across the Chinese border. Most of this brilliant plan was Donald's thinking and involved complicated code words to indicate my location and problems – all, in his view, absolutely essential in case things went wrong.

The CTS refused to tell me where I would stay in Canton or the telephone number of their chosen hotel.

'Why not?' I asked.

'Sorry, we have no information,' was their standard response.

'What about my official guide who is to meet me off the train at Canton?' was my reasonable enough follow-up question.

'Sorry,' came back the reply, 'we have no information.'

The other standard response to any question was 'Please wait.'

So Donald and I worked out our communication plan. Once I was ensconced in my Canton (Kwangchow) hotel I would try to 'phone Hong Kong. Assuming that worked – and everything else hinged on being able to call Donald from Canton – we arranged an elaborate coding system of words, which he would then translate into suitable English and file the copy to London.

In fact it wasn't necessary – but it was a damn good scheme. To my astonishment the cable service out of Canton worked perfectly well, and to my amazement not a single word of my stories was censored. But, of course, I didn't know the full extent of this non-censorship until, months later, I was back in Hong Kong. Donald could never communicate the good news to me – for obvious reasons.

That first trek into China lasted a couple of months, and was by any standards a remarkable journey. I visited agricultural communes, factories, collective farms, schools, hospitals, and many homes. My Chinese language skill was virtually nil, even though, gradually, I collected a range of words that enabled me to pick up various elements that my interpreter chose to ignore. My base was the Tung Fang hotel in Kwangchow. From there each day, usually starting around 6.30 am, my guide/interpreter would phone my room, 454, to check the day's programme. A car was provided to take both of us for many miles around the Kwangchow area. Sometimes we stayed overnight in a simple shack-like building with primitive facilities. At the Tung Fang hotel, which was administered by the People's Liberation Army (as, indeed, was practically everything else), even the waiters were soldiers hardly disguised. The telephone and telegraph/cable system was visibly a military installation with uniformed soldiers manning the switches. Outside the hotel the grounds were patrolled day and night by PLA men with rifles at the slant, and ready. There was no pretence about the fact that China was then being controlled by the PLA. The hotel was built by the Russians before they packed their bags and left in a huff. It was situated on the edge of the city in what had been a rather upper-grade residential area of Canton in pre-revolutionary China. My room was basic but functional and equipped with a life-saving electric fan (made in China) and a mosquito net draped over the bed. Both were absolutely essential. The heat was draining and, at night especially, the mosquito presence had to be protected against.

All roads leading to the city centre were lined with hoardings – as were the walls of the hotel itself – proclaiming the enemy: American imperialism. The halls, lobbies and walls in the ground of the hotel were sprayed with slogans condemning the United States for its war in Vietnam. Great posters with giant lettering showed the smiling features of Chairman Mao, with that unforgettable face mole helping him to look like the father of the nation. Then there were slogans denouncing Liu Shao-chi and the 'capitalist roaders' in language that was far more abusive even than the phrases denouncing the Americans. The slogan to beat them all was a caption under the picture of Liu Shao-chi who, we were instructed, led the 'running dogs of capitalism'.

This was the Cultural Revolution at its most grotesque, absurd level. The climate was one of tension, and at times I felt a creepy solitude descending. Yet there was also a huge paradox. During my stay in the Canton region the centre of the city was full of capitalist traders from West Germany (Germany was still divided), France, Austria, Scandinavia, Japan – and Britain. They were exhibiting their goods at the Canton Trade Fair, which was a curious mix of a propaganda shop window to demonstrate to foreigners that Mao's China was determined to develop a modern industrial base and to encourage western businessmen into favourable deals with Communist China. Early beginnings for the China of today.

The trade fair was in full swing during my visit, which enabled me to discuss its value and purpose with a variety of business groups from all over Europe – especially the Germans, Austrians and Italians, who seemed to be particularly well in with their Chinese hosts. Some of them had been travelling to the Canton Trade Fair for a decade and had established a strong rapport with the Chinese. They all found it worthwhile – even more so as a base to be kept open for the future as China developed. What particularly fascinated me was their indifference to what was going on inside China – Cultural Revolution *et al*. Their attitude was best summed up by a German businessman who shrugged: 'What Mao does with his own people is his business. I'm interested in securing a business base in this country, which in another ten years is going to be a world economic force.'

Everywhere I travelled – and I guess I covered much of the region in a few weeks – I was under the guidance (control might be a better description) of my interpreter, guide and mentor Hsi Tsuo-hsin. He was 35, married with one child (the permitted ration) and employed by China Travel Service, which, of course, was a branch of the Beijing Foreign Office. Hsi came from a peasant family in Kwangchow province, and he awkwardly confessed as we grew more informal that his mother, who lived in his birthplace village about 100 miles from Canton, remained an ardent Buddhist. Did this count against her? I enquired. 'No,' he said because his mother was also a revolutionary and devoted to Chairman Mao. Yet she saw no reason to depart from her spiritual beliefs. Hsi had no problem with that paradox. He sighed: 'It is all part of our deep tradition,' he explained. 'I believe it is correct that it should remain like that. We must do nothing to discourage those beliefs even if the younger generation, like me, cannot share them. Our older people believe in these things. We must leave them alone.' I wondered whether this was for my ear or whether he actually believed it. I was never sure.

Hsi had been through his Cultural Revolution 'penance period'. He did two and half years as a labourer on a commune in central China and had only recently returned to his old job as an interpreter for the CTS. He told me that during his work on the land where he 'learned how the peasants lived' he had been paid by the CTS, though he had not been allowed to have his wife with him. She was sent to another commune to do her penance. That seemed to reinforce his purity. Certainly, any hint of western-style admiration for the opposite sex brought a severe rebuke on my head. When I remarked on the drabness in the way even the most attractive Chinese girl dressed herself – no make-up, baggy trousers, shapeless Mao-style tunic – he rounded on me with a severe lecture: 'We believe in plain living,' he preached, 'without show and display of rings or jewellery. We don't approve of vulgarity – that is a symptom of capitalism, and China has turned its back on such things.' (Tell that to the young Chinese of today!)

He grew increasingly stiff and agitated about my remark on the drabness of clothing: 'What would our peasant women say if visiting women turned up in our villages wearing fancy clothes, bright dresses or' – horror of horrors – 'make-up?' Hsi was really quite trenchant about my observations. He felt obliged to correct my 'western imperialist values'. 'Surely,' he protested, 'it is not drabness to dress simply and neatly. That is the correct way. If our women were to do anything else it would simply mean that we were back on the road to capitalism. Vanity, selfishness, personal greed would be back again. China will never take that road.'

I often reflect back and wonder how Hsi Tsuo-hsin is coping with contemporary China. Probably like all his other comrades who were then assuring me that there would never be any retreat from the teachings of Chairman Mao and his little Red Book, which they all held in their tunic pockets at that time. China in the early 1970s was certainly no mannequin parade. The one exception, even then, were the children. They were invariably well turned out with colourful clothing, well cared for and exceptionally healthy-looking. The schools, of course, were marshalled like military establishments, like all other main institutions. Military drill was an essential part of the school curriculum. On my numerous visits to schools in towns and villages I witnessed the daily drill of the children holding wooden rifles, girls as well as boys. This was still more strongly the case in the universities where the older, more traditional lecturers and professors had been bundled off to the countryside, where the peasants would (according to the official gospel) be able to teach them the basic concepts of Mao's socialism, his 'return to basics'. Revolutionary committees were in charge of the universities, where normal lectures and studies had been replaced by organised recitals from Mao's Red Book.

The great Cultural Revolution was breaking the back of China's Communist Party elite – and fragmenting the entire social fabric of the nation. Mao's unique form of ideological immolation in which he uprooted his own system in an extraordinary spell of destructive cleansing eventually left China bereft and deprived the entire nation of at least ten vital years. Modernism, technology, academic and intellectual achievement, even industrial productivity as well as basic education were all simply cast aside in Mao's frenetic and perplexing attempt to sweep away any political opposition within the Communist Party and to purify his ideal. But an ideal of what? That was a question never put, because everyone lived in fear.

Unleashing thousands of Red Guards to vent their youthful violence against a system that they themselves had helped to establish, and which their fathers had fought and died for, was an act of irrational self-destructiveness on a scale that even today cannot be adequately measured or explained. In the context of a religious war against all personal and political weaknesses – as defined by a small elite around Mao – there are few parallels in history. Can Mao's Cultural Revolution be compared with the Crusades? Or the Hundred Years War? Or the tumult of classical Greece? Or the Essenes of ancient Hebraic times? To look for such parallels seems pointless. Looking back on that first, astonishing, experience of Communist China, I cannot but marvel that they have recovered so well. What is equally remarkable is that the ideas of Liu Shao-chi, which Mao castigated, banished and quashed, were in most senses the very same ideas later to be developed with such success by Deng Shao-ping and which Deng's successors have further advanced to bring China to the status of a considerable world power and to the brink of super-power status.

For me the mystery remains. How could one man, even if he was urged on by his even more curious wife, Chiang Ching, establish and wield such terrifying power and influence? Of course, it led to his own destruction and those of his immediate circle. In those final insane years of his life Mao turned his own achievements upside down and laid waste to his own dream. The paradox today is that he helped to create the kind of 'capitalist roadism' that he so feared would destroy his dream. His exceptional achievements in liberating that vast nation and leading his armies through one of the most astonishing revolutions of our time were then simply turned inside out and upside down – deliberately.

An act of sheer madness? Or bewildering mystery? Who knows. What I do now reflect back on is my search in those early travels for some clue, some light of explanation. I was certainly seized by the sheer enormity of China's task in trying to drag itself into the contemporary world. Population growth alone had already become an insuperable problem – or so it appeared to me. A peasant population, four-fifths of the whole, seemed to be beyond the practical reach of the party and even the Revolutionary Committees who then dominated the countryside and communes. The PLA, of course, were omnipresent to ensure that trouble anywhere was quickly suppressed. China was a military encampment, since it was probably the only method by which its rulers could ensure control.

Mao himself was, of course, a peasant at heart, and his thoughts and writings, even when couched in Marxist phraseology, always reflected his background. It is possible that Mao's instinctive feeling, even in earlier years, came to terms with the sheer size of the task he had set himself and that he saw the entire operation as a huge gamble. There are many Chinese I have since befriended who are convinced that Mao fell into a state of despair at the magnitude of the challenge, and shrank from the notion of China emerging into a modern world power that would inexorably be drawn into a global capitalist system; that he could not bear the thought of his successors treading that path; and that he experienced his own profound disillusion when he realised what had already transpired in the Soviet Union under Stalin.

The ageing, feckless MaoZedong (Mao Tse-tung) was by then surrounded by Madame Mao's Gang of Four who flattered and deceived him as they planned their own future control. Despite the numerous books written in the last thirty years the whole business of Mao remains a mystery wrapped in an enigma, to use Churchill's famous description of Stalin's Soviet Russia. I am always reminded of Edgar Snow's interview with Mao whom Snow revisited shortly before his death and Mao's riveting description of himself: 'I am only a lone monk walking the world with a leaky umbrella.' Perhaps it wasn't modesty, false or otherwise. Perhaps it was Mao the poet and even The Monk in search of paradise lost.

*   *   *

I knew when I entered China in 1971 that I might well suffer, inescapably, a feeling of inadequacy in trying to describe such a nation in turmoil. My self-doubts never really departed. The more I saw the less clear I was of what I was actually witnessing. The more I moved around China and talked with others the thicker became the mist.

I did try to describe it all to the readers of the *Daily Mirror*, and somehow it was said to have made sense. I am not so sure. A thousand stars burn brightly in the sky and we can all see them, almost palpably touch them with our imagination. Yet the closer we are drawn to their glow the more difficult it becomes to discern what we are actually seeing. That is precisely how I felt about my own reporting on China.

The paradoxes never ceased. My copy from China was not censored by the zealots of the Cultural Revolution; I was never aware of being followed or bugged, though I am sure I was; no questionable move was made to make life difficult for me; I was regarded as an oddity by all and sundry, and not least by the female room attendant of room 454 in the Tung Fang.

I had made the gross error of buying some dried plums from the hotel shop only to discover that they were simply inedible. So I dropped them into the waste basket in my room. Each evening I found the bag of plums back on my room table, neatly rewrapped. I attempted disposal five times – always with the same result. Finally, I gave up and simply left them on the table to rot. Visiting the Canton Trade Fair I lost a button from my jacket. It wasn't much of a button, but evidently it was identified as belonging to a westerner's jacket. Enquiries must have been made about a wandering westerner around certain trade fair stalls that day: result – the button was returned to me at the hotel the next day. Moral? Detective work during the Cultural Revolution was very efficient and effective. The endless series of paradox and enigma never ceased.

Eventually I returned to Hong Kong, for a long and splendid discussion with Donald Wise. Donald, who had not been into mainland China, was riveted by the stories but not surprised. Dick Hughes simply shrugged and snorted: 'Well, what did you expect?'

In all my subsequent visits to China I have never known quite what to expect and I have not been disappointed.

11   Prepare for Revolution: In Britain?

If, as I believe, 1979 was *the* watershed year in post-1945 British politics, then it seems to me that the story line effectively began with Heath's victory in the general election of June 1970. Or, to put the emphasis slightly differently, with the defeat that June of Harold Wilson's Government rather than the victory of Heath's Conservatives. The 1970 election was very much a vote of 'no confidence' in Wilson's Premiership more than a positive choice in favour of Edward Heath and his party. A whole raft of reasons leads me to this view – mostly based on Harold Wilson's failure to capitalise on his overwhelming success in the 1966 election. Certainly the failure to tackle trade union reform in 1969 and the ignominious retreat from 'In Place of Strife' were primary factors.

The 1970 election was the first step toward Thatcherism and the break from the post-1945 consensus. It took another nine years for that fully to develop, but the signs were evident throughout the Heath premiership and still more so in the years that followed the fall of the Heath Government in 1974.

By another of those strange twists of chance and circumstance, it was the election of the Heath Government in 1970 that brought me into a new and closer relationship with government than I had previously experienced. Given the political tone of my writing this indeed was an odd paradox. The explanation, however, is quite simple. I was then a *Daily Mirror* journalist rather than a *Daily Herald* or Odhams' *Sun* man. That made all the difference. The Cudlipp *Daily Mirror* was in a quite different category. No Conservative Government could ignore the country's largest-selling daily newspaper regardless of its pro-Labour stance. The paper's influence was such that quite soon after he arrived in Downing Street Edward Heath made the first move to get on to closer terms with Hugh Cudlipp. Heath knew – and his advisers certainly were in no doubt – that no incoming prime minister could afford to ignore the thrust of the *Mirror* rather as, in a similar way in more recent times, Tony Blair knew – and again was firmly advised – that neither he nor his government could afford to ignore Rupert Murdoch's *Sun*.

By 1997, of course, Murdoch's *Sun* had replaced the *Daily Mirror* as the most important mass circulation national paper on the Downing Street agenda pad. But in the 1970s being part of the *Mirror* political culture meant, by definition, that we had access to sources and individual Cabinet Ministers that were not so readily available to other newspapers. Of course, the Conservative-supporting newspapers had their own special connections with the Heath Government, yet even that political 'family mafia' linkage did not diminish the importance with which Heath's ministers regarded the *Daily Mirror*. During the critical years of the Heath Government – and, come to think of it, they were all fairly critical – I therefore had links with ministers and senior civil servants on a regular basis.

Of course, it was forever necessary to be on guard against being 'used', always an exceptionally difficult judgement to make. When one was being briefed by a minister or a senior civil servant it was never clear just how much of the truth was being coated with the sugary temptations of what is now known as 'spin'. There is no ready-made formula for the avoidance of the inevitable trap – just the simple rule to be forever on guard and sceptical of the helping hand of officialdom. The period from the Heath Government's election in 1970 right through the 1970s required scepticism of a very high degree. It was an extraordinary time to be reporting the changing mood of British political life.

In the first frenetic 18 months of the Heath Government the purpose of the Conservative Cabinet was to put some flesh on the bones of 'Selsdon Man' – the original image of the Heath administration. The essence of this species was to take Britain back to a prewar, certainly pre-1945 economic agenda. 'Selsdon Man' had emerged from a pre-election meeting of Tory cardinals at a country hotel near Croydon, the Selsdon Park Hotel. Out of that ambience stepped a new-style Conservative leadership armed with an overtly abrasive social and economic programme consisting of a hard-line market economy approach, cutting public sector spending, lowering taxation, coming down with a heavy hand on the public sector industries in which the unions were particularly strong and, first among the priorities, 'taming' the unions. In effect it was precisely the formula that nine years later became the mantra of Margaret Thatcher.

In his memoirs Heath denies that Selsdon presaged the Thatcher epoch (*The Course of My Life*, 1998). Yet the truth is that it was Heath's Selsdon agenda that Thatcher used to justify her attacking Heath after he made his famous U-turn in 1972 – something for which she never forgave him. It has to be remembered that it was the Heath Government that came up with the first legislative programme of reform of the trade unions. It was the 1971 Industrial Relations Act which led directly to the first great clash between a postwar Conservative Government and the trade unions. It was also that same government that in January 1972 presided over the first unemployment figure of over one million that Britain had experienced since prewar. Heath himself was always repelled, as he points out in his memoirs, by the prospect of any return to mass unemployment on a prewar scale.

So how do we explain this odd phenomenon of Edward Heath, the liberal Tory, the caring, sensitive son of a Broadstairs building worker, who rose through a state primary school and Ramsgate Grammar to an organ scholarship at Balliol College, Oxford, and yet, aware or not, actually laid the foundations for the Thatcher revolution, which later he so profoundly despised: how do we explain that? So, pause for a moment to take Sailor Heath on board. I grew to admire the man even though he is far from easy to actually *like*. Yet I developed an admiration for his integrity and honesty as well as his sense of history, which carried something of the resonance of a younger Macmillan, who was, of course, a figure from a quite different background and social milieu.

Like Macmillan's character-forming experience on the Somme in the First World War, Edward Heath's views, if not personality, were hugely shaped by his experiences during the Second World War. He rose from an artillery gunner to a Lieutenant-Colonel commanding the 2nd regiment of the Honourable Artillery Company. As an Oxford undergraduate he joined the Young Conservatives: yet, the paradox again, he volunteered to go to Spain as an observer of the civil war and demonstrated his sympathies for the anti-fascist Republican side when he reached Spain. In fact, it was where he first met a young Liverpudlian who was in the International Brigade – Jack Jones – though it wasn't until years later, when he was prime minister, that Heath and Jones jointly realised they had first met on the Ebro front in Spain. There was another factor in Heath's earlier influences: he witnessed the distress of mass unemployment during the 1930s even in his own, relatively protected home area of Kent. It all added up to a strange alchemy of political contradictions that remained with him throughout.

Heath entered Downing Street when least expected. Almost everyone believed that Harold Wilson would win a third term in June 1970. He thought so, and so too did most of his entourage. I have explained earlier how my own warnings, filtered into Downing Street via Marcia Williams (Lady Falkender), were dismissed as unnecessarily alarmist. Moreover the opinion polls all pointed to a Wilson victory. Labour's lead over the Tories was variously given as ranging from 8.7 per cent (Marplan in *The Times*) and 4.1 per cent (NOP, *Daily Mail*) down to the 2 per cent predicted by the *Daily Express*'s Harris poll. These poll figures would have given Labour a majority of anything between 20 and 100 seats. Only one major poll, Opinion Research Centre, published on polling day by the London *Evening Standard* gave the Tories a lead – of 1 per cent. In fact the swing to the Conservatives was 4.7 per cent, described by *The Times* as 'the most surprising upset of overweening electoral prediction in the western world since Harry Truman defeated Thomas Dewey for the American Presidency in 1948'. There was a huge abstention, which particularly affected the Labour vote. Turnout was 72 per cent, the lowest since the war and the lowest on record until the 1997 General Election. This was in spite of the fact that the electorate had increased by 1,800,000 as a result of the vote being given to 18-year-olds for the first time.

It was a severe jolt to Harold Wilson personally and to the whole Labour movement. But George Brown, whom I reported for much of the campaign, was instinctively correct in his forecast. He felt, at an early stage, that it was 'going wrong' – principally because of the trade union issue and the retreat from 'In Place of Strife'. He lost his seat at Belper, which he had held for 25 years, and Aneurin Bevan's widow, Jennie Lee, saw her 11,000 majority at Cannock turned over to the Tories. She too had served in that constituency for 25 years. Something was happening.

It was happening to the newly elected Heath Government as well. A month after the election Heath lost his Chancellor, Iain Macleod, at 56, victim of a heart attack while preparing his first Budget speech. Macleod's death left a vacuum that was never filled and without doubt left a vacancy in the Heath team that eventually helped Margaret Thatcher to become leader.

From that point we were plunged into a series of political/ economic/industrial crises, which, as I know from my own reporter's notebook from the 1970s, scarcely ceased until Margaret Thatcher took over in May 1979. What an extraordinary decade that was, as it shifted through the Heath years, then back to Harold Wilson in

1974, on to Wilson's resignation two years later – an event which still puzzles so many – and finally to Jim Callaghan's three years at the helm in a period of ceaseless tension before the lady with the handbag grabbed the nation's attention.

Toward the end of 1973 as the miners' dispute brought the Heath Government to the brink of collapse, or at least of believing they were about to face disaster, a senior civil servant at the old Ministry of Labour (Department of Employment) called me in for a chat one evening.

Sir Conrad Heron, as he later became, had just been appointed Permanent Secretary at the department following a long career in the industrial relations section of the old Ministry of Labour. He knew every stitch of the fabric in that department and had taken over as Permanent Secretary from the late Sir Denis Barnes. Conrad invited me one evening for a drink and a private chat during which the thrust of his conversation was that the country could well be 'on the brink of revolution'. It was an astonishingly frank and open insight into his thinking about the industrial crisis that then affected the nation, with a three-day week having been proclaimed by the government because of the miners' strike.

But Conrad went beyond the miners' strike situation. He spoke with dramatic candour about the events that had led up to the 1973/4 miners' dispute. The first element in his list of disasters was the collapse of Heath's Industrial Relations Act of 1971. He saw this as a major setback in the programme to bring some order and sense into industrial relations; moreover it had also increased the feeling of power among the unions. They had in fact defeated the government. Then he listed the government's various U-turns on industrial relations circa 1972 and 1973, the development of a wage restraint policy that had cracked wide open under the miners' pressure; and the oil crisis of 1973, which had quadrupled oil prices and precipitated the miners' pay dispute. The issue of 'Who governs Britain?' had become the favoured cliché-question of the moment.

Heron and I were alone in his room at 8, St James's Square, the old headquarters of the ministry. 'I have to tell you,' he said, 'that we must prepare for a possible revolution in this country.' Heron talked in quite measured terms. He wasn't blustering or melodramatic. That was not his style. He was a quiet, careful, judicious man. He had reflected for a long time on the information that was available to the department through the various intelligence sources of government. He felt I should know how he saw the scene. I signalled to him that I was utterly sceptical about all this – which he readily confessed was no surprise to him. He knew I would find his conversation unconvincing. Even so he insisted that this was his honest assessment about the dangers now facing the country, not so much from the miners, he emphasised, but 'from groups who would be prepared to exploit the current situation'. He didn't specify or identify these 'groups' but assumed I would need no great help to follow the line of his thinking.

I left him feeling confused and quite unable to write on the theme. Not that I distrusted Conrad Heron: quite the opposite. I knew him to be a very cautious, precise and vastly experienced civil servant of absolute probity and integrity. That's what baffled me about this dramatic information. Why, I kept asking myself, should Conrad of all people talk like this? Maybe he really did believe it. I am still not sure.

Not long before that meeting with Conrad Heron I had arranged a private lunch at the Ivy Restaurant with the new minister drafted into the department by Heath to tackle the miners' crisis – Willie Whitelaw. He had been brought back to London from Northern Ireland by Heath because Downing Street had lost confidence in the previous occupant, Maurice Macmillan. I thought this was grossly unjust to Maurice Macmillan whom I liked and felt was doing all he could to handle a situation that had become untenable for the government as a whole. But Macmillan carried the can for all the government's failings. So Heath summoned Whitelaw from Belfast to take over at St James's Square.

Within days of his arrival I fixed up a private lunch for Whitelaw to discuss the miners' strike and its implications with a group of us from the *Daily Mirror* – including the editorial director Sydney Jacobson (later Lord Jacobson), the paper's chief leader writer, Deryck Winterton, and myself. We discussed a possible 'peace formula', which I myself suggested to Whitelaw. The National Union of Mineworkers had rejected the latest offer from the Coal Board – a 13 per cent across the board pay increase. The NUM leaders believed they had the government on the run and could see the potential for a significant victory so they brushed aside the 13 per cent offer, even though it burst through the government's pay policy like a torrent breaking down a matchwood dam. An overtime ban, which, arguably, was as effective as a strike, began in November (1973) and the following day, 13 November, the Cabinet declared a State of Emergency, prohibiting the use of power for advertising signs, flood-lighting of all sporting events and limiting the domestic use of electricity. One month later, on 13 December, Heath announced a three-day week as industry began to shut down. Peter Walker at the Department of Industry prepared for petrol rationing. The country was sliding into a state of siege.

This was the atmosphere surrounding our lunch with Whitelaw in the first-floor private room at the Ivy. He pleaded with us to have the *Mirror* do all it could to help 'bring some sanity back into this terrible situation'. I then suggested the 'peace formula' (based on phasing in concessions to the miners over a period), which Willie Whitelaw said he would take to the Cabinet's crisis-committee. I think he did this, but the information I received later suggested that it was probably too late for such a compromise. It was a bleak Christmas for the Heath Government, with an even bleaker New Year to follow. In the period between Christmas and New Year came the first really serious suggestion of a snap general election on the single issue of 'Who governs Britain?' It was around that time that Conrad Heron called me in for his chat: prepare for revolution.

*   *   *

Earlier in the year, in August to be precise, before the miners' dispute exploded and when the Heath pay policy was still more or less intact, despite the opposition from the TUC and individual unions, I was invited to meet the Prime Minister at Chequers. The Middle East oil crisis had yet to break out.

One Friday morning I was sitting in my room at the *Mirror* when a call came through from Robin Haydon, the Prime Minister's press secretary (the late Sir Robin Haydon). Would I like to have a talk, off the record, of course, with the Prime Minister?

I was staggered, to put it mildly. 'Well, yes, Robin, I would be delighted; but tell me, will this be exclusive to the *Mirror*?'

'Well, not quite,' Haydon replied. 'What we have in mind is that three of you, *Financial Times*, *Guardian* and yourself, come over to Downing Street about lunchtime and then we drive out to Chequers to see the PM.'

Snap, I said, and arrived at Downing Street to find John Elliott of the *Financial Times* and Keith Harper of the *Guardian* joining up with me. We were driven out to Chequers in a government car along with John Pestell, a colleague of Robin Haydon. It was a very hot day toward the end of August, shortly before that year's Trades Union Congress.

The three of us speculated on why Heath and his advisers had invited us. Was it because we had been specially selected as journalists likely to influence events at the forthcoming congress? Maybe. Or perhaps it was part of a wider programme of Downing Street PR designed to help Heath influence the press over Britain's entry into Europe, which he had achieved in January of that year?

And maybe there was something else: Ted Heath had changed a great deal since the days of Selsdon Man. From the spring of 1972, when the U-turn was launched and the Industrial Relations Act was allowed slowly to become marginalised in favour of the famous three-stage incomes and prices policy, the Prime Minister's style had changed perceptibly. So had the government's policies. A remarkable new Industry Act was introduced by Peter Walker (Lord Walker) in June 1972 giving the government wide new powers to intervene in industrial development, and to offer rescue packages to 'lame-duck' industries such as Upper Clyde Shipyards and Rolls-Royce. Out of the mould of this extraordinary new programme a new Ted Heath had also emerged. It was a Heath who beckoned the trade unions to join him at the highest levels of government in discussions on how to solve the nation's economic problems. In short – the most astonishing U-turn of recent political history had begun. It was even claimed that Peter Walker's new Industry Act gave the Conservative Government wider powers of intervention in the economy than the Attlee Government possessed after 1945.

By the summer of 1973 – as we reached Chequers – Heath had already developed a powerful friendship with all the main figures of the TUC and especially with men like Jack Jones, Hugh Scanlon and Victor Feather. One almost expected to find the three of them at Chequers sipping drinks when we arrived. But no, the Prime Minister was alone on the terrace waiting to greet the three journalists as we arrived.

Pestell had already informed us on the journey to Chequers that the Prime Minister had set aside the entire afternoon for us. In fact we spent nearly four hours with him in a long, relaxed discussion, which embraced almost every aspect of domestic social and economic policy and, indeed, touched notably on the future of Britain's relationship with Europe – a subject inescapable in any discussion with Edward Heath at any time. I shall never forget my own surprise when the Prime Minister stepped through the French doors to greet us on the terrace. He was dressed as if he had just climbed off his yacht. He wore a bright blue-flowered open neck shirt, white cotton sailing trousers and matching canvas deck shoes. He greeted us warmly as we sat down to tea and scones. I remember making a mental note of how exquisitely comfortable were the garden chairs on the Chequers terrace.

Heath led the discussion by opening on the subject of Europe and how he saw Britain's future relationship in Europe. He emphasised how vital it was to have a third airport around London despite the opposition from so many vested interests. Heath's own preference was for the Thames estuary site, which, of course, was later abandoned. He was scathing about the City's failure to think into the future on such projects, the narrowness of the financial establishment and their short-term, selfish approach. His condemnation of the 'capitalist inward-looking City establishment' could easily have come from a radical socialist.

We moved on to the subject the three of us had anticipated – the forthcoming Trades Union Congress. I asked him why the talks with the TUC had broken down. He looked disconsolate. But he answered with remarkable candour. 'We simply couldn't deliver what they were asking for,' the Prime Minister said.

The TUC had asked the government to guarantee action to control prices and curb excess profits in return for supporting a third stage of the government's pay restraint policy. 'We couldn't go that far,' Heath insisted and at the same time hinted that even if he had been prepared to do a deal with the TUC he wouldn't have been able to carry his Cabinet colleagues. That was a fascinating insight into the battles that we had suspected were going on inside the Cabinet.

Heath was also remarkably frank about his personal relationship with the TUC leaders. He praised Vic Feather's qualities: 'Without him,' he reported, 'I doubt whether the TUC talks would have come this far. He paved the way and fought hard to keep the dialogue moving forward.' He also confessed a warm appreciation of Hugh Scanlon's leadership and a regard for Scanlon personally: 'I like him. He's very open; very honest and straightforward. I know where I stand with Hugh.'

Yet his reaction to Jack Jones was not what I had expected from reports by Jones – who previously had admitted to me privately how much he had grown to admire Heath. Even so the Prime Minister spoke about Jones almost with awe: 'Jack is a very tough negotiator' – well, we all knew that, I thought to myself – 'the toughest of them all. He wants action on prices and he won't be shifted from that view. In fact I think he even irritated some of his TUC colleagues by his tough demands. I put it to him, alright Jack, what do you want the government to do? Control prices in every shop? If so – how would *you* do it? You tell me.' Heath went on to describe Jones's reaction: 'All he kept on saying was, you've got to do something about shop prices.'

There was a pause in our dialogue as the butler moved the tea. The Prime Minister suggested we might like something stronger so we went on to whisky, which helped to shift the conversation further along the informal path.

I looked at him (I was sitting on his right). His florid features were burnished by the hot afternoon August sun. His heavy-jowelled face nestling, almost, on his chest. Very little neck. Indeed, the neck was like an Elizabethan ruff swollen at one side – a glandular condition – and he was overweight. Behind the public façade one could sense the image of a lonely man, uneasy with his political colleagues, uncertain, perhaps, even about his basic conservativism. Through his shaded eyes and the drooping lids here was a prime minister who clearly found it extremely painful to reach out to the world. Much of his emotional energy seemed to be absorbed precisely in trying to do that.

Europe, of course, was his obsession, which was hardly surprising since he had only lately taken Britain into the European Community. At the same time he was starkly critical of the British attitude toward Europe. 'Trouble with the British,' he lectured, 'is that they don't seem to be able to keep a steady course for long. They shift about. They ...' – it was always 'they', hardly ever 'we' – 'They seem to lack the ability or the will to get down to things and keep at it, certainly in peacetime. That's our big problem. I suppose ...' he drifted off, almost self-reflectively. 'I suppose it's also a problem of leadership.' He stopped. For a moment there was a complete silence so that we actually heard the birds chirping ... then, 'Well, I'm going to keep trying. That's my main aim from now on ...'

He spoke about the nature of the country's social divisions and deplored them – in industry, in the schools, in society at large. He was severely critical of British management, whom he regarded as 'poor and unimaginative', and said he suppported more worker involvement in running companies. When I put it to him that the public school system had a great deal to answer for in terms of Britain's social divisions he didn't demur. 'I agree,' came the quick response. His abiding consolation as prime minister was already evident. He had 'taken Britain into Europe'. As we moved from the terrace he turned to me and glowed, 'Well, at least, we'll go down in the history books as the government that took Britain into the Market.'

It was clear that he didn't really want to break up the party. By then we were all on relaxed first-name terms. As we moved into the house he said: 'Come and have a look round the place.' He had recently refurnished and refurbished most of the rooms. There were new carpets and modern curtains; a good deal of the old furniture had been replaced. He gave us the guided tour, encouraging us to admire his taste in style and design – which we did. Toward the end of the day – we had been there well over three hours – we went into the magnificent main lounge, a huge room running the length of one wing of the house.

I noticed his hi-fi system and casually mentioned it to him, enquiring how it performed in such acoustics. 'Would you like to hear it in action?' he immediately enquired as if he had been anxiously awaiting the cue. 'What would you like to hear?' Mozart, I replied. He leapt at that, congratulated me on my selection, and sprang to animation in a manner that our earlier political discussions had failed to excite. So Mozart it was – and we stood, midway between the speakers, just the two of us (my two colleagues had drifted off elsewhere). I was standing to his left, and as the music captured and dominated the room I glanced at his profile in the shadows. He stood, as if militarily to attention, transfixed by the music, staring into a middle distance, effectively unaware that he was in the presence of anyone else but W.A. Mozart. At that moment he seemed to me a deeply vulnerable figure, albeit quite relaxed and at peace, set apart from the strange, tense, competitive, anguished world in which he spent most of his life. I felt, then, momentarily, I had discovered the genuine Edward Heath, the ordinary chap; that he had emerged, briefly, from behind the mask and the façade in which he spent most of his political life.

*   *   *

It is sometimes overlooked that the Heath Government actually had to deal with two great miners' strikes, the first of which certainly forced the historic U-turn of 1972 and effectively broke the Industrial Relations Act of 1971. That was the miners' strike in which Arthur Scargill, then still a little-known figure in the Yorkshire area of the NUM, first rose to national prominence when he organised his notorious 'flying pickets'. The dispute was finally resolved after a

Court of Inquiry under Lord Wilberforce, which gave the miners virtually everything they had asked for including a 21 per cent pay increase. There remains vividly in my mind the picture of the miners' leaders, Joe Gormley and Lawrence Daly, emerging from Downing Street at the end of February 1972, triumphant at having won even more from the government than Wilberforce had recommended. Lawrence Daly's immortal quote was: 'We've now finally won back what we lost in the 1926 General Strike; our dignity. We've got our own back.'

That moment changed the entire political climate of the period. The late Sir Denis Barnes, Permanent Secretary at the old Ministry of Labour, knew then that the game was up for his plans to reform Britain's industrial relations. The 1971 Act, which he helped to design alongside Robert Carr (Lord Carr), the Secretary of State, and his deputy minister Sir Geoffrey Howe (Lord Howe), was effectively in ruins. Barnes still felt anger, fury, deep disappointment at what he believed the country had forfeited when the Wilson Government and Barnes's minister, Barbara Castle, retreated from 'In Place of Strife'.

In fact by the spring of 1972 Barnes was in despair about any government having the will and the courage to tackle the problem which he regarded the number one domestic challenge – reform of industrial relations. His constant theme to me during his years as head of the department was that 'something has to be done' to bring order and sense into British industrial relations. Indeed it was why, in the end, he lined up with Margaret Thatcher to advise her, just prior to his retirement, on how she should handle the trade union 'problem'. It all stemmed from his disillusionment after 'In Place of Strife', his profound gloom over the events of 1972, and his belief that neither Harold Wilson nor Edward Heath 'had the guts' to take up the challenge.

I thought then, and I still believe, that Barnes was placing far too much emphasis on the reform of industrial relations, the unions etc., and too little on the extraordinary changes that were already becoming evident in the technology of industry and the rising fear of insecurity on the shopfloor. But what is still interesting about his view is that it came from someone who had hitherto been a highly liberal thinker, much in favour of government doing all it could to assist social reform.

Denis Barnes came from a pre-war Manchester working-class background. He had been picked out and indeed tutored by Ernest Bevin when Bevin was Churchill's wartime Minister of Labour; and, like so many others, had fallen under the spell of the great trade union leader. But Denis became increasingly soured by what he saw as the negative attitude of postwar trade unionism. That was why, ultimately and I think sadly, he devoured the Thatcher message. Barnes was typical of a number of first-class minds in Whitehall who chose a similar route. It also helps to explain the attitude of men like Conrad Heron, very much a Barnes protégé.

After his retirement from Whitehall Barnes wrote a book (*Governments and Trade Unions*, published in 1980) with a colleague, Eileen Reid, which remains a classic in the analysis of the British industrial scene of 1964–79. In it he confessed his serious doubt as to whether any government would have the nerve to carry out the reforms he had advocated. In fact he doubted whether even Margaret Thatcher would go through with such a programme.

The real problem with Denis Barnes's analysis was that he misjudged both Mrs Thatcher and the ultimate damage that such draconian reforms might lead to. He also overestimated the political power and influence of the trade unions; but, then, that was not an error of judgement exclusive to Whitehall mandarins. Certainly, when I sat listening to Conrad Heron that evening late in 1973, I felt I could also hear the lament of Denis Barnes.

*   *   *

There was no doubt that a substantial coterie of the Whitehall Establishment frowned on Heath's U-turn and the development of his close association with the trade union leaders of the day. They might have been prepared to tolerate discussions in Downing Street, but what many of them resented was Heath's personal bid to come to terms with them, not least his periodic private dinner parties at his personal flat in Albany, Piccadilly ('The oldest block of flats in England and probably the most exclusive,' as it is described). Here the Prime Minister entertained leaders of the TUC as he sought to persuade them to join in a consensus with the Conservative Government. In his memoirs (*Union Man*, 1986), Jack Jones describes one evening with Heath in Albany when Victor Feather called out to the Prime Minister – 'Play the Red Flag for Jack,' at which Heath 'cheerfully played Labour's national anthem ... it put a seal on a jolly evening,' wrote Jones. Still more telling is Jack Jones's summing of Heath's attempt to do a deal with the unions and his ultimate failure:

With a little more patience [in 1972] he [Heath] might still be leader of the Tory Party today [that is, in 1986] ... So why did Ted Heath go to the country [in 1974] when he was close to reaching an accommodation with the unions? Those of us who had got to know him well felt keen disappointment when he lost the leadership of his Party. At the outset I thought he represented the hard face of the Tory Party but over the years he revealed a human face of Toryism, at least to the union leaders who met him frequently. It is doubtful whether the public gained that view of him partly because, as he himself admitted at one of the Downing Street meetings, he was a bad communicator. Amazingly he gained more personal respect from union leaders than they seemed to have for Harold Wilson or even Jim Callaghan. (Jones, 1986: 261–2)

The events that eventually swept away the Heath Government in February 1974 are now part of the legend in modern British political life, second only to the 1979 'Winter of Discontent'. It was the second of the three great miners' strikes that led to the fall of the Heath Government in a sequence of events that began not long after my memorable visit to Chequers.

It is worth a brief recall of those events. In September 1973 the NUM put in a claim for a pay rise of 'up to 40 per cent'. In anticipation of this claim Heath had met the NUM's President, Joe Gormley, in Downing Street in mid-July for a private discussion at which Gormley sought to reassure the Prime Minister that he was not in favour of such a high demand and certainly did not want a rerun of the previous year's bitter strike. What Gormley wanted was an updating of the 1972 Wilberforce settlement. But Gormley failed to hold his powerful executive. They insisted on pressing ahead with the full claim, and four days after the Middle East war broke out, sending oil prices through the roof, the NUM leaders rejected a Coal Board offer of a 13 per cent pay rise.

Gormley returned for private talks with Heath before the end of October, and promised the Prime Minister to try again to persuade his executive to accept the Coal Board's offer. He was turned down. By then the full impact of the Middle East crisis and oil price inflation had become apparent. In mid-November the NUM started an overtime ban. The following day – 13 November – the government declared another State of Emergency, even though there were nearly eight weeks' supply of coal stocks. And, as I have described earlier in this chapter, it was at this juncture that Willie Whitelaw suggested the lunch with the *Daily Mirror* at the Ivy Restaurant, followed not long afterwards by my dramatic meeting with Conrad Heron.

The crisis deepened into January, with the Cabinet and its crisis-committee virtually in permanent session. There seemed one last possibility open to the government, and this was proposed by the TUC leaders who asked for a special meeting of the National Economic Development Council (NEDDY). It met on 9 January 1974, and the TUC offered a formula to help the government out of its logjam: 'let the Coal Board and NUM resume negotiations and reach an agrement and the TUC will pledge that other unions will not exploit any miners' settlement as an argument in negotiating their own pay deals'. In short, the TUC pledged to regard the miners as a 'special case' and not use it as an example. A piece of paper to this effect was passed by Sidney Greene (Lord Greene) – the railwaymen's leader and then chairman of the TUC economic committee – to Heath's Chancellor Anthony Barber (Lord Barber) who was in the chair.

He showed it to the Prime Minister's Principal Private Secretary, Sir Robert Armstrong, sitting alongside. Armstrong (Later Lord Armstrong of Ilminster) scribbled a note, which, in effect, advised Barber; 'Don't touch it.' Armstrong, who later became Margaret Thatcher's Cabinet Secretary, didn't trust the TUC to deliver. Barber nodded. Yet even after that piece of drama Heath refused to give up all hope. He called in the TUC the next day to test whether the offer could be guaranteed. Len Murray (Lord Murray) had just taken over as TUC general secretary from Victor Feather, and he urged the Prime Minister – 'trust us'. In fact Murray put the pledge in writing to Heath in advance of the Downing Street meeting. It was always Murray's view that Heath himself would have taken a gamble on the TUC word, but the majority of his Cabinet colleagues were unpersuaded, as were most of Heath's senior civil servants.

The Prime Minister continued to keep open the wires to Len Murray and even held further informal meetings. But nothing changed. The pressure to hold a snap election had become irresistible, and from that point it was largely a question of when the general election would be held. About a third of the Cabinet wanted it as quickly as possible – 7 February was the original favoured date because that would have been three days after the result of the miners' strike ballot was due. But Heath decided to delay and call it for Thursday 28 February. He was still fighting for time. The miners' strike ballot was announced on 4 February – producing an 81 per cent vote in favour of striking. The pits were to be shut down from 10 February.

In the country the tension rose as each side declared political war on each other – the miners' vice president, Michael McGahey, a Scottish Communist, denounced the Tory Government as 'the enemy', while various ministers went on record to describe the whole dispute as a left-wing miners' plot to destroy the Heath Government.

In fact Heath was never in favour of testing the voters with a 'Who governs Britain?' slogan. But he was trapped. All avenues to a peaceful solution seemed closed. Within his Cabinet two members, Sir Keith Joseph and Margaret Thatcher, urged him to 'fight the miners openly' rather than go to the country. Their view was that the government should 'stand up to the challenge and take on the miners', and reinforced their argument by claiming that it was cowardly to hide behind the voters. Yet, to the end, Heath was desperate to avoid a bitter confrontation. There is enough evidence to show that the whisperings about 'a revolutionary situation' had reached his ears and had unnerved him. That certainly explains the delay in calling the 1974 election, which subsequent academic studies claim to have been his fatal error of judgement. To quote one distinguished source:

Heath's decision to delay the election by three weeks probably cost him the election. He consulted widely with party officials, Cabinet Ministers and private advisers and went along reluctantly with the majority view. He paid a heavy personal and political price for the decision. (Kavanagh, 1987: 231)

Nor was Harold Wilson in favour of an election to find out 'Who governs Britain?' He was all too well aware of the dangers in such a precedent. Wilson tried hard behind the scenes to bring the miners back to the negotiating table but was told by Gormley to 'stay out of it'. After that Wilson left the intermediary work to Len Murray and the TUC, but he remained ready to intervene if he could and deeply worried about the political implications of the miners' dispute. Nor did he believe that the Labour Party would benefit from a general election in February. My own conversations with him at the time left me in no doubt that he thought he would lose that election.

* * *

So was Conrad Heron correct? Was revolution in the air?

Certainly there were plenty of people in high places who were thinking similarly, in industry and the military establishment as well as the civil service. We know that there were numerous weekend salons being held in country houses where captains of industry, city financiers and the military elite gathered to exchange sombre views about what the country may be moving toward. Private security groupings were being formed at that time, most notable being GB75 run by Colonel David Stirling, founder of the SAS. One influential company of stockbrokers, Kitkat Aitken, actually had its entire staff join up with the Territorial Army because of the City's fear that the nation was under threat. It was a mood that actually carried over into the Wilson Government of 1974 and ran through much of the 1970s.

My own view is that most of this melodrama was quite deliberately inspired to encourage a view at the top of the social ladder about Britain being under a dangerous threat from the left and especially from militant trade unions. It was a view which Margaret Thatcher stoked still further after her election to the Tory leadership, and before 1979, when she described Britain as being on the verge of becoming an 'Eastern European Republic' – i.e. a communist state. I believe that Ted Heath himself was aware of this calculated attempt to whip up hysterical reaction as a kind of 'counter-revolutionary' blast. The industrial climate was volatile, without doubt; there were certainly elements within the trade unions ready to go on to the streets and cause trouble as well as to exploit all genuine industrial grievances. But in my opinion these constituted a minority without political significance and hardly any threat beyond breaking a few shop windows. Everything was, of course, in a state of social and economic turbulence leading up to the age of Thatcherism.

12 1973–4: For All Our Tomorrows

The great political crisis of Christmas and New Year 1973/4 would have been quite enough to be going on with without an additional input of dramatic news from my own base at the *Daily Mirror* – Hugh Cudlipp announced that he was to retire at the ridiculously youthful age of 60. Fleet Street was stunned, and so were we. He had celebrated his sixtieth birthday on 28 August and had been knighted. He seemed at the peak of his creative energy and power. But behind the façade of a glittering reputation as King of Tabloid journalism, a Prince of Fleet Street and still in charge of the most popular national newspaper in the land – behind that mask there was an unease that few realised. Perhaps his exceptional sense of the public mood, which for so long steered his instinct about what the readers want, had now picked up something else: that the whole Fleet Street scene was about to undergo fundamental change. He never admitted this in precisely those terms, although he was deeply aware that the Murdoch 'invasion' had changed the entire game of popular journalism and that he, despite all his past achievements, was unsure how to play the cards in future.

Cudlipp publicly declared that it was time for someone with a fresh outlook to take over the great newspaper empire of Mirror Group Newspapers, and announced that it would be 'unpardonable vanity to go on editing popular newspapers after the age of 60'. That sounds even more absurd today than it did at the time – and it seemed pretty absurd then. But in January 1974 Hugh Cudlipp decided to go. It sounded like a trumpet call to a Fleet Street revolution. And it was.

The truth is that one had already begun down in Bouverie Street, where Rupert Murdoch was producing his *Sun* and shaking the cobwebs off every preconceived Fleet Street notion. The Cudlipp instinct, which, frankly, we all then viewed with profound scepticism, was in truth pretty accurate. It was indeed the end of an era, and in his bones, or his instinct or whatever, Cudlipp sensed it. What timing: what a moment to jump ship, at the very moment when a miners' strike was about to topple a Conservative Government. Of course, he didn't know that – though I have always had a feeling that he sensed something of the kind was about to explode. The sense of drama never left Hugh.

Cudlipp's departure from Holborn Circus prior to the 1974 election left a huge gap on the bridge at the *Mirror*. He remained on the premises in a suite across the connecting bridge to the Mirror Group's auxiliary building in Fetter Lane. He remained there during the election and indeed for some time afterwards and was constantly in touch with his chosen successor at the helm, Sydney Jacobson, but he did not interfere with the political direction of the paper, much as he would have liked to have been back in charge. With what amounted to monumental will-power he resisted the temptation, in defiance of Oscar Wilde's maxim. So the *Daily Mirror* was firmly in the hands of Cudlipp's closest friend and colleague.

Sydney Jacobson himself was a remarkable figure. Born in South Africa, schooled in London, he had done much of his early apprenticeship as a reporter, then rising to assistant editor, on *The Statesman* in Calcutta, where he worked with another young journalist, Malcolm Muggeridge. Sydney joined the army at the outbreak of war and had a distinguished war in which he won the Military Cross. He met Cudlipp after the war shortly after both were demobbed, and then joined Cudlipp on the old *Sunday Pictorial* (*Sunday Mirror*). I first met Sydney when we were both covering the first postwar meeting of Sir Oswald Mosley's British Union of Fascists – he for the *Sunday Pictorial*, me for the *Sunday Express*. We remained firm and close friends until his death in October 1988.

Sydney had one of the sharpest and most sophisticated political minds in British journalism. He had been at Cudlipp's side for many years as adviser, chief lieutenant and *eminence grise*, but, most all, as personal friend and confidant. He was political editor of the *Mirror* at the peak of its circulation and influence in the 1950s and early 1960s and then moved across to edit the *Daily Herald* when the paper was acquired by Mirror Group, remaining with the Odhams' *Sun* as editorial director until it went to Murdoch.

For the *Mirror* the 1974 election was as crucial, in terms of its future competition with Murdoch's *Sun*, as it was politically for Heath and Wilson. The *Sun* had begun its new life under Rupert Murdoch and his first editor, Larry Lamb, by supporting Labour (in the tradition of its inheritance), but by 1974 it was already beginning to turn away from Labour and the trade unions. The *Mirror* remained steadfast albeit occasionally critical. In command of the scene in February

1974 Sydney Jacobson put everything he had into the campaign to back Harold Wilson and the Labour Party. He was on deck virtually for 24 hours a day throughout the campaign and assembled a team around him similarly dedicated. I was fortunate in being appointed by Sydney to be his close lieutenant as well as continuing to write daily pieces for the paper. Alongside was a dear colleague, the late Deryck Winterton, who was the *Mirror* chief leader writer as he had been under Sydney at the *Herald*.

There can be no question about the impact of the *Daily Mirror* in that 1974 campaign. Each day the paper's editorial thundered out the message that Britain needed a new government under Wilson to extricate the country from the existing industrial chaos.

The three-day week was a crippling economic burden although, ironically, productivity in some key sectors of industry actually increased during that crisis period. Jacobson kept up the paper's relentless barrage against the Heath Government right up to polling day on 28 February, when Jacobson produced a poster-style front page in huge 60-point type, which read:

FOR ALL OUR TOMORROWS VOTE LABOUR TODAY.

It had an astonishing impact. The front page of the *Daily Mirror* was used as a poster – which was Jacobson's intention – in Labour Party committee rooms throughout the land as well as in the front windows of thousands of homes. It is pretty certain that the paper's front page had more impact on the voters than any other national newspaper on that polling day. Many observers have since compared its influence with a previous famous *Mirror* front page in the 1945 General Election when the great cartoonist Philip Zec produced a memorable drawing of a wounded British soldier handing on the beacon of victory and peace with the caption, 'Here you are – don't lose it again'. Jacobson's 1974 message seemed just as powerful on the day. In fact, there were reports of Conservative Party activists actually burning the front page of the *Mirror* that day as a public demonstration of their anger.

It is always dangerous and certainly foolhardy to make too many fanciful claims about any newspaper's influence, in an election or at any other time. But it is a fair assumption to claim that the *Daily Mirror* that day did have a significant effect on the result. This claim is strengthened by the statistics of that extraordinary election. In their study of the 1974 election, David Butler and Dennis Kavanagh

(1974: 1–17) examine the unusual depth of uncertainty among the voters: their findings are worth repeating:

> The evidence of a long term decline in strength of partisanship was substantial. In 1964 44% of people said they were very attached to one of the two main parties. By 1974 that figure had dropped to 27%. The status of politicians had fallen too. People were ready to vote for the lesser evil in a sceptical mood with a new cynicism about the outcome.

The Butler/Kavanagh survey also showed that the 1974 Labour poll of 37 per cent was its lowest postwar vote at that time. In 1983 it was, of course, still lower. The survey also revealed that the 'class content' of voting attitudes showed the 'sharpest decline' in February 1974 while the Liberal vote increased by 12 per cent, which was the single biggest change in the percentage share of the vote for any party between one election and another since 1945. Yet with 20 per cent of the vote the Liberals had only 2 per cent of Parliamentary seats. In fact the February 1974 election was decided by a handful of voters in several marginal constituencies – Carmarthen, Sowerby, Stockport, Preston and Portsmouth. Something of the order of 500 votes in these five constituencies decided the fate of the Heath Government (see the *Observer*, 22 September 1991). It was that close. How political history swings on such tenuous hinges of chance. Denis Healey (Lord Healey), commenting on all this, wrote in his autobiography (1989) that 1974 was 'a watershed in British politics. The electorate was trying to tell us something. But, was anybody listening?'

Labour emerged as the strongest single party with 301 seats against the Conservatives' 297. The Liberals won 14 seats, Ulster Unionists 11, Scottish Nationalists 7, Plaid Cymru 2 and others 3. For several days the whole future of 'which Government, what Government?' lay in the balance. Ted Heath remained rooted in Downing Street, trying to persuade Jeremy Thorpe and the Liberal Party to form a government with him. He was finally turned down. On 4 March – four days after the election – Heath finally resigned office and the Queen called on Harold Wilson to form the new government.

It was his third administration – and, as I have reported earlier, he did not expect to be back in Downing Street. During the whole of that election period I had worked closely with Wilson, chiefly as a link with Jacobson and the *Mirror*. I spent a good deal of time with Wilson, who had briefly taken a house in Lord North Street after losing the 1970 election. We were often together either alone or with Marcia Williams, sometimes with Joe Haines. It was important both for the *Mirror* and the Labour leadership that the liaison should be close and intimate. It was my role to ensure that the link worked smoothly.

But while the campaign at the paper was driven forward with dynamic energy by the Jacobson team, the same could not be said of the Labour Party campaign. It was struggling. Moreover, the more I saw of Harold the greater became my anxiety about his mood. He was far from enthusiastic about the election campaign, and his health seemed questionable. He had a bad cold and a painful stye over an eye. He appeared to me to be run-down, tired and wearied. His mind was still alert, especially after a bit of stimulating discussion but it lacked the razor-sharp quality I had known in the 1960s. His lethargy was apparent. His eyes looked strained and heavy. In fact he appeared to lack any obvious enthusiasm to take office again.

I had no idea then that I might be witnessing the first significant signs of a deterioration that was to become apparent sometime later. But on reflection it becomes pretty obvious that the signs I was picking up at that time were the first indications in the serious decline of Harold Wilson. Hindsight mocks us all.

Even as he took office he had few illusions about the problems ahead. In his mind, as we now know quite clearly, Harold Wilson had had enough. Mary Wilson certainly had, and she refused to move back into Downing Street. Wilson was then still only 58. But he had already experienced eleven years as party leader and five and a half years as premier. He knew his own limitations and, more potently, the limitations of office in such circumstances as existed in 1974. To preside over a minority government, even more constricted than in 1964, was not an attractive proposition. He also had few illusions about the internal conflicts within his own Cabinet. One account of the pressures hanging over Wilson is worth recalling. It came from Bill Rodgers (Lord Rodgers) in a review of Roy Jenkins's memoirs, *A Life at the Centre* (1991). Rodgers (*Observer*, 22 September 1991) describes a dinner party at Jenkins's home in March 1974 a few days after Wilson re-entered Downing Street:

> I recall a gloomy supper at the Jenkins's home in Ladbroke Square when the outcome of the 1974 election was known and a depressed twitchy gathering of his [Jenkins's] friends ... learned of his immediate future. This was to have been the year when,

according to his strategy a 'temporising Labour leadership was to receive its just reward in the shape of a lost general Election'. Instead Harold Wilson formed his second Government and Roy Jenkins returned unwillingly to the Home Office where he had once served with distinction. In the next two years his standing as Wilson's natural successor seeped away and on Wilson's departure James Callaghan pulled ahead of him to win the ballot.

The Jenkins group, largely consisting of the old Gaitskellite wing of the leadership, not only desired Wilson to lose the 1974 election; they seriously believed it was the only path by which to rescue the Labour Party. They had no confidence in the government, their own, that Wilson formed in March 1974. Here was yet further evidence that the road to the break-up of the Labour Party, which followed in the early 1980s, and the path to Thatcherism, was already well advanced in 1974.

For Rodgers, as for Roy Jenkins, the Wilson 'victory' of February 1974 was effectively the end of the road for their ambitions. By the time Wilson went back to the electorate in October 1974, seeking a workable majority, Jenkins had departed for Europe. His hope, his ambition and, at one period, his near certain conviction that the leadership of the Labour Party was within his grasp, had disappeared in that February election. He had little or no idea about the thinking that was already going on inside Harold Wilson's mind about resigning the premiership. That was the closest-kept secret of all. A short time after taking office for the third time as Prime Minister Wilson told a selected handful of people around him – Marcia Williams and Arnold (Lord) Goodman were the two most prominent people taken into his confidence – that he intended to retire on his sixtieth birthday, 11 March 1976. No one in the Cabinet knew: not Jenkins, neither Healey, nor Callaghan, who would eventually succeed a younger man.

The other dominant element in Wilson's mind at the time was to hold a second general election in the autumn of 1974 in the hope of securing an overall, working majority. In the meantime he had no option but to slog it out, for at least seven months, without any majority at all. At odd moments when he felt particularly depressed he would confide to close colleagues like Barbara Castle that he had had enough. 'Can't go on forever, you know Barbara.' What is remarkable is that he actually succeeded in turning that 'unworkable' interim government into a good deal more than mere survival on a political life-support machine. With Michael Foot at the Department of Employment, Denis Healey as Chancellor and Callaghan in the Foreign Office, the government began to look interesting and, at least, functional.

Michael Foot (known to the satirists, not too unfairly, as 'the minister for the trade unions') settled all the outstanding disputes, including the miners, by agreeing to most of what the unions had been demanding. The inflation rate rocketed beyond 27 per cent and was then slowly brought down to 8 per cent after about two years of the Social Contract: ah, yes the Social Contract; the phrase that seemed to leap somehow from Rousseau out of Jack Jones or Tommy Balogh (Lord Balogh, the famous Hungarian-born economic adviser to Harold Wilson). For three it years seemed a possible life-line for the Labour Government despite the ridicule that was frequently piled on it by friends and foe in almost equal proportions. That now almost forgotten concordat between government and unions, which, despite all the subsequent cynicism, did in fact have a considerable success. Above all it demonstrated that government and unions could actually operate an agreed policy on wages for a limited period and in the face of enormous internal strains, especially within the trade unions. In fact the Social Contract deal of the 1970s was not all that far away from what Ted Heath came so close to achieving before the oil crisis and miners' strike led to the collapse of his government.

The Social Contract – which claimed numerous authors when it seemed to be succeeding and only detractors after it failed – was primarily the brainchild of the Transport Union leader, Jack Jones. He put forward the tentative idea in a speech to the 1971 Labour Party conference by proposing a 'joint policy' for economic and social reform to be worked out between the Labour leadership and the trade unions in time for the next election. That was how and where it all began. Jones has always been hesitant to make the claim of original authorship, but in his personal conversations with me he has always accepted that without his speech of 1971 the Social Contract, probably, would never have materialised.

Jones is on record (see his memoirs, 1986) with the admission that it 'never occurred to me to call it a social contract at the time. I used phrases like "a blueprint" or an "agreed platform" ...' While in Opposition Wilson set up a special committee to discuss Jones's proposal with the TUC leadership. These discussions were held at the same time as, indeed almost in parallel with, the negotiations going on between the Heath Government and the TUC. Heath certainly was aware of this, which made relations within his own Cabinet oft times even more difficult. Jones was also having some tense moments with his Labour Party friends. 'In many ways,' he writes in his book, 'it was like negotiating a collective agreement with the highly experienced political leaders – Denis Healey, Barbara Castle, Shirley Williams, Jim Callaghan and Harold Wilson amongst them – seeking to make sure that they did not give too much away.'

But Jones became convinced that the deal – it acquired the label, Social Contract, sometime in 1972 – could work and would eventually become the key factor in determining the success or failure of the next Labour Government. So intricate and detailed did these discussions become that Wilson and later Callaghan suggested that Jones himself should join a future Labour Cabinet, much in the way his predecessors, Ernest Bevin and Frank Cousins, had done. But he declined. Where his influence was ultimately decisive was in the appointment of Michael Foot as Secretary of State for Employment in 1974: that was largely done on Jones's nomination. In fact it was a sensible and practical decision to put Foot into that department, though he had no previous experience in that area. Yet since the whole basis of the Wilson Government in 1974 was to establish a working relationship with the trade unions it was logical to build it on the foundations of the Foot–Jones friendship, which was both political and personal. To be sure, it offered a natural and irresistible bait to the Conservatives, in Parliament and press, but that was the gamble Wilson had to risk.

For seven months between February and October 1974 the Wilson Government lived on its nervous energy and a precarious Parliamentary balancing act made tenable by a strange political paradox: the Conservatives were in no mood for another quick election, they were deeply divided, disaffected about their leader, Ted Heath, and convinced that eventually the Wilson Government would make such a hash of its special relationship with the unions that it would collapse ignominiously under the pressures of a future economic crisis. That was a prescient scenario. I can well recall discussions with Tory leaders at the time – Willie Whitelaw, Sir Keith Joseph, Geoffrey Howe, etc. – who were quite content to let the Wilson Government grapple with an 'impossible' economic climate, inflation, pressure from the IMF and cuts in social spending etc. – all, in their view, eventually preparing the way for a return to Conservative Government. Having experienced the trauma of the

1973/4 winter crisis the Tory leadership had no insatiable desire to snatch the thankless task away from Wilson.

Heath recognised the force of this scenario – but also saw beyond its superficial attraction to the dangers, as he correctly perceived, of a more extreme form of Toryism taking over. Heath tried again, in the summer of 1974, to bring the Liberals into an alliance with him; he put to them the concept of a centre coalition, which might get trade union support in the event of failure by the Wilson Government. He saw himself as a Tory leader seeking to heal the wounds of a deeply divided, and politically confused, British electorate. But that was not what the Tory power groups had in mind as they conferred, regularly and secretly in their weekend country salons, re-echoing the fears that Britain was seriously in danger of becoming 'an East European state'. The ground was being solidly prepared for a Tory leader to replace Heath, a new figure who would cast aside the Keynesian policies of postwar, the social–economic consensus, all talk of working with the trade unions and such corporatist ideas as incomes policy. The intellectual storehouse for Thatcherism was in full preparation *before* the second General Election in 1974.

*   *   *

Wilson's problems in taking over in March 1974 were enormous. The economic cost of inheriting the industrial climate could hardly be measured at the time. In Denis Healey's first Budget as Chancellor he raised income tax and increased corporation taxes, adding a chilling warning about more tax increases to follow. He made no attempt to conceal the brutal truth about the nation's economic condition. What he did not reveal – but disclosed later in his memoirs – is that the Treasury had got its figures hopelessly wrong. It is worth quoting the crucial passage from Healey's book (1989: 380–1):

> For my first budget three weeks after I took office the Treasury gave me an estimate of the PSBR in 1974/5 – leaving aside all the fiscal changes later in the year – which turned out to be £4,000 million too low. This was the equivalent of 5.4% of that year's GDP. The magnitude of that one forecasting error was greater than that of any fiscal change by any Chancellor in British history. Two years later, in 1976, the Budget estimate of the PSBR was £2,000 million too high; and in November that year I handed an estimate to the IMF which turned out to be twice as high as it should have been.

If I had been given accurate forecasts in 1976 I would never have needed to go to the IMF at all.

That amounts to a sensational political disclosure the significance of which, to this day, has not been fully recognised. With uncharacteristic generosity Healey exonerates the Treasury mandarins from culpability. 'I found it difficult to blame the Treasury for these mistakes, though others did,' he writes. 'None of the independent forecasting bodies had a better record.'

Even so, the implications of Healey's revelation puts a different gloss on the state of the nation inherited by the Wilson Government, good and bad. The agenda pad was overfull: Wilson began by trying to 'renegotiate' the terms of Britain's membership of the EEC, a process destined to be long and tortuous – and arguably still going on. Michael Foot had to unravel and amend the Heath Government's Employment Act and unscramble what remained of the Industrial Relations Act; the TUC under Len Murray began detailed work on the Social Contract. The concept of a National Enterprise Board, as an instrument of government intervention in industry, was being developed. The backwardness of British industry, not least across substantial areas of its senior management, had already been largely exposed by Heath (his famous phrase about 'the unacceptable face of capitalism' etc.), who developed a profound contempt for the protected operations of the City of London.

For years there had been under-investment across the entire field of industry – private as well as public sector. Even the better areas of British industry lagged well behind most of their foreign competitors in research, development, training and indeed often in enterprise itself. The NEB, which Wilson set up in 1974, was created to generate a new energy and drive into British industry, to encourage mergers and to help provide state assistance where it was required. The real problem was that there was no distinctive economic strategy but merely a tactical commitment to a broad concept. Wilson excelled in tactical manoeuvre but was weak in longer-term strategic planning. George Brown's grand dream of a National Economic Plan, having collapsed in 1966, was never revived.

At the Department of Industry Tony Benn, rampant with his radical ideas, was blocked at every turn – if not by Wilson directly then by his senior civil servants, who regarded him as a 'revolutionary nut case' (a phrase actually used to me by one of Benn's top civil servants at that time). Benn's White Paper in 1974, which set out his concept of a radical industrial policy equipped with planning agreements to be discussed between management and shopfloor in all the major industries, fell to earth with a thud after Wilson declared it 'sloppy and half-baked'. It was indeed sloppy, but it also contained some sparkling ideas that could have been developed, improved on and certainly implemented. It was effectively the end of Benn's attempt to inject some socialist thinking into industrial planning.

Wilson's antipathy to Benn derived partly from the formidable campaign waged by the Confederation of British Industry against the White Paper. Some of the CBI leaders were deeply involved with the weekend salons already preparing the ground for the post-Wilson period. At that time my close CBI contacts were telling me, in confidence, about these weekend meetings and the agenda – which, effectively was to devise a political strategy to stop Britain becoming – that phrase again – 'an East European Republic'. When I expressed some scepticism about this kind of alarmist talk my objections were always dismissed as naive. 'You simply don't realise the dangerous waters we are running into' was the usual response. Benn himself provided a classic focal figure, a kind of unconscious accessory to the destabilising propaganda that was then flooding across (sometimes cascading over) the Wilson Government. Everywhere it turned the government seemed to run into impediments.

My own mind, in those times, inevitably referred back to that conversation, months earlier, with Conrad Heron. Even I began to wonder whether there was some part of this puzzling political canvas that required deeper explanation. Could they – whoever *they* were – be right? Was there a serious, lurking danger that we had all missed, or underestimated? A book published in 1991 seeks to offer a partial answer. Two left-wing journalists, Stephen Dorril and Robin Ramsay, suggest (*Smear: Wilson and the Secret State*, 1991) that there was a serious plot to destablise the Wilson Government, but not from the left, rather from the right. They argue that there were numerous groupings, including extreme right-wing factions, paramilitary 'security' organisations, influential businessmen and City financial tycoons, bankers as well as representatives from the security services – all gathering, not necessarily in one community, at various times to discuss what should be done to 'stop the rot'. The Dorril/Ramsay book argues (p. 288):

Thatcherism grew out of a right-wing network with extensive links to the military–intelligence establishment. In our view Mrs.

Thatcher's rise to power was the climax of a long campaign by this network which included a protracted de-stabilization campaign against the Labour Party during 1974–76.

A good deal of this certainly chimes with my own experiences at the time, both inside Whitehall, when I was seconded to work with the Prime Minister in 1976 (see next chapter) and in my work as a journalist for the *Daily Mirror*. It also reflects Hugo Young's claim in his book on Margaret Thatcher ('One of Us', 1989) that 1974 was, in his phrase, 'the hinge year for her as well as her party'. Of course it was. Heath was defeated in two general elections; the Conservative Party were in turmoil, dissatisfied not only with its leader but with the entire lack of direction in Britain's political affairs, including the way in which the Heath Government had managed the nation after the 1972 U-turn.

Yet my own, perhaps more eccentric view, is that the collapse of the postwar consensus really started in 1966 when Harold Wilson, with a commanding majority of nearly one hundred, failed to face up to the social and economic challenges that had become all too evident. That in turn led to Ted Heath's 1970–74 failure, the Wilson/Callaghan inheritance of February 1974 and the terrible final crisis years of the 1970s with Callaghan's Government desperately trying to cope with what was an impossible situation. Even so I do not – cannot – underestimate the significance of that extraordinary year of 1974.

There was, in my considered view, a serious attempt by some groups to undermine, destabilise and remove the Wilson Government. To some extent we now have the dubious benefit of the evidence from Peter Wright's book *Spycatcher* (1987). But even if we dismiss much of Wright's story as tainted evidence from a soured former Intelligence officer, there are aspects in the Wright book that clearly mesh with other pieces of detailed evidence of which I am aware and which I will discuss in the next chapter. Some of these elements are inevitably linked with Harold Wilson's dramatic resignation in March 1976.

But in the meantime, in that almost phoney political period between the two elections of 1974, Wilson did struggle hard to keep the show on the road. Tired and depressed as he clearly was, nonetheless there was a residue of that determination which ten years earlier had elevated him to a point no other political figure on the stage was able to reach. The bitter disappointment, and, to be sure, the final blow to his confidence, came in the election of 10

October 1974. Labour gained a mere 17 seats, which left them with an overall majority of 3 – effectively back to 1964. Wilson needed a minimum overall majority of around twenty and had counted on getting at least that. He was shattered by that result. He tried to put the best gloss on a grim situation and told the *Daily Mirror*, 'I should have liked a bigger majority, naturally, but the present position is perfectly viable.' He knew that was nonsense.

At the *Mirror* we again had pulled out all the stops. The paper ran a very good campaign for the Labour Party, and on polling day Sydney Jacobson repeated his poster front page of February – FOR ALL OUR TOMORROWS VOTE LABOUR TODAY. But it didn't have the desired impact. In fact it appeared to have far less effect as a pulse quickener than its original. Something deeper was going on inside the body of British political life and in the minds of voters.

13   Inside the Whale:
A Journalist in Whitehall

The scene was the press table in the Winter Gardens' ballroom at Blackpool, July 1975. The occasion was the biennial delegate conference of the Transport & General Workers Union. The speaker was Jack Jones, the general secretary. The subject, the Social Contract – and what the trade unions needed to do to rescue a beleaguered Labour Government from impending disaster. The press table was full of reporters, industrial and political correspondents, editorial opinion writers, columnists, even the odd editor concerned not to miss the drama of the moment. Tension was high in the hall and aroused among a wide audience throughout the country already informed about the crisis in Whitehall. I cannot recall a more capacious press table at any previous trade union conference.

Jones had just concluded his speech, which contained the astonishing proposal that everybody's pay rise should be limited to £6 a week. He was insisting that something as dramatic, indeed unique, as this was now inescapable if the unions were to rescue the Wilson Government from disaster. It was a remarkable speech, made still more so because Jones, despite his towering authority, needed to fight his own conference: the TGWU had a long-standing commitment to oppose wage restraint of any kind. Despite that heritage Jones won the approval of his tough, critical conference, with some one thousand delegates actually giving him an ovation for a speech that could not have been sweet music to their ears. A considerable political moment had been recorded.

The Social Contract had been stumbling for a year while the economic crisis worsened by the day. Jones and the other TUC leaders recognised they had reached a crucial point. Something more than platitudes and phrases was needed – and quickly. Jones came up with the £6 idea – actually he wanted a bit more. He discussed it with Wilson and Healey and other Cabinet Ministers before putting it to the TUC leader, Len Murray, and then to his union conference. Jones had already bargained with the Chancellor, who wanted the figure limited to £5. Jones made a bid for £7 or £8. The compromise was £6. Healey had warned the TUC leaders sometime earlier that the pound was in grave danger and the IMF was breathing down his neck. In fact, the Cabinet was in turmoil, and only later did Jones himself become fully aware of how precarious was the Government's situation. He knew that a number of ministers were balancing on their toes, ready to resign – chiefly over the Treasury's demand that the government introduce an emergency package of measures to include statutory wage control and severe cuts in public spending. To Jones, with his memories of earlier crises involving Labour Governments, it sounded like 1931 all over again – but even more dangerous. Jones was effectively leading the TUC pack, and his authority, prestige and political standing was at its peak. With all this in his mind he proposed setting a figure for all pay rises to avoid statutory control. That's how the £6 idea was born.

Of course, the situation had been building up to this drama for some time. At the 1974 Trades Union Congress James Callaghan, then Foreign Secretary, was Labour Party chairman and the guest speaker at the TUC. He used that public platform to emphasise the importance of the Social Contract, which was under attack from some of left-wing led unions, who saw it merely as a new name for wage restraint. But Callaghan did something else in private – he again invited Jones (on Wilson's behalf) to join the government. Callaghan pointed out that one swift way of bringing him into the Cabinet would be for Jones to be given a life peerage. Jones dismissed the idea with contempt. He told Callaghan: 'I don't want to go to the Lords, and I don't want to be in the Government – but I'll help it all I can.' That was on the eve of the second general election in 1974, and Jones was as disappointed, and as profoundly surprised, as Harold Wilson and Callaghan that Labour failed to get a substantial working majority in that October 1974 election. It was all pretty desperate by the time the Transport Union leader, very much conscious of his role as a kind of commander-in-chief of Labour's trade union army, reached his own conference in Blackpool in July 1975.

I was sitting at the press table when a note was passed to me. It briefly read: 'Please call Joe Haines at Downing Street.' I did. Joe said: 'Can you come and see me at No. 10 as soon as possible? I have something important to discuss with you.' I explained that I was supposed to be covering the conference for the whole week, to which Joe replied that he had already been in touch with the editor of the *Mirror* and Sydney Jacobson. He hinted, vaguely, that the Prime Minister wanted me to do a 'special job' and wanted to talk with me privately – something that could not be discussed on the 'phone. It sounded melodramatic and mysterious.

I left Blackpool early the next morning and drove myself to Downing Street. Joe was waiting for me in his room and told me the full story. The Prime Minister wanted me to take on a special assignment for the government – to start and run a Counter-Inflation Publicity Unit. The function of the unit, which I would head, would be to explain to the nation just how critical the situation was and, especially, forge links with employers and trade unions to secure their combined support for this campaign. He told me that Wilson had already discussed this with the *Mirror* board and that the paper was agreeable to lend me on a secondment to the government, provided I approved the idea. Wilson had also told the *Mirror* that the government would provide guarantee cover for all my pension and employment rights while I worked in Whitehall and ensure that my salary was at least equal to that paid by the paper.

While I was with Joe Haines the Cabinet was locked in a five-hour session discussing the economic crisis. Joe left me alone from time to time to find out what was happening inside the Cabinet room and brought back updated reports. The point was that my role hinged on the Cabinet accepting the Foot–Jones bargain of a voluntary pay policy based on the £6 and rejecting Treasury pressure for a statutory wages limit.

Late that afternoon the Cabinet reached its decision – a statutory policy was rejected but it was a close-run thing. The Treasury fought zealously to the last minute, arguing that a voluntary deal would carry no confidence with the IMF. Once the Cabinet verdict had been reached I was called in to see Harold Wilson, who filled in more details about the job and promised me that I would be responsible directly to him and linked to him through his Downing Street secretary, Ken Stowe (Sir Kenneth Stowe), as well as Joe Haines. I would be given a special office in the Old Admiralty building, across Horse Guards' Parade, and a substantial staff to team up the unit. We discussed the whole nature of the task, the avenues I should tread, the people and organisations I should encourage to co-operate – CBI, TUC, and even prominent figures in the Opposition parties – and the budget I would have available.

It was exciting stuff, and I accepted the role. Even so I had still to discuss these details with two close friends – Michael Foot and Jack Jones. Both of them were crucial to whether I could carry out the task at all. And in those conversations I began to get an insight into how tough it was likely to be. Michael was delighted that I would do it, but warned that it would be a hard road to tread: there was still a lot of opposition within the government to the idea of such a unit, which originally had come from Barbara Castle. He warned me that several Cabinet members objected on principle but didn't list their names. I could guess.

My discussion with Jack Jones was even more difficult. He was still burning with anger at the Treasury attempt to build in a statutory policy, and he warned me that if there was even the slightest attempt to revive this he would walk away from the deal and have nothing to do with my unit. Jack also marked my card in advance of any discussions with other union leaders – 'beware'. What he meant was that there was still a great deal of work to do to persuade the government and some union leaders that his £6 policy was the way ahead. Of course, he would help me where he could – but warned that I would be on my own for much of the time. He was correct on all counts.

*   *   *

I joined Harold Wilson's team of advisers – incidentally, far fewer in those days than the contemporary Downing Street culture appears to require – at the beginning of July 1975 on leave of absence from the *Daily Mirror*. Wilson appointed me with the title of Head of the Counter-Inflation Publicity Unit and gave me a substantial free hand to set up my own staff team from scratch. But, of course, that would have been impossible without his help and advice and, similarly, the help and advice from Ken Stowe and Joe Haines, who gave me a quick learner's guide about potential hazards and provided me with a list of likely people to choose from. The late Charles Birdsall became my chief-of-staff. He had worked in No. 10 and knew the ropes. But more crucial at that stage, Charles had long experience inside the Whitehall machine (the Whale, as he called it after Orwell's aphorism), and had been press officer in various key departments, in particular the old Ministry of Labour, where I had first come into contact with him. Charles knew every nook and cranny of those Whitehall canyons. He had served under most governments since the Attlee days and had been especially close to Harold Macmillan when he was Prime Minister. I had no problem in welcoming Charles. I knew he would be immensely loyal and invaluable as a guide through the minefields out there. I was provided with a superb personal secretary in Jill Thompson from the Cabinet Office, and gradually we built up a strong support team.

Wilson in his personal briefing had charged me with the task of explaining (in *Mirror* language, as he put it) the whole point and purpose of the Social Contract and the terrible dangers of rampant inflation. He told me that I would get all the help he could provide in establishing close relations with the trade union leadership, the top employers and academics. He also assured me that I would get civil service backing, and any problems were to be reported direct to him, personally. 'My door is open at all times,' he promised, and I was answerable to him as Prime Minister and to no one else. Technically I was a member of the Cabinet Office team, but since accommodation inside the various office suites that link No. 10 with the rest of the Cabinet Office was limited he proposed I use some available space in the Old Admiralty Building across Horse Guards' Parade from No. 10. I was made a temporary civil servant with the rank of Assistant Secretary.

Then Harold Wilson asked me about a deputy and disclosed to me, for the first time, that Sydney Jacobson (already Lord Jacobson) was keen to help me if I wished. I was both flattered and amazed because I knew that Sydney had been approached, before me, to take on the job of starting and running the Counter-Inflation Unit – but had turned it down in favour of me despite the fact that he was just retiring from the Mirror Group. Wilson told me that although Sydney had turned down the top job he was willing to work under me, indeed he preferred it that way – a remarkable gesture, and tribute, from someone who only a few weeks earlier had been my boss at the paper.

Mind you, it was a typical Jacobson gesture. Here was one of the outstanding journalists of his generation, a man who, with great personal modesty, had steered Hugh Cudlipp through so many political minefields, having finally stepped down from running the Mirror Group papers, ready to help an old friend and colleague. Sydney was one of the finest friends I ever had in a trade where genuine friendship is never easy to establish nor to sustain into a lasting bond. He also wore his badge of courage with similar calm modesty. His wartime MC was indeed an acronym for Man of Courage. So we began yet another partnership in what was, for both of us, a somewhat foreign field.

The Treasury allocated the unit an annual budget of two and half million pounds – quite a sizeable chunk in 1975 – that was then approved by Parliament. Compared with some of the subsequent allocations to similar governmental bodies our budget was small change – for example, about one-tenth the money given to ministers for their publicity operations during Margaret Thatcher's period (especially to Lord Young's various departments). Even so I felt it adequate for our immediate task, which was to draft, print and circulate to every household in the country a booklet explaining the nature of inflation and the reasons why we were in existence. Sydney and I wrote the booklet over one weekend and had it agreed by the Prime Minister within 24 hours. Most of the rest of the budget went on several waves of press advertising – in the regional as well as the national daily newspapers.

My principal task at that time was to win the support from both sides of industry in the shape of text messages for advertisements backing the work of the unit and supporting the government's counter-inflation measures. Most of the trade union leaders gave me their support without much difficulty, but it was often hard-going with some of the top employers, who were cagey about being associated with the detailed policies of the Wilson Government. In persuading most of them to do so I concentrated on the crisis facing the nation, regardless of which party was in power, and to their credit the great majority of senior employers accepted that challenge. Only a few demurred.

One of the key factors was getting the support of the Confederation of British Industry through its then Director General, Sir Campbell Adamson, who showed great tenacity and audacious courage in persuading his council to back the campaign. In fact what was developing was an unusual degree of cross-party, indeed cross-ideological, support for the policy of the Wilson Government. One of the most delicate tasks was to hold behind-the-scenes discussions with the Conservative Party in Opposition. Margaret Thatcher had been elected leader of the Conservative Party not long before my appointment and the creation of the Counter-Inflation Unit. She had condemned the whole concept, and indeed in a Commons debate my own role had been compared with that of Dr Josef Goebbels, a somewhat absurd parallel but indicative of her deep hostility toward the Wilson Government.

Harold Wilson himself was anxious to soften this hostility and suggested, very privately to me, that I might try to have confidential talks with senior Conservatives to see if there was any possibility of cushioning Thatcher's abrasive attitude. I suggested Willie Whitelaw, whom I knew quite well and liked very much. Harold nodded, though he stressed the absolute importance of keeping such contacts under wraps. Only the two of us should know – although I persuaded him that I should inform Sydney Jacobson.

I had several private meetings with Willie Whitelaw, usually at his home in the morning. I showed him proofs of the newspaper advertising campaign before the ads were published and kept him informed of the unit's other activities. He was always appreciative and promised to do what he could, behind the scenes, to 'persuade Margaret to tone down her opposition'. At the same time he made it clear that he was speaking in a personal and private capacity and not on behalf of the Conservative Party. Willie privately was always very encouraging; after all, few knew the problems better than him. Much to my amazement, we somehow managed to keep these contacts to ourselves.

Not that my relationship with Whitelaw deterred Mrs Thatcher from continuing to attack the work of the unit, and indeed the whole concept of the Social Contract, which she consistently ridiculed as the 'Social Con-trick'. Even so by the end of 1975 the unit was showing signs of some real success, although I was encountering problems in various corners of Whitehall where elements at the top end of the civil service showed their disapproval, even their cynicism, at what we were trying to achieve. Nor was this confined to civil servants. Some members of the Cabinet were scarcely more helpful. This applied on the left, with Tony Benn, as much as on the right, with Roy Jenkins.

Benn had been moved to the Department of Energy after his bitter experience at the Department of Industry, where he was replaced by Eric Varley. Tony and I had always enjoyed a friendly relationship, and I admired much of his work, his openness and his unorthodoxy. But his relationship with Wilson had soured. Benn was opposed to a whole range of policies. His plans for a radical industrial and economic strategy, for industry-wide agreements between unions and employers, for a much swifter move toward extending public ownership in key areas of the economy – all this had been swept aside by Wilson, never to return. He regarded the entire Wilson operation as a 'sell-out' and bracketed the counter-inflation policy along with the rest. So although Tony continued to be friendly enough on a personal basis I could get no support at all from his department – which, after all, was a key sector. Roy Jenkins, at the Home Office was not in such a vital economic sector. Yet his political support would have been enormously important – alas, it never came. He resented Wilson and especially his own return to the Home Office rather than the Chancellorship or, still more his real preference, the Foreign Office. Jenkins showed his contempt for Wilson and the No. 10 entourage at every step. I knew I would get no help from that quarter.

Naturally, the Permanent Secretaries in all the main departments of Whitehall were fully aware of these tensions – and in their own interest played to them. The Counter-Inflation Unit was small fry, a mere gnat in the jungle of lions, tigers and serpents, though this never prevented them including the gnat in their big-game hunting when the mood carried them in that direction. In several of the inter-departmental meetings, which were held to discuss co-ordinating the work of the unit across a whole range of Whitehall ministries, senior civil servants would regularly lay down their booby traps.

There was one particular meeting held in the Cabinet Office to which I presented a paper – couched, I had assumed, in the usual Whitehallese routine gibberish – proposing greater inter-departmental co-operation in support of the Counter-Inflation campaign. I argued my case at the meeting and pointed out some glaring omissions – for example, there was scarcely any ministerial drive to involve the nationalised industries in the campaign; nor was there any policy to co-ordinate public sector pricing. I suggested – it seemed so obvious to me – that there ought to be far more co-ordination if the government's counter-inflation policy was to succeed. Around the table sat top men from the Treasury and Departments of Trade, Industry, Prices, Employment and Energy. I could sense a certain rigidity as I spoke but took it to mean no more than routine Whitehall emotions on display. Moreover I knew I did have *some friends* among the gathering.

Came the responses – and they were almost entirely negative, derisive and destructive. In particular there was one top mandarin from the Treasury who seemed to have a clear message to me written across his passionless features: 'What have we here? Who is this journalist upstart that Wilson has imported into our midst, trying to tell us how to run our affairs? ... Co-ordination indeed, what poppycock: he'll be asking us for our support if we're not careful.' It needed no special intuition on my part to sense the brittleness, the hostility and the contempt coming from that quarter. The more sophisticated opponents simply turned to me and used the old technique of spraying inertia with a charm offensive. Their long training in fencing provided a wonderful script for doing nothing while demonstrating an absolute willingness to do all in their power to help.

'Well, yes, what a splendid idea,' they smiled with Sphinx-like subtlety, 'I think we should look at your proposals very carefully and consider the implications for the government and the industries concerned. It is a most interesting idea ...' Then there would be silence followed by ... silence.

I was never sure whether this calculated inertia, resistance by inaction,was an expression of *political* opposition to the government or, more likely, a personal grievance against the Prime Minister's style or, still closer to the truth, the long-polished characteristic of the civil service culture based on the assumption that almost all radical change (by the left or the right) must be treated with considerable suspicion if not outright disdain.

Margaret Thatcher faced something of this when she took office in 1979; Clem Attlee certainly encountered it in 1945, although it was easier to contest in the immediate postwar ethos; Wilson certainly faced the problem in 1964, and by 1975 it had become a defined art.

The Prime Minister was kept informed of my difficulties and sympathised. Several times he personally intervened to my benefit, though I felt it was absurd to call for his assistance every time I met with obstruction. But Wilson did something else to help my unit – he called me in to attend Cabinet committees where the counter-inflation policy and programme was involved. At that time this was a highly privileged gesture. Very few of the outsiders brought into the entourage were permitted to sit on Cabinet committees. So I found myself at the Cabinet table alongside Chancellor Healey, Employment Secretary Michael Foot, Environment Secretary Tony Crosland, Trade Secretary Peter Shore and Prices Minister Shirley Williams, with the Prime Minister in the chair.

Of course, I realised that Wilson was doing this principally to help strengthen my credentials within the Whitehall machine and, in particular, to help win positive support for my work among senior civil servants. That is how the system works. The message would travel (as Wilson knew only too well) around the circuit that Goodman was attending Cabinet Committee X or Y or Z; the Permanent Secretary in Department Gobbledygook would make a mental note – perhaps even write a brief minute to his Deputy Secretaries and a nod and wink would follow. Yes Minister would then come into operation ...

The truth is that the Treasury never willingly supported the voluntary system of restraint on which the Social Contract was based. They had never abandoned their original role of demanding statutory enforcement of wages policy with strict sanctions and penalties. Denis Healey went along with that at the outset but then retreated. His book (1989) omits many of the details about the fierce battles that took place inside and outside Cabinet during June and July 1975, though he does accept that he was committed to a statutory policy. He also admits (pp. 394–5) that Wilson warned him earlier that:

> he would support me on anything I wanted – except a statutory incomes policy. He was determined not to repeat the humiliating fiasco of Heath's attempt to use legal sanctions against the dockers in 1972.

Healey's account of what happened in those crucial weeks in the summer of 1975 is inexcusably one-sided. A far better version is told by Joe Haines (1977: 59–65). I have already explained how I was sitting in Joe's room in No. 10 during the five-hour Cabinet battle on Thursday 10 July 1975 when the climax was reached between the choice of a statutory or voluntary incomes policy. It was at that meeting that Michael Foot threatened to resign if Healey got his way over a statutory policy. And if that had transpired it would have spelled the end of the Social Contract – and, of course, the whole idea of establishing a Counter-Inflation Unit. Indeed, it might have precipitated Harold Wilson's resignation at an earlier stage. Healey never forgot – nor forgave – Wilson for blocking the Treasury on counter-inflation policy; nor for a number of other policy decisions, which he regarded as symptomatic of Wilson's weakness and lack of direction.

The Chancellor was never disposed to give my Counter-Inflation Unit much credibility – which, I suppose, is hardly surprising in the circumstances. I had several one-to-one sessions with him, and one occasion I tried to persuade him (at Wilson's suggestion, though Healey never knew this) to lead a team of Treasury and economic ministers on a tour of the shopfloor in various parts of the country in order to sell the government's counter-inflation policy. The case I put to Denis was quite simple: 'show your face on the shopfloor and meet the rank and file of the trade union movement; demonstrate at first hand your commitment to the Social Contract; speak to them candidly about the nature of inflation and how it could undermine all their own aspirations; open your heart – and then listen to their questions.'

My message to Denis was based on a conviction that touring a number of factories would enhance the government's reputation among its own supporters and even impress its critics. But Denis wouldn't have it. 'Too risky,' he replied. 'We would become exposed to attacks from the militants, the Trots and all that lot; and the press would pick it up. It would do the Government no good at all.' Healey's view was that such a tour would end in disaster for the government. He wouldn't touch it with a barge pole. I tried hard to persuade him that it was worth the gamble. I admitted, sure there was a risk but, then, the entire Social Contract was based on risk. He wouldn't be shifted.

Without the Chancellor's open and active support I knew it would be pointless trying to persuade other ministers to pick up the challenge. The idea collapsed. I reported back to Wilson, in private, of course. He shrugged, without being surprised. He was disappointed but not fazed. He told me that there was very little he could do because he could hardly 'instruct' his senior ministers to go out into the country against their wish. Yet he still tried to encourage me not to be disappointed by this failure of a mission to the Treasury, and made generous noises about the success of the campaign in other areas, and pointed me in directions where still further successes might be achieved. That was typical of Harold Wilson. He would always try to say something positive no matter how bleak the outlook, part of that Walter Mitty temperament.

At the time I did not appreciate the full extent of the deep personal hostility between Wilson and Healey. To be sure, I knew they didn't exactly like each other – but then, very few members of that Cabinet actually liked each other. What I had not fully recognised was the depth to which the Wilson–Healey hostility dominated their relationship.

In early February 1976 I tried again to revitalise the unit and its campaign. Marcia Williams (Lady Falkender) arranged for me to have a private one-to-one with the Prime Minister in his Lord North Street house one Saturday evening – the venue and time specifically chosen to avoid the presence of any civil servants and even any other member of the entourage. Marcia was on hand but didn't stay in the room while Wilson and I talked. A few weeks earlier I had written a paper for his eyes only about the whole future process of the unit. The paper took account of all the problems, obstacles and the kind of sabotage – yes, I put it as strongly as that – that we had encountered. He asked me a number of questions, including my assessment of ministers as well as civil servants; he asked me what I would suggest in terms of future strategy and what, in my opinion, were the options open to him. He said he would reflect on what we had discussed and certainly gave me the impression that he agreed with the general thrust of what I was arguing – which, basically, was for the kind of overall co-ordination (including the public sector industries) that I had tried to push at an earlier stage. I left Lord North Street that night feeling a bit more heartened. What I did not know was that I had had one of the last in-depth policy discussions with Harold Wilson before his resignation.

*   *   *

A very small group of people knew that Harold Wilson would resign his premiership on 16 March 1976. I was not one of them.

I felt dismayed by that since we had developed a close relationship. I believed, at the time, that Harold ought to have taken me into his confidence as he had done with other things. But I subsequently discovered that the majority of his Cabinet had, similarly, been kept completely in the dark. There were very few exceptions. Denis Healey had far greater cause for anger – he discovered the impending drama when he went into the Downing Street toilet immediately before the Cabinet meeting and stood in the stall alongside the Prime Minister. Wilson then told Healey in a kind of side-whisper. 'I was flabbergasted' the former Chancellor says. Michael Foot had no idea until he heard it from Wilson at Cabinet.

Callaghan was an exception: Wilson had indicated his intention to go five days before the announcement when he gave the Foreign Secretary a lift back to Downing Street on 11 March 1976. It was immediately following a debate on public expenditure in which Denis Healey came under severe attack from Labour backbenches – so severe that it forced Healey to pause in mid-speech, turn on his critics and roar above their clamour: 'And you can go and fuck yourselves.' That was not reported in *Hansard*, but it was a decisive factor in Wilson's mind when, carrying Callaghan back to Downing Street, the Prime Minister turned to his Foreign Secretary, tapped him on the knee and solemnly declared: 'The job's all yours, Jim. He's [Healey] had it now.' It was Callaghan who told me that story. Then again, according to Sir Kenneth Stowe, Wilson had already signposted his intentions to Callaghan as far back as the election for party leadership following Gaitskell's death.

After defeating Callaghan in that leadership election Wilson told Callaghan that in the event of him becoming Prime Minister after the next general election he, Wilson, did not intend to 'stay too long'. He then told Callaghan that he had no intention to 'overstay his welcome in the party'. Of course, such things have been said before by prime ministers in waiting – only to be quickly forgotten once the trappings of power and the aura of No. 10 fall across their shoulders. In fact it wasn't until that brief car ride between the House of Commons and Downing Street, that March day, that Callaghan seriously began to count his chickens. So when, much later, I was briefed by Ken Stowe about the range of circumstances, thinking, pressures *et al*. that were playing on Wilson's mind before he finally decided to go, I realised that my objections to having been kept so completely in the dark were misplaced *amour propre*.

When the moment came I was sitting in my room at the Old Admiralty preparing the next phase of the Counter-Inflation campaign. It was a call from Sir Kenneth Stowe's office in No. 10. A tremulous voice simply said: 'Harold's resigned.' Adding for measure: 'It's on the wires, now.' My secretary, Jill Thompson, normally unflappable, marvellously and effectively in control, rushed into my room shouting: 'Have you heard?' she screamed. 'The Prime Minister's resigned.' Everything stopped and fell into a chill of bewildered silence. Belief itself took a holiday. I looked across toward the back entrance to No. 10, bemusedly, to see if smoke was seeping out of the windows. But on that March morning in 1976 the outward scene was one of absurdly routine tranquillity. Only inside Downing Street, and every other corner of Whitehall, were there scenes of utter confusion.

So why did he go? From the moment I joined his entourage it seemed to me that Wilson was far from being a healthy man. Only some time later was I to learn the whole truth behind that accurate observation. The Prime Minister had suffered a heart spasm, which went completely unreported, during the first economic summit conference at Rambouillet, near Paris, as early as November 1975.

Part of the reason the story never leaked was because the Napoleonic castle at Rambouillet was turned into a fortress for the inaugural economic summit of world leaders under orders from the French President, Valery Giscard d'Estaing. The idea of staging annual economic summit conferences came originally from Giscard, and he was determined to endow the event and its launch with mystery as well as a touch of French pomp and grandeur. The media were kept well away even from the servants' quarters (Giscard plainly knew the techniques of press reporters and their skill at tackling the lesser lights). Unlike all subsequent economic summits, which became largely media events, Rambouillet was kept very much under wraps except for the official communiqués. So Wilson's heart spasm did not leak.

The Prime Minister was already unwell before leaving for the summit conference, and decided to take his personal doctor, Joe Stone (the late Lord Stone), with him. Before leaving Downing Street Stone warned Ken Stowe not to load the Prime Minister with too much work. In fact Wilson had been talking with Joe Stone for some time about his workload being excessively burdensome (an uncharacteristic confession from the workaholic Wilson). Stone recognised at once that such an admission from his old friend was very strange, and disturbing. Stone underlined this point to Ken Stowe as they left London for Rambouillet. And in the 'plane to Paris Stowe gently suggested to the Prime Minister that he might ease up on some of the workload flowing out of the red boxes. Wilson nodded without comment.

Ken Stowe recalls that the Prime Minister did not seem to be at ease. He knew Wilson so well and he could sense an inner strain. And in my subsequent conversations with Sir Kenneth, who had a close and warm relationship with Harold Wilson throughout his tenure, the former Downing Street secretary was never in any doubt that the signs of strain, tension and tiredness were already well advanced. That was immediately before the heart spasm. In fact Wilson took Stowe into his confidence about his retirement plans shortly before the Rambouillet summit. This is what Sir Kenneth has since told me:

> He called me into his room [at No. 10] in November 1975 and disclosed his intentions. But I do not believe it was really part of any long-term plan he had. To this day I don't know how many others he had taken into his confidence: not many, I imagine.

To the best of my knowledge there were only about half a dozen people who knew – or who later claimed they knew; they included the late Arnold (Lord) Goodman, Marcia Williams (Lady Falkender),

Joe Haines, Bernard Donoughue (Lord Donoughue), the late Harold (Lord) Lever and, of course, Mary Wilson.

So where lies the truth behind the enigma, as it is still regarded, of Harold Wilson's resgination?

The theories and the speculation still surrounding his departure are likely to continue endlessly. Nothing that has already been written will satisfy an insatiable curiosity, especially among those who are convinced that, lurking somewhere in the undergrowth, there is a Le Carré scenario. Is there, then, a well-buried scandal; was it connected with his somewhat odd and dubious bunch of friends and contacts, some of whom were given honours in the famous 'Lavender List'; was there a spy riddle in the woodwork; a sex-shocker; maybe a bit of everything?

I believe the real explanation is altogether more prosaic. Wilson had simply had enough. He quit because he was a sick and tired man who had come to recognise that he was no longer able to contribute significantly in trying to resolve intractable problems. In short, he had done as much as he felt he could; he had been round the circuit of the same problems, usually recurring in similar form even if disguised as 'new problems'. He was also surrounded by intrigue – not that this is in any sense unusual at the centre of power – and had grown weary of trying to placate, or even excite, some of the warring factions around him. He was often in despair at their antics. One of the extraordinary aspects of the Downing Street scene when I first stepped into the pit of intrigue was that it had all the trappings of a medieval court. One could almost sniff the whisperings of treason behind the pillars of state. Seasoned advisers smiled when I mentioned my impressions. Their reply was typical of the ambience: ''Twas ever thus,' they nodded wisely and added, presciently, 'and always will be.'

But what I remain convinced about is that Wilson was the focus of a security sub-plot, which had as its Alice-in-Wonderland aim the destabilisation of the Wilson Government. I have already referred to the crazed and highly charged atmosphere of 1974. Something of this hung over into the Wilson period, and I believe that Harold Wilson did become the victim of a naive, certainly deranged, unofficial conspiracy in which some members of the Security and Intelligence services (not confined to MI5 or MI6) were involved. I can only reflect my own gut instincts on this issue along with some confidential information from people I can trust and who were certainly in positions that would enable them to have had access to secret files.

Some of this has been admitted by Peter Wright (1987: 267). Wright has disclosed that a range of people working closely with the Prime Minister in Downing Street were burgled in the strangest of circumstances. That is true: I was among them. My home was burgled at the same time as about a dozen other members of Wilson's entourage. The items taken were merely token – though my files were disturbed and there were other highly unusual aspects to my burglary, which, as I assumed, were meant to be 'messages' that I had been listed. Valuables, jewellery, cash, electronic equipment (generally a first target in 'real' burglaries) were all left untouched.

I mentioned the burglary to Marcia Williams the next day, to which she responded: 'So why should you expect any different treatment from the rest of us here?' It is easy to dismiss the oft-claimed paranoia of Lady Falkender, because she has consistently claimed to friends that 'They' were out to destroy Wilson ... whoever 'They' might have been. Lady Falkender has several times delved into great detail when insisting, to me, that the evidence in support of her allegations is 'overwhelming'.

Be that as it may, I find it less easy to dismiss other information that I have been given by senior civil servants who worked closely with the Prime Minister at that time. I accept that my refusal to disclose names must invite suspicion of the veracity of what follows. That cannot be helped. One very high-level source has repeatedly assured me that there 'is a lot in the Peter Wright story'.

It is also known that Wilson called in the head of MI5 at the time, Sir Michael Hanley – this was in 1974 after the second election – and expressed his anxieties to Hanley. He was given absolute assurance from the head of the home security service that there was no truth in any of the allegations, 'so far as he knew'. There was no plot to destabilise the government, Sir Michael reassured the Prime Minister. There is no reason to doubt Sir Michael's word that he 'knew nothing' about any of this. But another senior civil servant has told me the following extraordinary story:

Sometime during 1974 the Prime Minister went into one of the numerous ante-rooms inside No. 10 to talk with a couple of his senior advisers. Their room overlooked the Downing Street garden, which opened onto the back of Horse Guards. The PM sat down facing the window, with a full view of the garden wall which fringes Horse Guards. Wilson pointed to the wall and said, quietly and without any degree of hyperbole or drama: 'They could do it, you know. They'd need only a few commandoes to scale that wall and they could surround the place quite rapidly. It would be quite easy. They could do it.' The two advisers, both senior civil servants, were stunned into silence. They stared at the Prime Minister who just smiled, seemed quite calm as he shuffled out of the room leaving two Mandarins shaken into astonished silence.

It is a story one can believe or disbelieve according to inclination or even taste. But my informant is satisfied that when Harold Wilson made those extraordinary (perhaps the word 'sensational' would, for once, be appropriate) observations he was quite sober, of sane mind and not, as far as my informant could assess, under any unusual pressure in government. I can only report what I have been told in good faith as well as concealing his source.

Of course, all these charges have long been dismissed as the absurd melodramatic wanderings of a strange period in British political affairs. Certainly when Jim Callaghan took over from Wilson he steadfastly refused to hold any inquiry into any of these allegations. So the curtain fell across the whole saga.

It may well be the case that this whole business of intrigue, mystery, spy-drama stuff, hidden pressures, the whisperings behind the pillars etc. etc. – all perhaps did accumulate into one of the elemental factors that helped Harold Wilson make up his mind in March 1976. Perhaps. But even so it would have been only one factor among so many others. I remain quite certain that it was far more to do with his general state of health. He went, as I have said, because he was exhausted. Not yet the extinct volcano of Disraelian proportions, though perhaps not far removed at that juncture. Mary Wilson had long been pressing him to fix a definite retirement date, and he promised her he would do so. He was, after all, an ageing sixty with that birthday approaching on 11 March 1976. Could he have gone on? There are some who believe he could and should.

One notable voice who believed – and still does – that Harold Wilson should, and could, have continued is Lionel Murray (Lord Murray of Epping) who was general secretary of the TUC at the time. Len Murray has told me:

> I find it difficult to believe that he went just because he was tired. I didn't get that impression in my dealings with him at the time.

Objectively I couldn't see the reason why he should have been tired of being Prime Minister. Nor do I see why he should have been so despondent. Many of us thought we were beginning to see some light at the end of the tunnel in 1976. Inflation was coming down and we were coming to terms with pay policy. Of course, it is true that he had probably promised Mary that he would go at that time ...

Lord Murray's view is important because he was seeing the Prime Minister virtually daily at that time. The TUC were scarcely out of Downing Street. Even so there were pressures on Wilson of which even the TUC were unaware. Wilson's problems, the pressures on his time and energy, the conflicts and tensions were not confined to the Cabinet, or the Whitehall scene in general, but also within the Labour Party where the political battle had been raging for so long. Those years, stretching back to 1966, through the Heath reign, the miners' strikes, the whole of the incomes policy conflicts, plus Europe – all of these issues would place an almost intolerable burden on any political leader, even a healthy one.

Wilson's fight to keep Britain in Europe has never received the attention its importance merits. It was touch and go whether the anti-European group inside the Labour Party would succeed in undermining the Heath Government's decision to enter the European Economic Community. There was powerful opposition to remaining in the EEC from Cabinet Ministers like Peter Shore and Tony Benn, who was then campaigning for withdrawal. They had considerable backing from backbench Labour MPs and the trade unions. Wilson produced a master stroke in turning the tables on Tony Benn's proposal for a referendum – by accepting the Benn proposal for a referendum. Of course, Benn assumed a referendum would produce a vote to withdraw from the EEC. Wilson gambled on the reverse and won a remarkable victory in June 1975 – in the middle of his economic crisis – with a 2 to 1 vote in favour of staying in Europe. It is not fully appreciated that at the time Harold Wilson faced just as much dissension within the Labour Party as did John Major on the same issues within the Conservative Party some twenty years later.

Those who have made a speciality, even an industry, in detracting from Wilson's qualities have yet to answer the question: so who could have done better? Without a Gaitskell and a Nye Bevan, what credible name has been put forward? Denis Healey, Roy Jenkins? Neither would have been able to hold together the Labour Party as Jim Callaghan just about managed to do when he followed Wilson. In any event the mood of the country was already set in a trend toward the Thatcherism that was to follow and from which the Blair Government would eventually benefit.

Nor is it accurate to claim that Wilson had no vision. He did have vision – but lacked the imagination to turn it into an exciting political agenda. He did have profound radical instincts yet, sadly, lacked the ideological courage to match them. He did shirk hard decisions or, to put it differently, when finally he made up his mind to take tough decisions he too often allowed himself to be shifted sideways by expediency. None of these failings, weaknesses or whatever they may be, are unusual flaws in prime ministers of all colours. Above all Harold Wilson was, in my opinion, an outstanding leader of the Labour Party, with an immensely astute feel for what the British voter would stand for. He knew the Labour Party like an old glove. If there were flaws and question marks about Wilson, as there are, then the same can be said of the Labour Party itself, new, old or whatever prefix is adapted. And perhaps the same can also be said about the electorate.

14　Jim Callaghan Takes Over: 'Too Late at 64'?

On Monday 5 April 1976 Leonard James Callaghan kissed hands with the Queen and became Prime Minister of the United Kingdom. He was the first premier in the twentieth century to have held all four great offices of state – Chancellor, Home Secretary, Foreign Secretary and then Prime Minister. Quite an achievement for a boy who genuinely came from a working-class home and had not been to university – an unusual qualification for a Labour Prime Minister. Ramsay MacDonald was his only predecessor with such a clear-cut CV. Callaghan had more or less given up hope that he would ever reach the top of the greasy pole, though his ambition for the job was always pretty relentless. And like so much in political life – well, come to that, all life – it was largely down to time and chance, a phrase, incidentally, chosen by Callaghan for the title of his autobiography.

The election for Harold Wilson's successor took nearly three weeks during which the government machine was almost stagnant. It was a most unusual, if not unique period for British political life since no Prime Minister had resigned in mid-stream in quite the same circumstances. The Bonar Law resignation in May 1923, making way for Baldwin, was a quite different situation. Moreover, Callaghan was taking over from a younger man. The election required three separate ballots. In the first round Michael Foot topped the poll with 90 votes, Callaghan came next with 84, then Roy Jenkins with 56, Tony Benn 37, Denis Healey 30 and finally Tony Crosland with a mere 17. Jenkins, Benn and Crosland dropped out for the second ballot. Healey refused to drop from the list – only to collect a mere eight additional votes in the second count. He then, reluctantly, retired hurt to allow Callaghan and Foot to contest the final ballot, which Callaghan won by 176 to 137.

That result was significant for two reasons: first it produced a much higher vote for Foot than anyone had expected; secondly, there were already the signs of a split in the Labour Party that eventually led to the breakaway Social Democrat group in the 1980s. Those who were close to Roy Jenkins had effectively given up hope of influencing the course of events under Callaghan or Foot. They were biding their time, waiting for the ultimate crack in Labour's credible leadership, which they were certain would eventually emerge. Some who voted for Foot did so, quite clearly, because they believed the fissure would open more rapidly under his leadership than under Callaghan – precisely the same cynical approach that helped to win Michael Foot the Labour Party leadership over Healey in November 1980 and which preceded the launch of the SDP by the 'Gang of Four'.

Jim Callaghan was a different challenge for the cynics. He was tough and quite ruthless in wielding the axe, which he did immediately by sacking Barbara Castle from the Cabinet – Callaghan's vendetta against Barbara Castle had a long history, going back to the days of the Attlee Government and the mutual distaste, not to say hatred, had increased at almost every step.

The other major victim was Roy Jenkins himself, the man who had been convinced at one point that he was certain to succeed to No. 10 in any crisis of the Wilson premiership. Callaghan kept Jenkins at the Home Office to which Wilson had returned him. Jenkins was burning with frustration, and in September of 1976 he resigned from the government to take up the post as President of the European Commission in Brussels, never to return to the Labour Party. In fact Jenkins signalled his intention to quit the government within a few weeks of Callaghan moving in to No. 10. He has since been quite open and frank about his intentions and motive at the time. He confesses that he should have been 'more and not less disloyal in 1975' and tried harder to bring down the Wilson Government in favour of a kind of national coalition government that would have included leading Conservatives such as Ted Heath and Willie Whitelaw:

> A coalition of the Right of the Labour Party, Liberals and the Left of the Conservative Party might have done it [saved the country from 'gross inflation and subservience to the unions'] with much greater precision than the bombastic Manichaean Thatcherite revolution ... (1991: 425–6)

Indeed Roy Jenkins was well advanced in his efforts to achieve that coalition during the final days of the Wilson Cabinet – something Harold Wilson suspected without ever having the full details.

This was the climate in which James Callaghan began his three-year spell as Prime Minister, leading a government that was largely dependent for survival on support from David Steel's Liberal Party.

In one respect Callaghan was fortunate. The departure of Jenkins might well have sparked off a political crisis of vast proportions had Jenkins possessed the steely nerve to push his convictions to the limit. But he did not. He confesses as much in his autobiography. He simply didn't have the stomach for a full-scale power-battle within the Labour Party – either under Wilson or Callaghan's leadership. It was the crucial flaw in Jenkins's make-up and almost certainly the cause of his failure to become prime minister – identified much earlier by his then close friends Tony Crosland and Roy Hattersley (Lord Hattersley). Both of them had recognised the fundamental shortcoming in Jenkins's temperament and character, which led them to distance themselves from him.

Jenkins was always an intellectual dilettante: he never much liked the Labour Party despite effectively being born into it by way of his South Wales mining family roots. He recoiled from the brutish nastiness of political life where the sight of blood on the stone has to be borne with a philosophical shrug. Yet he was *not* an intellectual coward, as he demonstrated to his eternal credit and with much self-inflicted pain when he clashed so violently with his old mentor Hugh Gaitskell over whether Labour should support entry into the Common Market in the early 1960s. That was one of the most painful exercises in Jenkins's political life – but he didn't shirk from attacking his hero, Hugh Gaitskell. What he did not relish was the sniff of political cordite within the trenches of the Westminster jungle.

His background was filled with an ambivalence that cultivated a dichotomy between theory and practice. Jenkins was the child of a South Wales mining village, son of a former miner who became a Labour MP and eventually Clement Attlee's lieutenant as PPS to the Labour Prime Minister. The young Roy rose out of the local grammar school to enter Balliol College, Oxford, where he was a contemporary of Tony Crosland. When he eventually entered Parliament in 1948 as MP for Central Southwark – before moving on in 1950 to Birmingham Stechford – the young Jenkins was almost pulled to the left. In fact he wrote a memorably brilliant pamphlet for the Bevanite weekly paper *Tribune* on equality, then his favourite subject. That period faded quickly, notably with the dawn of the Gaitskell leadership when Jenkins's political hero succeeded Attlee. Gaitskell was the star in the firmament on whose glow Jenkins's future was seen to be linked. From that point it became an almost commonly accepted nostrum among political journalists that Jenkins would one day succeed Gaitskell as leader of the Labour Party should anything unexpected happen to the leader. And when that 'something unexpected' did happen Jenkins's frustration never ceased to show.

In later years those who had been unashamed admirers of Roy Jenkins – though not necessarily close to him personally – coined the aphorism: 'here was a man whose talent was squandered by his ego'. Possibly: I am less convinced.

The difference between Roy Jenkins and James Callaghan could scarcely have been greater – despite the fact that both of them came, originally, from deep working-class roots. In chemistry, style, intuition, and of course education, they were poles apart. From the start of their adult life the two men could well have belonged to different political parties. Callaghan's 'universities' did not contain the word Oxford; his apprenticeship, after leaving school at 16, was the trade union movement, a somewhat different avenue of life from that offered by the Junior Common Room at Balliol.

Callaghan, who joined the Inland Revenue as a teenager, soon became an active trade unionist and eventually the youngest full-time official of his union, the Inland Revenue Staff Federation. That was his job when the Second World War broke out and Callaghan joined the Navy. He came from a naval working-class family in Portsmouth. His father, a chief petty officer in the First World War, died when Jim was a boy of 9. His mother struggled to bring up a small family, an elder sister and Leonard James. They were intensely patriotic, non-comformist, and suspicious of 'outsiders'. The young Leonard did well at school, might easily have gone on to university in other circumstances – but the family were far too poor to contemplate such luxuries, and there is no doubt that this sense of deprivation had a lasting impact on Callaghan's later life and especially his resentment toward university-trained intellects by whom he was surrounded in the Wilson Cabinet of 1964 and later.

There is a fascinating story about how the young Callaghan became drawn strongly to socialist ideas – even intellectual facility – by the great Professor Harold Laski. As a young trade union official he was often in attendance at Civil Service Arbitration Tribunal hearings where Laski was equally frequently the nominee of the trade union side. So impressed was Laski by the potential of the young Callaghan that the Professor invited Leonard James to take an external degree at the London School of Economics, which Laski himself was prepared to supervise. Callaghan, grateful and flattered, said he simply didn't have the time to tackle such a challenge. But Laski didn't relax his efforts. He arranged for Callaghan to have a reader's ticket for the LSE library – and mentioned his name to Labour Party HQ as a future potential Parliamentary candidate. It was typical of Harold Laski – as I know from my own experience of that remarkable man. It was also the foundation stone on which Callaghan came to establish his political focus. From that point on he was an avid reader of Laski's books.

All of this helps to explain some of the paradox of Callaghan's later political tendencies, which, though they appeared to be well to the right, did in fact contain strands of radical left-wing views. It also helps to explain why so many of his old critics on the left of the Labour Party (excluding, of course, Barbara Castle) regarded Callaghan as a very good Prime Minister and were far more impressed by his work than with Harold Wilson whom many of them had originally supported. Almost everyone who served in Callaghan's Cabinets speaks warmly of his qualities as Prime Minister – including even Tony Benn. I certainly found Callaghan an extremely agreeable boss to work for in the short spell I had with him after Wilson's resignation. Different from Wilson, certainly; not as personally caring and responsive. But immensely perceptive, shrewdly reading the messages between the lines, and listening to advice. He wanted me to stay and continue to work with him. But, as I will explain, I felt I had had my ration of the Whitehall Whale.

*   *   *

Coming so late and unexpectedly to the highest office in the land James Callaghan had some advantages. One of his main advantages, to be frank, was that he was *not* Harold Wilson. In the eyes of the press, much of the Establishment, the mandarins of the City and in industry, and indeed much of public opinion Harold Wilson had become a discredited figure. Leave aside what justification there may have been for this overarching view, the unpleasant truth remains that Wilson had come to be regarded, especially by most of the Tory press, as devious, untrustworthy, questionable. I have already made it plain that I regard this assessment as largely unwarranted, a misjudgement and wrong. But it would be absurd to deny its existence.

Callaghan therefore took over with a good deal of comparative goodwill. His avuncular style, 'Uncle Jim' and all that, helped. He was an extremely effective speaker, both in the House of Commons and at Labour conferences, where his command of an audience was far more pronounced than that of a Jenkins, a Healey or even a Wilson. Callaghan, like Wilson, understood the idiosyncrasies of the Labour movement and could handle its irrationalities far better than a Jenkins or a Healey.

When he took over he had just passed his 64th birthday – exactly four years older than Wilson – but there was little outward sign of the ageing process. He was still quick to identify friends and foes; he possessed a swift reactive instinct in tackling difficult decisions. He could be moody, ill-tempered, gloomy and even pessimistic but was adept at being able to mask it all behind a *savoir-faire* earnestness. Healey – a particularly strong authority on the subject – regarded Callaghan as 'the best of Britain's post-war Prime Ministers after Attlee' (1989: 447–8). No doubt an exaggeration, but Healey subscribes to the view that Callaghan was a changed man from the Jim Callaghan he had known and worked with in earlier years.

There is a lot of truth in this, as I have reason to recall. After the 1970 General Election with Heath in No. 10 Callaghan actually considered leaving politics. He had a major operation (for prostate) and took a long time to recover. His confidence was sapped, as was his physical strength and energy. Around the time of his convalescence we met for a long talk, and he chose the moment to confess his dismay with the political scene in general. He spoke of its relentless grind, the never-ending pursuit of power and ambition common to all politicians hovering around the middle and upper reaches of the greasy pole. His conversation went like this:

'What is it all for?' He sat slumped in an armchair in the lounge of a London hotel where we met. 'Is it really worth all the travail, the anguish, the sheer nastiness?'

He answered his own questions: 'I'm beginning to think it isn't.'

Of course, these were rhetorical questions in a dialogue he, clearly, was having with himself. I happened to be present as he voiced them aloud. It might have been anyone else, given his mood of gloomy introspection.

It is a common experience of journalists to find themselves the recipients of this kind of deep inner reflective confidentiality from political figures. Nor is the experience confined to political leaders: all men of power or potential power (and possibly women too, though I am less sure of this) have this tendency to express their deeper self-doubts with certain selected people who are outside their immediate emotional turmoil. Journalists can provide a classic audience for this mood, which helps to explain why many journalists find themselves the confidants of people of power. Journalism trades in the language of power, the language of ambition, drama and the idiom of inner as well as outer conflict.

It is also true that the mood inside the Labour Party leadership after Ted Heath's unexpected victory in 1970 added substance to Callaghan's self-questioning. They were the days when the first rumblings of a possible fundamental split in the Labour Party were becoming audible. Much of that early rumbling came from Tony Benn, who began his own soul-searching operation by demanding to know 'what has gone wrong with Labour?' *Mea culpa* took centre-stage for a while, especially with Benn who seemed to undergo a mid-life change and, in a transformation that later brought havoc to the Labour Party, confessed that he felt the whole agenda of the previous Labour Government in which he served had been a retreat from the sacred gospels of socialism.

So when Jim Callaghan talked with some despair about the future there was some degree of objective as well as subjective alarm in his feelings. Years later, when I reminded Callaghan of our 1970 conversation, he confessed that he believed he had come to the premiership too late in life. This later conversation came in June 1989, when he was able to view the scene with some detachment. He then told me, in a soft and low sad tone, that it had been 'too late at the age of 64'. But, I reminded him, Churchill had been two years older than Callaghan when he took over a nation in crisis in May 1940.

'That was different,' Callaghan retorted. 'For me it would have been different if I had come to the job in my fifties. But I was 64 when I became Prime Minister. A lot of the steam had gone out of me. It was too late ...'

In this respect Callaghan's resentment of Harold Wilson remained deep. He was openly bitter that Wilson had not retired from the scene much earlier. He actually came to believe that Wilson should have gone after he lost the 1970 election to Heath in order to leave space for Callaghan to take over. Nor did Callaghan think that Jenkins would have been successful as a challenger. He shared the view of Jenkins I have already described – a man without the killer instinct whose weaknesses were all too palpable.

Yet, bitter though he was about Harold Wilson, Callaghan reluctantly admitted to his admiration. 'I must admit it,' he told me that day, 'Harold was very clever. Very clever.' The grudging confession came haltingly but was plainly meant. 'He was a remarkably bright person ...' The words fell from Jim Callaghan's lips like lumps of stone.

The change in the persona of Jim Callaghan once he became Prime Minister, which so many of his Cabinet colleagues detected, did not rob him of the old Adam. He did not lose his resentment of colleagues whom he had disliked or distrusted for most of his Parliamentary life. I have a suspicion that the metamorphosis was less pronounced than many of his Cabinet colleagues believed. Nevertheless Callaghan commanded a great deal of respect among his government colleagues during his three years at the helm. Michael Foot, an old political foe from the left, established a remarkably close and even warm relationship with the Prime Minister – and it was mutual. Healey, who probably understood Callaghan better than most of the Cabinet, had a number of similar characteristics – he could be ruthless, behave like a bully and was intolerant of criticism.

Even Tony Benn found Callaghan a considerable relief after his years of catastrophic relationship with Harold Wilson. Benn's diaries (1989: 557) reveal how he and the new Prime Minister tried to establish a new and healthier relationship, which worked for a time. Then it turned sour again and Callaghan considered sacking Benn from the government. Yet Benn was able to create a more positive relationship with his Prime Minister than was ever possible with Wilson. Benn may well have misread Callaghan's responsiveness but there may also have been truth in his reference (Benn diaries 1973–76) to Callaghan referring to Tony Benn on one occasion as: 'One of the greatest leaders this country has ever had – provided he behaves sensibly.' Such compliments about Tony Benn were rare at that level of government.

I sat through those interregnum days of the changeover from Wilson to Callaghan with a feeling of astonishment at what I perceived to be going on around me. It was often impossible to find a rational explanation. I discovered, to my consolation, that numerous senior civil servants were finding it equally difficult. Again I resorted to the wise counsels of Sir Kenneth Stowe. He took the view that it had been an act of exceptional courage for Wilson to resign when, and how, he did: handing over to his successor without a bloody internal revolt inside the Labour Party. Stowe again referred back to the appalling tensions surrounding Wilson in the months leading up to his departure.

He also compared Wilson's courage with previous examples where prime ministers had overstayed their political credibility simply to stop an old enemy within the party hierarchy – Macmillan stopping

Rab Butler, Churchill remaining in his chair until Anthony Eden was almost too ill to take over. Thatcher, of course, was forced out in the end by Michael Heseltine's manoeuvrings in what produced a near-Shakespearean drama for John Major to reap the benefit. But, as Stowe always insisted to me, the Wilson handover to an *older* man was comparatively unique and a demonstration of a civilised and democratic process.

*   *   *

I was called in to see the new Prime Minister a couple of days after his succession, and he immediately invited me to remain with him and continue my work at the Counter-Inflation Unit. Ken Stowe remained with him as his private secretary, but Joe Haines had gone. Tom McCaffrey (Sir Tom) took over from Joe as the Prime Minister's press secretary, having been with Callaghan in a similar role at the Foreign Office (Joe Haines had been Wilson's press secretary from January 1969 to April 1976). Ken Stowe and Tom were with Callaghan when we met to discuss the future of my unit. The Prime Minister said he had a high regard for the unit's contribution to the government's programme; he valued its work and would like to see me develop the operation beyond its present frontiers. This sounded very encouraging to me, especially after my earlier problems.

He then asked me if I wished to remain as head of the unit beyond the 12-month secondment agreed with the *Mirror*, to which I frankly told him that I was still undecided. I would quite like to continue to run the unit if it could obtain more muscle and authority, which, I told him, I now believed was essential not only to do its job but to help overcome the kind of opposition I had encountered. I carefully and discreetly told him about some of the difficulties I had experienced and how, despite Harold Wilson's best attempts, the unit's work had been impaired. He did not appear surprised to hear my story. He recognised the hurdles. I then told Callaghan that my newspaper were pressing me to return, and this was strongly tempting given the frustrations of my job at the unit. Jim Callaghan again urged me to stay – but told me to take my time to reflect on the options.

In May 1976 I told the Prime Minister that I had decided to the return to the *Daily Mirror* when my 12-month stint with the unit was completed at the end of July. He said with what I took to be genuine regret that he would be very sorry to lose me – and then asked me to recommend a successor. Was there, he asked, anyone in Whitehall I would suggest? Perhaps someone I knew and admired in the Government Information Service? I told him that in my opinion there were only two names I could offer him from within the Whitehall compound – Keith McDowall, who was then head of press and information at the Department of Employment, and Bernard Ingham, who was then at the Department of Energy working with Tony Benn.

Callaghan said he would prefer an 'outside name'. Was there anyone I could suggest from my friends in the media world? What about Peter Jay as a possible successor? I was shocked at Callaghan's suggestion, and told him so. So, too, was Tom McCaffrey. Jay was the Prime Minister's son-in-law, married to his daughter Margaret. Jay was then working for London Weekend Television and earning a high salary. I put it to the Prime Minister that even if the idea had been politically acceptable – which neither Tom McCaffrey nor myself believed it to be – it would be unlikely that Peter Jay would accept the job, not least because it would involve a substantial salary cut. Jim Callaghan was not quickly impressed with either argument, but finally accepted our view. All this process was, of course, to be repeated a short while later when Callaghan appointed Jay to the Ambassadorship in Washington on the suggestion of his then Foreign Secretary, David Owen, which once again Tom McCaffrey opposed.

The Prime Minister then made another startling proposal: 'What about Hugh Cudlipp succeeding you?' I was amazed. Lord Cudlipp had retired from the Mirror Group before handing over to Sydney (Lord) Jacobson, who was still working with me. Meanwhile Hugh had moved on to take up a high-profile role in television with Lew Grade (the late Lord Grade). My reaction to Callaghan's proposal – after recovering from the shock suggestion – was to say: 'A brilliant idea, Prime Minister, but do you really think Hugh could be tempted?'

I pointed out that the kind of detailed work involved in running the unit was not the kind of thing Hugh would enjoy. Callaghan dismissed my objection (of course, I am now convinced that he had already sounded out Hugh). He claimed that Cudlipp would be delighted to take on the role as a figurehead. He could then take a more public profile than I had been allowed to project, and this would be the attraction to Hugh. So it was done. In the final weeks of June and into July 1976 I had the extraordinary experience of handing over my job to my old boss, Hugh Cudlipp. With Sydney Jacobson staying on briefly to help his old chum over a few Whitehall hurdles, the paradox was total.

Hugh treated the whole business with characteristic disdain. He could see the fun as well as the irony. Detailed work could be left to Charlie Birdsall and others while Hugh could take on the stage-performance bit and keep in touch with 'Jolly Jim', as he liked to describe the Prime Minister. In fact the unit lasted only a brief time after that. A few months after my departure it was closed down, with the government claiming, somewhat emptily, that its task had been completed. No one believed that. But, as I had anticipated, Hugh found the role frustrating, and he told Callaghan that he saw no point in him continuing to play the Whitehall Clown. So it was all closed down – another interesting experiment had withered on the vine under Whitehall's insecticide.

When I packed my bags to return to Holborn Circus in August 1976 Jim Callaghan was generous with his compliments and personal bouquets. He offered me gongs, which I turned down. He was disappointed but understood my argument, which was that I did not think it right for working journalists, especially those still at the trade, to accept honours from any government. The Mirror Group had already received numerous honours, though it should be emphasised that these went to journalists who were about to retire or, as in the case of Bill Connor (Cassandra) were dying.

Honours and recognition from one's journalistic peers are one thing, taking them from a government, even from a government with whom one is in sympathy, seems to me to diminish the true function of journalism and the credibility of the journalist. Mrs Thatcher dished them out like confetti to her journalist supporters and admirers. It may have secured their loyalty – though this was there in any event – but it reduced their credibility at the same time as diluting her much-proclaimed purity of purpose. For my part when, in 1998, I did weaken by accepting the invitation to take a CBE, I had long retired from active journalism. Even so I was deeply uneasy and unsure about accepting the invitation from the Blair Government, and I remain dubious as to whether I ought to have given the nod. As far as I am concerned the whole business of an unreformed honours system remains absurd.

There was another personal problem that I had to face when I moved into Whitehall from the *Daily Mirror*. In March 1974, a few weeks after he returned to Downing Street, Harold Wilson appointed me a member of a new Royal Commission on the Press. Its chairman was the late Morris Finer QC, an outstanding lawyer. But the commission was scarcely off the ground when Morris tragically died after a sudden illness. His place was taken by Professor Oliver Ross MacGregor (the late Lord MacGregor of Durris), a sociologist who was already a member of the commission. We began work toward the end of 1974. Six months into the commission's work, which was entirely enthralling for me, I found myself seconded into the Whitehall Whale.

Immediately I was confronted with a tricky dilemma. Several MPs raised the issue in the Commons about my so-called 'dual role'. How, they demanded to know, could the government justify appointing me to head the Counter-Inflation Unit while remaining a member of the Royal Commission on the Press? One of the interlocutors was the late Tom Driberg MP, journalist, left-winger and fastidious forager after such morsels of high principle. Of course, he and the others were perfectly correct to challenge me – or rather the government – on this issue. It was, to be sure, a delicate balance, and I myself spent a lot of time wrangling over whether it was proper to continue to do both jobs. I put it to Harold Wilson and Sir Kenneth Stowe, and sought their advice. Both of them, separately, told me they were quite certain that it was proper and legitimate for me to continue to do both. They insisted that there was absolutely no conflict of interest, or principle, since despite my government connection I remained, fundamentally, an independent journalist, still with the *Daily Mirror* and merely on secondment to the government. So I agreed to stick with both.

Whether my work with the Royal Commission was worth the hassle I am less sure. When it reported in the summer of 1977 the final document included a Minority Report written by the late David Basnett (Lord Basnett) and myself. We both agreed that the majority report, much of which was acceptable to both of us, failed effectively to address some of the main problems facing the press – especially the increasing commercial pressures already evident throughout the media; the concentration of ownership of the press, television and commercial radio; and the question of quality and standards of journalism so profoundly affected by the circulation warfare that was daily becoming more pronounced. Our Minority Report predicted that these pressures would become larger issues in the years ahead and ultimately threaten to undermine a healthy development of a more diverse and democratic press.

Three other members of the commission agreed with Basnett and myself, and came close to signing the Minority Report, including the late Lord Hunt (John Hunt of Everest fame). In the end they bowed to MacGregor's persuasion that he wanted as much unanimity as possible. David Basnett and myself would have preferred not to have a Minority Report. We knew full well that Minority Reports simply gather dust. I myself appealed to MacGregor to put more teeth into his final version so that we could avoid a split. But he wouldn't budge. In my view that left the final report weakened and ultimately ineffectual. My hunch is that we would have had a more critical, sharper, more visionary report had Morris Finer survived.

As it was the MacGregor Report changed nothing and ended with a whimper. But working with a Royal Commission was a marvellous education in the processes of wheels grinding slowly, even if ineffectively. We were all offered Cabinet-style red boxes with our initials engraved in gilt. A regal gesture to conceal the truth – that most, if not all, Royal Commissions are confidence tricks. Harold Wilson, who in his time appointed quite a few of them, once described to a Trades Union Congress (in 1964) the futility of Royal Commissions. 'Royal Commissions,' he observed, 'are appointed to spend years taking minutes.' It was a perfect description, as I discovered during my service to the Royal Commission on the Press.

Nor is this to deride the staff work involved in such an undertaking. The members of that commission staff team were first-class people, and much of their research was of outstanding quality in an academic sense. They, along with the members, had to read and try to absorb immense amounts of material pushed before us; we sat through countless sessions of oral evidence; we had deep and profound debates among ourselves about the functions, limits and future horizons of a democratic press, and whether the control of newspapers by the Northcliffes, Rothermeres, Beaverbrooks and Murdochs of this world could ever fully be squared with a diverse, free and democratic media. Marvellous intellectual exercise in chasing rainbows. It all went nowhere. Professor MacGregor finished up as a life peer and others went on to join the queue of the great and the good. Alas the report, the third Royal Commission on the Press since the war, ended up at the back of some Whitehall filing cabinet, no doubt waiting for the eternal shredder.

*   *   *

My other reflection on that period of working within what George Orwell almost certainly meant when he wrote about The Whale, is on the dilemma of being a poacher turned gamekeeper, even if temporarily, and the effect this has on the psyche of the journalist. A few had done it before in varying capacities and many more have travelled the road since my spell. During the Thatcher reign the traffic was extensive, albeit highly selective and far greater than under any previous Prime Minister – that is until Tony Blair's Government took the traffic to new heights. There are good and bad, positive and negative aspects to it, of course. There I was, after spending years trying to extract secrets from politicians, civil servants, industrialists, financiers, union leaders *et al.*, suddenly finding that I too had secrets to protect from the press. That I too was in the midst of some Wagnerian Ring of intrigue, power-play, love–hate, calculating deception and having somehow to handle the immoderate ambitions that surround and penetrate the business of democratic government. I was no longer at the ringside, as an observer free to indulge in the luxury of criticising those who 'do things'; but there I was taking part, assisting with, plotting alongside the masters of the game-play. If, I frequently reflected to myself, this was democratic government in action God knows what authoritarian rule must be like.

One refers, idly and in cliché terms, to the 'centre of power'. Yet in practice much of this is fiction or, perhaps at best, a mirage. A prime minister does have enormous powers in theory, often in practice too, and certainly vast patronage at his disposal. Yet, in reality, the limitations are also enormous. Not so much because of the checks and balances of the textbooks but, far more, because of the number of sheer practical obstacles that stand in the way of getting anything done effectively and certainly quickly; the individual bloody-mindedness, the personal animosities and the unique mass of bureaucratic barbed-wire entanglements often present far greater problems than the proverbial checks and balances. It is true that prime ministers have the power to override, to order, to instruct. Yet at each stage and in every phase of that process there are hidden obstacles, some quite unconsciously laid, others prepared with the tender shrewdness that comes from generations of experience in stonewalling. It is, of course, perfect 'Yes Minister' territory. All governments eventually discover that there are real and substantial difficulties in follow-through action.

The best prime ministers are those with the ability to delegate and then trust their teams to keep a watchful eye and a monitoring check on decisions. The real problem is that the complexity of the modern state is such that this textbook ideal is frequently almost impossible to achieve. It did not take me long to discover these truths. Moreover, there is another dilemma for the journalist – or any other category of 'stranger' – on a temporary trip into the Citadels of Whitehall. To what extent, I can still wonder, does the experience scar one's independence of judgement as an inquisitor? Does it leave lasting damage? The answer may well be 'yes' since having witnessed the problems from 'the inside' and inevitably acquired some sympathy with the practical difficulties of running modern government, it is less easy to ridicule with conviction. Conscience and memory play a kind of subconscious censorship on the critic.

The entire fabric of the state machine is so similar to Alice in Wonderland, even if it is a more rational and explicable Alice. The subtle relationships built up within the civil service after generations of incestuous mutual protection are easy to question and even condemn. Yet there is merit in the system as well as the inevitable administrative corruption. It is an extraordinary web, and once trapped within it, it becomes all too tempting to develop spiders' feet and settle for what is feasible and on offer. Kafka opened our eyes and minds to it all long ago; but then, even earlier, so did Shakespeare. For the journalist caught up in this fabric, a tapestry of interlinking and interlocking threads that oft-times lace into every corner of life, it is very hard to cast off the image of Kafkaesque bewilderment.

Having tasted the scene inside these zones of clinical power it is not at all difficult to imagine the power-play that operated within the great Courts of history from Alexander the Great and the Borgias through to the Courts of Stalin, Mussolini, Hitler, Mao – or any other. Where there is no democratic system, however susceptible to corruption, no open press and Parliament, despite their limitations, to prevent those in command from using the triggers of power simply to shoot each other with live bullets rather than whispers of intrigue, then tyranny exists. Of course, all systems, including democracy, inescapably contain elements of authoritarian rule. But it is almost always a less efficient form of authoritarianism. Moreover, while corruption is an important flux in a democracy just as in a tyranny, the advantage remains that in a democracy corruption is so much easier to expose.

Government, any government anywhere, treads a rough road. Yet in truth it is no different from any other 'centre of power', be it in the media, academe, finance, industry, commerce, the arts and even the church. All prime ministers, like all chief executives, vice-chancellors of universities, football club managers and certainly powerful theatrical agents, have their groupies. The label changes in time but hardly ever the substance. All holders of power and influence throughout history have felt the need for a Praetorian guard whose duties can stretch far beyond the role of a protective shield or carrying an angry spear. The 'guard' can contain all elements – militia, sorcerers, clowns, propagandists, poets, musicians, performers, mistresses and certainly a sprinkling of journalists or, in biblical times, ancient scribes. They are all there to be 'used'. They know that and so, too, do their masters. Flattery plays a crucial role in all this since vanity is the simplest pedal to press.

It is no doubt all part of the great fabric of pretence and counter-pretence that is as much an integral unit of democratic government as of all else. David Lloyd-George of recent times was one of its supreme practitioners; Winston Churchill was no sloth; even modest Clem Attlee had a pretty shrewd notion of how and when to pluck the strings of the flattery fiddle. They have all done it – Macmillan, Gaitskell, poor Anthony Eden. The few who didn't because they were not very adept at deception, were also failures elsewhere. But, in the end, it's the best we have and we might as well put up with it, flaws and all. The alternatives are much less pleasant as Winston Churchill once explained so vividly.

15   Return of the Native: Back to the *Mirror*

When I returned to the *Daily Mirror* in the late summer of 1976 it was already clear to me that I was leaving a government in grave economic difficulties. Perhaps even on the road to disaster. Frankly, it required no great expertise or prescience to identify those signs. However, my discussions with both Callaghan and Healey prior to my departure, then of course in strict confidence, had given me a privileged insight into some of the acute problems ahead. The need for an incomes policy and price restraint was no less than it had been in the previous years, but the difficulties in trying to hold employers and unions to a disciplined policy were growing more difficult with each day. Callaghan in particular was very concerned to keep the Counter-Inflation Unit alive, but I knew – and so did he – that it would be doomed to impotence without the extra muscle and sinews I had long recommended, but had failed to achieve. In fact, what was to transpire over the next two years exceeded in gloom anything I had imagined when I returned to Holborn Circus to pick up where I had left off as industrial editor and to take up a new all-embracing role as an assistant editor of the *Mirror* as well as resuming a regular weekly column.

The paper was then in what I can only describe as its 'post-Cudlipp era'. There was a good deal of unease and a lot of uncertainty around largely owing to the immensely enterprising, though outrageously provocative, competition coming from Murdoch's *Sun* under the editorship of Larry Lamb (on whom Mrs Thatcher was later to bestow a knighthood). A former *Mirror* man, Larry Lamb's audacious artillery barrage at the launching of the new *Sun* had both scared and horrified the *Mirror*'s executive team. And by the time I came back Murdoch's new baby – then nearly six years old – was already making serious inroads into the *Mirror*'s circulation, and there were clear signs of panic in the editorial boardroom. Mike Molloy had been appointed editor of the paper while I was away in Whitehall, and a previous editor, Tony Miles, had taken over as editorial director, the post once held by Hugh Cudlipp and Sydney Jacobson.

Of course, the paper was then under the commercial supervision of its proprietors, Reed International – the paper manufacturing group that had at one time been a junior partner in the *Mirror's* overall grouping, IPC (International Publishing Corporation) in the days of Cecil King. Sir Alex Jarratt was chairman of Reeds and, a few years later, he was to be a crucial figure in Robert Maxwell's takeover of the Mirror Group. But in those pre-Maxwell days, on my return to Holborn Circus, the paper still retained very much of the old Cudlipp journalistic culture, if not the special flair and flavour that Hugh Cudlipp's presence always injected. It also had a remarkably loyal readership much of which had remained with the paper from wartime and immediate postwar years. But, of course, this was an ageing readership, and the trick was to attract younger, new readers in a fierce fight against Murdoch's *Sun*, which had already succeeded in winning over a substantial slice of a younger, sexier, less serious audience: an audience, which, to be brutally frank about this, was far less concerned with politics, international problems or even social welfare and much more devoted to the nipple count. It was a formidable challenge.

I have already discussed, in an earlier chapter, the phenomenon of the old *Daily Mirror*: how it had its readers, which was a legacy of the paper's role in wartime as the 'Squaddies' Gazette', with Jane prancing across the page in near-knickerless attire and the special relationship the *Mirror* established with all the troops. It was then little short of the troops' own platform. I cannot recall ever going into a NAAFI or a mess hall without seeing the majority of my fellow RAF lads holding a copy of the *Daily Mirror*. That kinship continued in the postwar years, if with some wavering, almost until Rupert Murdoch launched his *Sun*.

It was Hugh Cudlipp's genius, when he took over the paper from Guy Bartholomew after the war, that he was able to read and understand the mood of the 1950s and 1960s and turn the paper into the largest-selling popular daily in the world. He achieved that with a brilliant mix of popular journalism, humanising the daily drama of life in postwar Britain, raising laughter out of the trivial, and presenting the most serious and complex subjects in a form of outstanding journalism that the ordinary reader could understand and indeed react to. The paper reflected the man – brash, but a brilliant campaigner; an unusually sharp sensitivity to the needs, anxieties, problems of ordinary people; an insatiable appetite for fun, but not banal ridicule; a penetration of suspect reputations; and, often a surprise to those on the outside, an obsessive concern for accuracy and the proper use of the English language.

Cudlipp was never an easy task-master, not easy to please; he could be very tough about casual, slack journalism and with sloppy journalists. Above all, however, he was an inspiring commander-in-chief more than a 'first violinist', the soubriquet that a bitter Cecil King handed out after he had been dethroned as the orchestra's conductor. Working for Hugh Cudlipp's *Daily Mirror* was a badge of pride that its journalists wore without any bombast, censoriousness or extra-territorial claims on old Fleet Street.

There are periods in the life of all great newspapers when its journalists feel that sense of inner pleasure at working in a particular ambience – it was true of my earlier period on the *News Chronicle*; it was also true of my many old chums on Beaverbrook's *Daily Express*; it was certainly true of the *Manchester Guardian* troops. And under Cudlipp that was the mood at the *Mirror*. Such was the legacy he left and to which I returned, in 1976, to find a paper now fighting for its life against Murdoch's *Sun*. And quite apart from the other factors, mentioned above, what was astonishing to *Mirror* journalists was the success Murdoch had achieved in somehow persuading *Sun* readers that his paper was the heir to the old *Daily Herald* and even the Odhams' *Sun* – this despite the fact that Murdoch had already turned the paper against the Labour Party. For years there were countless readers of the Murdoch *Sun* who baffled the market research experts by clinging to this misconception. All of which made the task of the *Mirror* that much more difficult not to say oft-times perplexing.

* * *

Back at Holborn Circus I briefed Mike Molloy and Tony Miles on what I believed to be the looming political and economic crisis. I broke no confidences in terms of state secrets, and told both of them that I was not in possession of any great secrets of state that might be revealed in the paper. What I did offer them was my distilled impressions built up during my period in Whitehall. The main point I tried to put was of a government in dire difficulty and in need of considerable sympathetic understanding from the *Mirror*. It was an odd feeling to be returning to active journalism while still conscious of wearing a kind of Whitehall hat to explain and defend the Callaghan Government. It was far from an easy switch of loyalty, and I have little doubt that both Molloy and Miles were wary of what they probably considered, with some justification, a government propagandist. I am sure they viewed me with friendly dubiousness as someone who had 'gone native' in Whitehall. Even so it didn't take too long before I was back in a *Mirror* stride.

By the time the 1976 Trades Union Congress met in Brighton the crisis had already hit the government. Unemployment was rising above one and half million and the 5 per cent pay 'norm' agreed earlier as the acceptable level for the second stage of the Social Contract was already in trouble. The CBI were also changing step. They had a new Director General in John Methven who was threatening to withdraw from co-operation with the Callaghan Government. He was later to become a strong supporter of Mrs Thatcher. The unions were bitter in their complaints about rising prices, increasing unemployment and the pay limit. A mood of disillusion was beginning to develop. By the autumn of 1976 pressure on sterling mounted to dangerous levels. Methven at the CBI echoed the fears and deep reservations of his powerful industrialist members – who clearly were reckoning on an imminent collapse of the Callaghan Government. He warned Callaghan that the government would run into 'an all-out war' with industry if the government persisted with the plan to introduce legislation based on Lord Bullock's report on industrial democracy – designed to give the shopfloor and unions a greater voice in management. The Bullock Report duly faded into oblivion.

By the time the Labour Party conference assembled for its annual display of self-immolation in late September 1976 the scene was one of despair. Healey has written, with some passion, about his own mood, and refers to the period from the party conference through to the year-end (1989: 428):

> The next four months were to be the worst of my life. Sterling came under pressure yet again in early September because there was industrial trouble at British Leyland and the seamen were threatening a strike. There had already been a big outflow of sterling balances in the second quarter. I had to raise interest rates by 1.5% to 13% so as to get gilt sales moving. After a short respite the pound fell below 1.70 dollars on Monday September 27th.

In Blackpool at the Labour Party conference Callaghan was so concerned at the deteriorating situation – there were large demonstrations against unemployment outside the headquarters' hotel – that he phoned Healey, who had remained in London ready to fly to the IMF conference in Manila. The Prime Minister asked his Chancellor to cancel the Manila trip and hasten to Blackpool to take part in the economic debate. The RAF flew Healey to Blackpool, and I was in the hall when he arrived by the side door looking considerably shaken. Shortly afterwards he strode up for an allotted five-minute spot – the conference entitlement for speakers at the rostrum – and amid howls of jeering and booing the Chancellor cried out: 'I come from the battlefront ... and I do not come with a Treasury view ...'

It was characteristic Healey courage. He refused to budge from government policy of spending cuts, a 5 per cent pay norm and taxation policies already announced. He contemptuously dismissed his critics' demands for a siege economy and shouted his defiance, pledging the government to stand by its policies and promising to 'win through'. He left the rostrum amid uproar. The mix of cheers, boos, jeers and cries of 'resign' was deafening. Healey just waved it all aside, stretched out a comradely hand to the conference and was off back to London en route for the IMF. Healey writes in his book about that moment: 'For the first and last time in my life for about twelve hours I was close to demoralisation.'

With my refurbished *Daily Mirror* hat firmly fixed by now I wrote about the Blackpool scene and its implications with a mixture of sadness, grimness and gratification that I was not still in my old Whitehall job. At that point the Callaghan Government appeared to be a very short lease. Its narrow Parliamentary majority was ever more precarious despite Liberal support. Looking back at that period, the remarkable thing is how Jim Callaghan was able to hold on through the year and 1977/8 and, amazingly, appear at least on the surface to be gradually strengthening his and the government's position. Of course it was an illusion – albeit an illusion that was superficially persuasive.

At the Tory Party conference a week later the hotel lobbies and bars were full of the gossip about the imminent collapse of the Callaghan Government. Margaret Thatcher's advisers told her to prepare for an immediate general election. Edward Heath was at private dinner parties hinting to political journalists that he was in touch with Roy Jenkins about a possible National Government. Margaret Thatcher, hearing about these dinner parties, dismissed the Heath–Jenkins rumour factory with a contemptuous wave of her handbag. Her speech to the Tory conference was: 'Prepare for power', and she blamed the trade unions for most of the nation's troubles.

'Socialism is on the way out,' cried Margaret Thatcher at that 1976 conference as she unfurled her banner in preparation for the ultimate charge of her Light Brigade. Heath's rumour factory and its adherents were banished from sight. It didn't require a great deal of insight to recognise the writing on the wall.

I kept open my Whitehall doors as best I could in the circumstances. Most of the Cabinet Ministers I had worked with were prepared to see and talk with me, often at quite short notice, although mostly on a private and confidential basis.

One of my first calls after the conference 'crisis' season passed was to visit Denis Healey. It was November, he was back from the IMF and all that, and looked astonishingly fresh and buoyant. He joked and told stories against himself and confessed, scarcely a blinding revelation, 'You know, this is a bloody awful job. You've got to put up with tension from your colleagues in government, the Parliamentary Labour Party, the TUC and, bloody hell, practically everyone else ...' He paused for a laugh.

'But I have to say,' he continued with a touch of uncharacteristic grace, 'the TUC lads have been exceptionally good, especially Jack Jones and Len Murray.'

What of the great crisis? 'Well,' he told me, 'things are a bit better, a bit easier, now.' He paused again and added slowly, 'Jim has been bloody difficult lately but it's getting better and I have agreed that I should soldier on in this job till next summer [1977].'

It was the first time I had heard of Callaghan's plan to switch Healey from the Treasury to the Foreign Office in a straight swap with Tony Crosland. I knew that both had enviously eyed each other's office for a long time. Healey perhaps now more so than Crosland. Who, I reflected, in his rights senses would covet Healey's job at that moment? I have little doubt that this is why Callaghan shelved the idea and ruffled Healey's feathers – to protect Crosland at the Foreign Office. When Healey told me that he had 'agreed to soldier on' what he really meant was that Callaghan had told him he *had* to stay where he was for the time being. I learned the truth later from the Callaghan camp – which was that Healey should remain at the Treasury at least until the summer of 1977, by which time the economic deluge would have been dammed with the help of the IMF and the immediate crisis subdued if not overcome.

Of course, all this was overtaken in February 1977 by the sudden death of Tony Crosland – a severe blow to the Callaghan Government and indeed the whole Labour Party. Yet another potential leader had been cut down at an early age. Crosland, 58, died on 19 February 1977 after a massive stroke. Callaghan reeled under that blow. Crosland had been a firmament in his Cabinet, much stronger in character than Roy Jenkins, better versed in economics than Healey, and intellectually probably the strongest and most rigorous member of Callaghan's team. He was never afraid to take an unpopular line in Cabinet, challenging the orthodoxies of the right as well as the left. He was frequently, perhaps surprisingly, alongside Michael Foot in expressing serious doubts about the wisdom of Treasury policy. He was a tower of strength in that government – arguably the one individual Callaghan could least afford to lose.

In my 'diary of talks' with Cabinet Ministers at that time one individual stands out for special attention not least because he was so magnificently indiscreet, albeit in confidence – Harold (Lord) Lever. At the time of the great Healey crisis, circa autumn 1976, I went to see Harold in his luxurious Eton Square mansion apartment. He was as generous a host as he was a journalists' friend. We sat in his sumptuous office/library/study on the first floor overlooking the Square, him in his favourite easy chair on the right of a classical fireplace. He mused about the government in which he served as Chancellor of the Duchy of Lancaster, a kind of elder-statesman role without any specific portfolio, though ever available to help out with his advice and practical assistance as a trouble-shooter.

He and I had been friends for a long time, and he confided in me about his anxieties. He was very gloomy about the state of the government, believing that Denis Healey and his Treasury team were on the wrong track and too easily and readily accepting the IMF's recommended medicine. Lever argued for a more adventurous, even riskier, course of reflation in order to restore some confidence in industry, which he described as being in a 'dreadful condition'. He was in favour of active intervention to reduce unemployment and regarded Treasury advice to Healey as 'entirely negative'.

Lever told me he was trying to persuade the Prime Minister and his advisers to embark on a different, more positive policy and had put in several papers to this effect. Yes, he admitted, this would require additional borrowing powers. 'Nothing wrong in borrowing to invest in the future,' he told me. 'That's how all businesses operate in the most successful economies.'

I had never seen Harold Lever so angry about his colleagues and their lack of political fighting spirit as well as economic courage. He went through a list of his Cabinet colleagues – past and present – with these comments:

Roy Jenkins: 'A big disappointment. He's obsessed with anti-Wilson feelings.'

Jim Callaghan: 'Jim hasn't got Harold's quality of mind. He lacks confidence in his own abilities ... but he's much less devious than Wilson.'

Harold Wilson: 'Well, I still like him. But the trouble is that, even though he has now gone, he is devious to an absurd degree.'

Denis Healey: 'In the grip of the Treasury, and I simply don't trust their judgement.'

Michael Foot: 'He's the one with the most courage.'

I am not suggesting that Harold Lever's assessments are beyond question; far from it. I would not agree with some of his judgements. But that is scarcely the point. Here was a senior member of the government discussing the character, nature and quality of a number of his closest Cabinet colleagues at a critical moment in the life of that government. Moreover, the Lever summary chimed with a good deal of what I had been hearing from some senior industrialists.

Frank (the late Lord Kearton) Kearton, then still head of Courtaulds, echoed much of what Lever had told me when I saw him shortly afterwards. Kearton claimed that most of his friends in the City were as critical of the Treasury as Harold Lever. But Kearton went on to a quite different tack – and was even more damning of the City's financial centres of power and influence. 'The City is obsessed with trying to preserve its international connections quite regardless,' Kearton claimed. 'They are not nearly concerned enough about helping British industry. Ted Heath was quite correct in his attack on them in the early 1970s. Nothing has changed since then.'

When I began to piece all this together, couple it up with my experience in Whitehall, add a pinch of what I knew was going on inside the Tory Party after Margaret Thatcher's succession and then try to look ahead into the crystal ball, there was a distinctly uneasy feeling in my stomach that things were not going very well in this Britain of ours.

*   *   *

The brutal truth is that although the situation did appear to improve in the two and half years that followed it was an illusion. Nothing substantial, certainly nothing fundamental changed, before the fall of the Callaghan Government on 3 May 1979. The surprising feature, as I have mentioned, remains that the Callaghan Government lasted as long as it did. A number of his own Cabinet members were certainly among the most to be surprised at that – not least Shirley Williams (Lady Williams), whom I saw a few days after the death of Tony Crosland. The fascinating aspect of my talk with the then Mrs Williams was the contrast it provided with Denis Healey with whom I had talked the previous day. The Chancellor had just concluded a series of negotiations with the TUC on the third phase of the Social Contract (which, by then, was simply a euphemism for wage restraint), and he was much cheered by the progress made in discussions with the union leaders.

Shirley Williams's view was very different. She told me that day, in February 1977, that she was convinced that it would be 'almost impossible' for the Callaghan Government to continue beyond November 1977. By then most things she could see on her horizon would conspire to bring them down. When we had our one-to-one talk there were no civil servants present in her office at the Education Department to where she had just been moved from being Secretary of State for Prices. She was much more at home in Education but that did not dispel her gloom. Her Cabinet role had been expanded to include such things as the Bullock Report on industrial democracy and worker participation – but she confessed straight away that she saw this as a kind of albatross. Of course, she wanted to see progress made toward industrial democracy; but given the weakness of the government, the fierce opposition from the CBI and the divisions even within trade union ranks she knew it would be a pretty hopeless operation. She also confessed that the Cabinet was in a fearful state of tension and disarray. Almost all members were at a loss to know how to handle what they knew to be a crisis of confidence in the Labour Government. They didn't require the opinion polls to tell them.

Of course, it is important remember that, by then, Shirley Williams had pretty well lost confidence in the Labour Party. She was close to Roy Jenkins and much influenced by him. The seeds were already being sown for what was to happen when the 'Gang of Four' broke with Labour to form the Social Democratic Party in the early 1980s. With hindsight it is clear that Shirley Williams was well on the road to that milestone when I was talking with her in February 1977.

Yet in truth there were very few smiling faces to be found anywhere in the leadership of the government, Labour Party or TUC by the middle of 1977. Len Murray at the TUC did claim that he was 'more encouraged' by the signs of economic improvement by the middle of that year – but few then shared his optimism. Most of his fellow TUC leaders were dismayed and, at best, sceptical about the future prospect. The late David Basnett (Lord Basnett), leader of the GMB union, was savagely critical of Denis Healey, whom he described as a 'bullshit merchant' while Healey responded – privately, of course – by describing Basnett, a wartime RAF pilot, as 'weak and vacillating'.

Perhaps alone among the stalwarts who still believed it worthwhile to battle on was the man who had effectively designed the Social Contract – Jack Jones, the Transport Union leader. While Jones distrusted the Treasury he was far less critical of Healey personally. He was also tougher and more aggressive in his stance than most other TUC leaders. 'Never let the buggers know you're defeated' was his common expression to me when we discussed the political and economic crisis. His Merseyside realism, his refusal to concede, his deep political convictions seemed to defy the outward gloom. His exceptional personal discipline and the power of his union, then by far the largest in the country, helped.

It was Jack Jones, along with Len Murray, who between them ensured that the third phase of the Social Contract was signed by midsummer 1977. This produced a new and higher 'norm' of 10 per cent and a more flexible system to enable both sides of industry to negotiate exceptional cases and anomalies. At the time of that deal Denis Healey told me: 'The real problem with Phase Three will be to make it stick. The testing time will come at the end of this year.' His prediction was out by exactly 12 months. But maybe that was because Healey himself expected a general election by the autumn of 1978. 'That's what I am looking at now,' he told me in midsummer 1977. And indeed so, too, were a lot of other people who were to be dismayed when Callaghan postponed that target date and, instead, chose to go through the winter of 1978/9, by which time the Social Contract had collapsed across the wounded body of Jack Jones.

It all happened at the biennial delegate conference of the Transport & General Workers Union on the Isle of Man in July 1977, which was meant to be a set-piece platform for Jones's retirement as well as his final plea of support for a Social Contract that he knew, in his heart, was beginning to crumble. He had already told me a few weeks before that conference that it would be very difficult to sustain support. Revolt was growing among his members as well as from employers who found it impossible to conform to the rigid pattern of the wages norm. His ominous words, reflecting the entire spectrum of trade union leadership, were: 'We cannot go on carrying the burden like this': in short, the TUC could no longer carry the responsibility of sharing government. It was a fundamental turning point, perhaps in the entire development of the old Labour movement. Then came the defeat of Jones at his own conference. It was a severe blow to his pride as well as to his power base in the Labour movement, and indeed a unique experience for a TGWU general secretary, an emperor in his kingdom, to be defeated in this way by a delegate conference on such a critical issue.

Jones had been given advance warning of what was in prospect. Most of his national officers were warning him for some time that they simply couldn't 'keep the lid on any longer'. The Midlands area, especially in the motor plants, was already in open revolt. Ironically, this was Jones's old area in which, as a young organiser in wartime Coventry, he had built up one of the most powerful shopfloor organisations in the country. He was the advocate of 'shopfloor power', of shop stewards' rights, of industrial democracy at the grassroots. Now it was boomeranging on him. At this critical moment in his career, less than a year before his retirement, he was fighting to prop up a Labour Government to which he was deeply committed and yet which almost everyone recognised was probably in terminal trouble.

Jones's situation was pure pathos. I can still picture him during that critical debate on the Social Contract, a tense hall in Douglas, Isle of Man, a hot July day outside, ice cold inside. Jones was sitting on the platform, pale faced, biting his lip as delegate after delegate came to the rostrum to denounce the Social Contract – *his creation* – as a lamentable failure.

*   *   *

There were the usual cries of 'sabotage from the left' by various observers as Jack Jones went down to defeat. Even some members of the government attributed the collapse of support to an organised campaign by the Communist Party and groups still further to the left. To be sure, there was an element of truth in this insofar as the Communist Party, Trotskyist and Militant groupings had been campaigning against the Social Contract for a long time. Yet the truth is that it was a genuine rank and file revolt against pay restraint, albeit aggravated and spurred on by its organised opponents. Prices were rising by 15 per cent and the purchasing power of the average worker had fallen by 7 per cent in the two years of pay restraint. Jones did not deny these statistics but sought to argue for an 'orderly return' to free collective bargaining, the cliché demand of his opponents. That plea had no impact. After the vote, which was substantial, Jones looked badly shaken but tried to put the best philsophical face on the situation: 'Well, that's democracy isn't it? That's the answer to those critics of the trade unions who accuse us of dictatorship. It's the members who decide policy in our movement and that is how it should be.' Brave words – but in fact it spelled doom for the central pillar of the Callaghan Government's claim that it could work effectively with the unions and that this partnership would see the country through its economic troubles.

There was no panic in Downing Street when the news reached No. 10 – only a grim recognition that, this time, it was going to be a severe uphill climb to survive for much longer. Callaghan and Healey made it clear they would press on with the 10 per cent pay norm and refused to be deflected. The White Paper on pay policy (*The Attack on Inflation after 31 July 1977*, Cmnd 6882) was published before Parliament rose for the summer. In fact when the TUC September congress voted on the White Paper it was nominally accepted – with a large vote against, including the TGWU. Yet even those unions that voted to accept government policy did so with a heavy and reluctant heart along with warnings of dire consequences ahead. One union leader, Bill Sirs of the Steel Workers, actually used the phrase 'explosion of discontent' when he warned of what the trade union leadership could face in the months to come. In the light of what was to happen in the winter of 1979 the Steel Workers' leader could hardly have been more prescient.

The Prime Minister was a guest speaker at that 1977 Congress, and it was probably the most difficult appearance he had ever made at a trade union conference. He was frequently interrupted and challenged from the floor as he tried to insist that the government's policy was being pursued to 'protect your own interests'. The remark was greeted with whistles of derision. But Callaghan stood his ground. The government, he argued, was convinced that this painful period had to be endured to lift the country out of its crisis. Whether the unions and their members liked it or not the government would not be shifted.

'You have your responsibility,' he told that Congress, 'the government has its responsibility. Each of us will carry that out – but it must not lead to confrontation.' It was Jim Callaghan at his bravest.

He knew the score. The half-hearted standing ovation, the obligatory salute to a Labour Prime Minister, meant nothing and he knew it.

A couple of weeks later Callaghan repeated the unpleasant truth to the Labour Party conference, using still more forceful language. It had the same effect. By now the Prime Minister's exasperation with the trade unions was manifest. It was a clear indication of things to come, though few were prepared to read too far ahead into the crystal ball. It is only history that has now provided the text for Callaghan's successors, like Tony Blair, to read and take note.

The strange paradox to all this – still a year ahead of the *real crisis* – is that the third phase of the Social Contract actually succeeded to a far greater extent than any of the critics or sceptics had prophesied. Of course, there were numerous disputes along the way, the most serious challenge coming from the firemen whose strike spread into 1978. There was another major dispute in electricity generating – then nationalised – with a final settlement averaging around 17 per cent with a variety of subclauses on productivity to disguise the breakthrough. Numerous companies in the private sector followed a similar pattern but by and large the 10 per cent norm was the settlement for the majority of employees – at least on paper.

It is only too easy to scoff at all this and to ridicule any attempt to bring some order into pay increases. The fact is that while the problems raised are enormously complex it also remains the case that all governments try to discipline wage increases in their own particular way – either by monetary supply policy, as in Mrs Thatcher's case, which means high unemployment, or by the manipulation of interest rates against currency depreciation, which also leads to unemployment. Precisely the argument used by George Woodcock a decade before the Social Contract or indeed by Keynes even earlier. No government can escape the conflict, nor is there a simple lasting answer to the problem. Equally, no government should be condemned for trying to seek a civilised solution based on the mutual interests of corporate groups in society. That is what all postwar attempts at a rational solution have amounted to.

The weakness of the Social Contract, as of most of its predecessor formulae, was that it demanded too much from institutions outside government; it concentrated too much on the detailed settlement of wage claims and too little on trying to provide the social and economic infrastructure by which pay settlements, and boardroom salaries, could be determined more rationally. Perhaps that is asking too much; perhaps rational solutions to such complex and deeply conflicting issues are beyond the capacity of democratic government. The jury remains out on that question.

Margaret Thatcher's 'incomes policies' were determined not by rational argument but by a return to mass unemployment. Vast industrial changes to the structure of the British economy and especially to traditional industries were introduced. Legislation against the trade unions was brought in specifically to shift the power of decision-making away from the unions and back to full-scale dominance by management. The sinews of traditional industries such as coal, steel, shipbuilding and heavy engineering were torn apart and the state sector, within which so many of those sinews were sewn, ripped open. The trade unions were effectively rendered impotent as the membership drained away and funds dried up. And yet even the Thatcher Governments, with the strength of national support mostly behind them, were still unable to combat inflation nor in the end modernise the economy without huge injections of foreign investment. The challenge remains for contemporary government no matter what labels may be attached to so-called 'new' nostrums.

*   *   *

Toward the end of 1977, in November, the Prime Minister invited a group us from what we might call the '*Daily Mirror* culture' to meet him privately at No. 10. Three of us were invited to spend an evening in private chat – the late Lords Cudlipp and Jacobson and myself. Jim Callaghan's press secretary, Sir Tom McCaffrey, was the only other present. The Prime Minister, we had been informed in advance, wanted a 'very private talk about the situation'. It certainly had its bizarre moments. We had been in Downing Street only a short time, sitting in the Prime Minister's study, when the lights went out – no one was quite sure whether it was a power failure or the result of the unofficial dispute in electricity generating. In fact there were two power cuts during our evening with Jim Callaghan.

The discussion revolved round the way the government's economic policies were working – or not. Callaghan confessed that wage increases overall were rising at a faster pace than the 10 per cent norm; he also admitted that the government's hands were tied by a whole range of circumstances – meaning, in particular, the IMF conditions for having baled out the UK economy. What worried him most was that many people might feel 'cheated' (that was his word) because they had fallen behind in the pay race against those with the guile or the muscle, or both, to extract more than their fair share. He was deeply conscious of the unfairness of the wage restraint policy, particularly in relation to the freedom of boardrooms to vote themselves extra income, often by dubious methods.

'What can we do about it?' he asked us plaintively. We could offer him few options he hadn't already considered. Yet, in spite of it all, Callaghan retained some optimism. He predicted that inflation would fall in 1978; that unemployment – then still around one and half million – would come down steadily. In fact he achieved both of those targets – albeit through the assistance that came from the IMF. It enabled him to survive through 1978 – but only just. It probably also provided him with a sense of dangerously false hope that he could go on surviving into 1979 when the next general election was due. That, ultimately, was his wrecking delusion.

16 A Nation in Discontent: Nothing at the End of the Rainbow

On a gloriously warm day early in May 1978 a group of senior journalists and editorial executives from the *Daily Mirror* were invited to lunch with the Prime Minister in Downing Street. At first it sounded like yet another close encounter between the so-called No. 10 powerhouse and Holborn Circus. But this time it was different: not just a few selected individuals but much enlarged on anything we had experienced before. The Prime Minister wanted the *Mirror's* editor to choose his team for lunch at Downing Street – a form of open invitation to the paper's senior journalists. So, in advance, we knew something special was on the luncheon menu. And so it turned out – quite a different event from the one in the previous November just described. This time it was the paper's current five-man policy-making team – Tony Miles, then editorial director of the Mirror Group; Mike Molloy, the editor of the *Daily Mirror*; Terry Lancaster, the paper's political editor; Joe Haines, the chief leader writer, and myself.

The Prime Minister knew that the five of us constituted the team that met daily to discuss the paper's editorial line and debate that day's editorial comment. He had hinted in his invitation that the editor might wish to choose the five policy-makers. On the journey to Downing Street we debated what the main item of discussion would be. The majority view settled for one outstanding issue – the coming general election. We were certain that Callaghan would want to test us out on the timing of this while, of course, keeping his cards still very close to his chest. We were only partly right.

In fact, the Prime Minister didn't really want to discuss the issue at all – certainly not in specific terms. Indeed, he made it very clear that he was in no hurry to go to the country. He received us in his private suite on the first floor and looked extremely relaxed, chatting amiably about the government's success in bringing down inflation ('do you realise we have almost halved the rate of inflation compared with the previous year'), reducing unemployment, easing pressure on sterling, which had regained much strength against the dollar, with reserves having reached a record £20 billion. Jim Callaghan beamed as he emphasised that the trade balance looked far healthier than it had for many years. No one referred to the IMF. Naturally enough he resisted any mention of such a sensitive subject.

As the wine flowed round the table – the Prime Minister drank only water – talk shifted toward the future. Someone round the table couldn't resist mentioning the word 'election', which Callaghan let slip by. His style was to stress the government's wish to be in a position to demonstrate to the country that it had been successful in bringing inflation under control by its policy of building up a broad consensus between employers and unions – a policy that had succeeded despite the critics and all the problems. 'We need time to let that sink in,' was the Prime Minister's line. Whenever the election occurred, he added, the government's case would be based on that achievement.

He glanced across the luncheon table and, with a confident smile, assumed all the Mirror Group papers would support him in that objective. He realised there were some doubts about the attitude of the corporate owners of the Group, Reed International. Callaghan had picked up vibes that the men who controlled Reed's were looking for a change of government – a matter on which Tony Miles sought to reassure the Prime Minister that, despite all the rumours about Reed International views, the Mirror Group papers would continue to support the Labour Party.

Callaghan then quickly moved away from even fringe talk about the next election and shifted to what was clearly his principal current concern – the government's pay restraint policy. He reminded us that the government was going for a fourth phase of the Social Contract despite all the signs of imminent breakdown. In his New Year message on BBC radio Callaghan had actually named the figure of 5 per cent before serious discussions had even started with the TUC. He had been attacked for that, and everyone knew that Denis Healey had run into severe trouble in his preliminary talks with union leaders.

With coffee being served and cutlery still rattling, Callaghan looked round the table at the *Mirror* team and carefully and deliberately declared his firm intention to make the 5 per cent norm stick. He chose an old tactic of moving round the table, asking his guests what they thought would happen to this critical fourth stage of the Social Contract. It took the *Mirror* team a little time to gather their thoughts. Most of them said it would be a tough road to tread but, well, it might work, though they had some doubts. They were carefully diplomatic. Joe Haines demurred – his doubts were stronger.

Callaghan turned to me and asked directly: 'Do you think the unions can deliver?'

'No, Prime Minister, I don't think they can,' I replied at once. I expanded on the theme by suggesting that, of course, the TUC leadership certainly *wanted* to deliver. But their difficulty was that they were now under the lash of pressure from their members who were increasingly in revolt against pay policy.

I reported a story told me by the late Tom Jackson, then general secretary of the Post Office Workers Union, himself a strong supporter of the government. A few days ago, I reported to the Prime Minister, Jackson told me about a recent tour of his South Wales region, a traditional stronghold of loyalty to Labour and the zone of Callaghan's own constituency of Cardiff. Tom Jackson had met with full-time officials and rank and file members to discuss government pay policy, and the reaction from them was violent opposition. In fact they told Jackson they were prepared to vote Conservative if there was no change in government pay policy. They were fed up, Jackson explained, with their union's timidity and the blind support their union leaders were giving the government.

The point of the story, I suggested to Jim Callaghan, was that in my opinion this was typical of rank and file attitudes throughout the country. It may be unpleasant news – but in my experience going round the country this was the reality of the current scene. My summary answer to the Prime Minister's question was not well received: 'I simply don't think it will be feasible, this time round, for the unions to deliver what the government is asking – irrespective of their own feelings as union leaders.' I told him across the table: 'We saw this with what the TGWU did to Jack Jones. They can no longer sell the policy to their membership.'

There was a silent pause. No one shuffled a chair. Then the Prime Minister waved an arm across the table and looked hard at me. 'Alright,' he retorted, 'if that is the case then I will go over the heads of the trade union leadership and appeal directly to their members – and the voters. We have to hold the line on pay or the government will fall.'

This was dramatic stuff. Callaghan's features were fixed in a mask of determination. Around the table the *Mirror*'s team remained silent. The only sound was the audible movement of a coffee cup. This was no 'fireside chat' in the style I recalled from the previous November's meeting with Jim Callaghan. It was a Prime Minister, firm-jawed, exasperated at the frustrations of trying to deal with so many conflicting interest groups, fed up with what he saw as weakness and lack of courage among the trade union leadership, convincing himself that what was now required was a bit of rough table-thumping to bring people to their senses.

He would go out into the country and tell the voters that this policy, his policy, was inescapably in the national interest and it was up to them to see it that way and support it. Trade unionists, employers, non-unionists, academics, the media, all of those critics out there, standing on the touchline of reality ... Jim would sock it to them. He also appeared persuaded that given an outspoken approach of this kind, telling the people the truth about Britain's economic situation, he could rally support and that the nation would respond by endorsing his stand when they were presented with the full facts.

We didn't realise it at the time but in retrospect it is quite clear that on that day in May 1978 the signposts were already being erected for the winter of 1979.

*　*　*

Shortly after the *Mirror* team visit to Downing Street the Prime Minister began his circuit of the trade union conferences to rally the troops behind the government. His theme was, as he had outlined it to us at the Downing Street lunch, defiantly hopeful. 'The Social Contract *has* worked and remains the centre-piece of Government economic policy,' he told one one of the white collar workers' unions, APEX (now part of GMB). 'The partnership has saved the country. It has rescued it – and the world knows that.' He praised the steadfast work of the trade union movement, its loyalty and courage. He told the delegates that he, better than most, understood the sacrifices, the frustrations, often the irritation – after all, he had been a trade union official himself. It went down very well. There was never any doubt about the skill and effectiveness of Jim Callaghan addressing a trade union or Labour Party audience. He could establish a profound rapport with his listeners.

But behind the flattery there was also a grave warning – not in so many words, but clearly written between the lines was this: 'You'd better stick to our partnership or you'll suffer the consequences in jobs and savage cuts in our social services if you allow a Tory Government led by Margaret Thatcher to return to power.' Of course, it wasn't put with such outspoken crudity but there was no mistaking the message behind the message. At conference after conference the Prime Minister wearing his trade union tie pleaded with the rank and file to help the government – 'your government' – to establish a 'new understanding, a new consensus, that will take us into the 1980s'. No matter the self-delusion involved, it was an act of considerable courage and political fervour at a time when the Cabinet's spirits were low.

Chancellor Healey's White Paper on the next stage of pay restraint was published in July, and the government made it clear that it would impose the policy across the public sector and also tighten up sanctions on the private sector. Companies who defied the 5 per cent norm would be punished. Roy Hattersley (Lord Hattersley), who was then Secretary of State for Prices and Consumer Protection, was given the unpleasant task of discussing all this with a hostile CBI. What he told them about the government's detailed plans only added to that hostility. When the CBI leaders asked him to spell out an example of the sanctions the government had in mind Hattersley offered the case of Ministry of Defence contracts with the private sector – then running at an average of a thousand contracts a month. Hattersley warned that this gave the government a powerful lever – and it would be used against companies defying the pay norm. There was a predictably bitter reaction to all this. Private industry virtually withdrew co-operation and counter-warned ministers that the whole edifice of government policy would begin to crumble. The leaders of the CBI were already looking with considerable confidence to being rescued from their dilemma by a speedy general election and the return of a Conservative Government.

Almost every serious observer then regarded an autumn election in 1978 as a certainty. For quite different reasons that was also the view of the TUC leadership. They prepared for the annual congress, in the first week of September, convinced that it would be a kind of pre-election platform. The Prime Minister was invited to speak and had accepted. The scene was set, in Brighton, for an election rally rather than a routine congress.

Jim Prior (Lord Prior) was then Shadow Employment Minister, a man very much in the Ted Heath mould, carefully discreet under the new leadership of Margaret Thatcher, but privately sympathetic to the trade unions and their problems. In fact he had already established an informal and warm relationship with most of the TUC leaders – largely on the assumption that he would shortly be in government dealing with them. He also established similarly close links with the leading industrial journalists for the same reason, and I came to know him well – and warmed to his informal, straight-forward dealings. In many ways Jim Prior was already exhibiting his deep differences with the Thatcher approach. Not that he was uncritical of the unions and some of their practices; but he retained a sense of rational balance, he tried to understand their problems and why they struck the attitudes that so often caused much public hostility. He did his homework, read his history and developed a genuine sympathy with many of the underlying feelings motivating trade union attitudes and prejudices.

Long before becoming Margaret Thatcher's first Secretary of State for Employment Jim Prior demonstrated to those of us in contact with him that he was not in favour of her extremes. Yes, he did believe in the need for legislation to limit some of the existing trade union freedoms – especially on strike balloting and picketing. But he saw this as a slowly developing, step-by-step policy and was strongly opposed to the blustering, destructive, near-military style crusade against trade union rights that became the trademark of the Thatcher years.

Jim Prior came to the Brighton TUC in 1978 to speak at a fringe meeting organised by Conservative Party trade unionists. Like the rest of us Prior was convinced that it was the first of his speeches in a general election campaign. The organisers of his meeting shrewdly – as they thought – chose to have their man speak on the opening day of the congress – Monday – the day before the Prime Minister's speech was scheduled. Everything seemed to be in place for the election to be announced – probably for early October.

Hardly anyone then knew that on the Friday evening before the TUC Jim Callaghan invited six senior TUC leaders to dine with him at his farm near Lewes, a few miles away. Even when news of this 'secret dinner party' began to leak out later in the following week it was still very difficult to discover what, precisely, had occurred there. The six TUC leaders who attended were sworn to secrecy, and for once the secrecy pact held – for quite a long time. The six were: Len Murray, the TUC general secretary; Moss Evans (who had succeeded Jack Jones to become TGWU general secretary the previous March); David Basnett (GMB), who was president of the TUC that year; Alfred Allen (leader of USDAW, the shop workers' union); Geoffrey Drain (the NALGO leader); and Hugh Scanlon, president of the AEU.

When, much later, I managed to discover elements of the dialogue around the table at the Callaghan farm that fateful Friday evening, it was clear that the Prime Minister had resorted to another of his question-time tactics. He asked each one of the TUC leaders: 'When do you think I should go to the country?' One by one they replied: 'Go now, Jim. Go this autumn. Don't wait until next year. We cannot guarantee industrial peace in the coming winter.' One TUC voice demurred: Hugh Scanlon (Lord Scanlon). He told Callaghan to delay the election until 1979. Even so the six men left Callaghan's farm that Friday night convinced that there would be an autumn election. The Prime Minister had said nothing to change their impression.

When, the following Tuesday, Callaghan delivered his famous speech to the congress containing the notoriously bizarre 'There was I waiting at the church' ditty the entire conference seemed utterly bewildered. That evening the bars were full of trade union delegates still baffled by the Prime Minister's curious message, which people were interpreting in numerous ways. Lord Callaghan now claims that his 'Waiting at the church' song should have provided the clue that he was postponing the election. It did no such thing. David Basnett, in the congress chair, never forgave Callaghan for what he regarded as a 'terrible deception'. When the truth came out after a meeting of the Cabinet that Thursday Basnett's reaction was that the whole congress had been a fruitless journey to Brighton.

At around 6.30 pm on Thursday evening, as the congress was about to wind up, the Prime Minister broadcast to the nation to declare that there would be no election in 1978. I was sitting in my room at the Grand Hotel in Brighton with my colleague Terry Lancaster watching the Prime Minister's television performance. The day before Terry had written a splash story for the *Mirror* predicting the election date – 5 October. This 'information' was leaked to both of us two nights earlier by Tom McNally, then Callaghan's close adviser (now Lord McNally, who joined the Social Democrats later). It turned out that McNally was no better informed than the rest of us.

Everyone had been wrong-footed. But, on second thoughts, maybe I should not have been all that amazed. A few days before travelling to the Brighton TUC my wife and I spent August Bank Holiday lunching with Michael and Jill Foot at their Hampstead home. Michael then told me, in the strictest confidence, that he was against an autumn election and believed the Prime Minister shared his view. His case was very much the argument of a Parliamentary purist – 'The voters have given us a mandate for a five-year Parliament; it would be quite wrong of us to run for cover now simply because we are facing serious problems.' An argument one has to respect – though I disagreed with it, as I made clear to Michael that lunchtime.

In the course of our visit Michael received a 'phone call from the Prime Minister. I happened to overhear some of the conversation at the Foot end of the line. Michael was telling Jim Callaghan that he should stand firm against having an autumn election. I continued to argue with Michael in favour of an autumn election but he persisted: 'No, it wouldn't be the right thing to do. We would be accused of lacking the courage to face the winter and that would go against us.' Brave words from a man of exceptional principle.

Lionel Murray (Lord Murray of Epping) has since described that famous farmhouse meeting as a deep embarrassment to him, personally, and the TUC as an institution. He told me in conversation in May 1991:

> Frankly I was astonished at the conversation we had that evening on the eve of the 1978 Congress. We should never have been invited to discuss that with the Prime Minister. The TUC did not want to be part of that discussion and Jim shouldn't have involved us in any talk about the timing of the general election. It had nothing to do with the TUC.

Here again it was the voice of strong principle. Although Murray was a powerful advocate of partnership with the Callaghan Government he nevertheless retained an even stronger belief in the special role of the TUC – in the Woodcock tradition – that it should never become too closely involved with the *function* of government. He believed that the 'Farm Summit' (as it came to be labelled) carried the TUC dangerously into the realm of a Cabinet function or, at least, would be so regarded if the story ever leaked out. And that this would be damaging both to government and the TUC since it would be exploited by the Opposition and certainly by the Conservative newspapers – as indeed it was. But this was not how Jim Callaghan saw it. From his point of view it was a shrewd piece of political strategy and demonstrated the readiness of his government to consult with the trade union leaders on even the most sensitive areas of political policy.

What was also interesting about the conversation I later had with Len Murray (May 1991) was the advice he gave to the Prime Minister at that 'Farm Summit':

I told him that we couldn't hold the situation that winter. We pointed to a yawning gap that was emerging in pay settlements between the public and private sectors. And I reminded him of what happened to previous pay policies under a Labour Government going back to Attlee's time. I recalled the collapse of the Cripps' policy in the 1950s when the private sector had given big rises well in advance of the public sector. I told Jim that this is where the crunch would come again in the winter of 1979. But he wouldn't shift his basic view. In any event I think he'd made up his mind about the election date before he saw us. He'd spent August studying Labour Party internal reports and research, and I am sure he'd already made up his mind to hang on because he didn't think he could win in the autumn.

Murray's predictions proved to be uncannily accurate to a fine point.

Long before the now legendary 'Winter of Discontent' it was pretty obvious to most observers that the Callaghan Government had run its course. But still more than that there was growing awareness that something deeper, more fundamental was beginning to shape the course of British politics. Hindsight confirms all that as obvious enough. But many observers had no need of hindsight at that time. There were sufficiently clear signs that the postwar dream, the rainbow land of postwar 1945 *et al.* ... that all that had come to a bleak full stop. Perhaps it couldn't have been avoided in any event. Society, the world, had moved on even if British institutions and indeed many of Britain's social habits had not. Perhaps 1979 was the end of an epoch that had been waiting in the wings for some years. There is, as previous chapters have argued, much evidence on that score. And perhaps in his own way, intuitively, Jim Callaghan, in his bones, knew that. Increasingly I became convinced of that.

It is hard, even from this distance, to be quite sure where the real crunch point came. Was it when Jack Jones was defeated at his 1977 union conference? Was it when the Prime Minister pulled the rug from under the feet of the TUC leadership at the 1978 Congress (as they went on believing for a long time afterwards)? Or was it in the closing months of 1978 when all hell began to break loose on the wages front?

There are those who believe the fabric began to shred around November 1978 when the TUC rejected Denis Healey's carefully prepared document on the 5 per cent norm – which, by then, had already slipped up to around 8 per cent in actual settlements. Various concessions were being made in the public sector by using the dubious device of 'productivity allowances'. The Treasury tried to oppose these so-called 'exceptions', as did the advisers around the Prime Minister. But ministers were choosing a line of least trouble, trying desperately to keep the lid on a boiling pot. Everything was being done to buy off trouble. Meanwhile both Callaghan and Healey were, by the day, becoming more angry and frustrated. Healey's so-called 'Joint Agreement' on continuing pay policy came before the TUC on 14 November. The economic committee met first and insisted that there should be no specific reference to a 5 per cent norm in the Joint Statement. Then there came a full meeting of the TUC General Council. They rejected the Joint Statement – even without mention of 5 per cent – and, by a single vote, threw it out.

The backdrop to this astonishing turnabout was no less bizarre since a number of key trade union figures were simply absent from the meetings. The Transport Union leader Moss Evans was on holiday; the Railwaymen's general secretary, Sidney Weighell, left the meeting before a vote was taken – to catch a train to Birmingham. Had either of them been present the chances are that the vote would have been reversed. As it was the TUC's rejection of government policy triggered a political explosion.

In his book *Prime Minister* Lord Bernard Donoughue, then a principal adviser to Jim Callaghan, writes (1987: 171):

Had the General Council been constituted of personal representatives of Mrs Thatcher it could not have acted more effectively in the Conservative leaders' electoral interests.

It was a mortal blow. Yet more was to come. Two weeks after Healey's document had been dumped by the TUC the Ford Motor Company demonstrated its contempt for the government's pay policy. The firm announced a three-stage deal that amounted to a pay rise of 17 per cent for the motor company's 40,000 workforce. Ford UK chairman, Terence Beckett (later Sir Terence, and Director General of the CBI), called a news conference in a West End hotel to explain why Ford felt it necessary to settle for 17 per cent. He even went to elaborate lengths to justify the rise as being 'within the intentions of the Government White Paper' – whatever that meant. But Beckett's real point was that Ford couldn't afford another major strike. He revealed that unofficial strikes in 1978 (and in 1977) had been running at over 600 a year. To have resisted union demands at that point, Beckett claimed, would have led to a major stoppage, probably official, which the company had already costed out as something of the order of £100 million. The pay deal would cost them £48 million.

The Ford deal rocked the government. The cabinet ordered sanctions against the company, but when ministers tried to introduce their sanctions proposals the House of Commons voted them down. Callaghan's thin majority, with Liberal support, simply couldn't sustain such controversial legislation. By Christmas 1978 the government's entire pay policy was in tatters. Settlements were, by then, averaging between 10 and 15 per cent. The end was indeed in sight.

*   *   *

It all seems long ago and far away as, of course, it is. Two decades have slipped by and we are now in a new millennium. Yet it remains a remarkable period, and nothing is lost by reflecting back at some of the extraordinary events that occurred during – and following – that 'Winter of Discontent'. It was – far beyond all the detail of industrial and political conflict, beyond even the measurement of economic damage – the moment when British politics changed perhaps for all time. Not simply the close of that 1945 epoch of romantic visions, of dreams and fantasies to which much of the earlier part of this book referred. It was a volcanic eruption: a fundamental shift in the political scheme. The fissues that had been manifesting themselves for so long finally snapped into huge ruptures of the political landscape. The triumphant Margaret Thatcher on the steps of No. 10 Downing Street in May 1979 marked that change, and still does. She was 53 then. Now she, and the nation, are a lot older, and perhaps, just maybe, a trifle wiser.

*   *   *

The story of what happened in the first few months of 1979 has passed into national legend. But it is worth a brief recall. As Prime Minister Callaghan, slightly sun-tanned, stepped off the RAF VC 10 from gloriously warm Guadeloupe into a shivering January England, he returned to a country frozen economically as well as climatically. It was virtually paralysed as much by myth as substance. By then, indeed, myth had become so entangled with reality that it was almost impossible to separate the two. Callaghan did *not* say, when he was interviewed in the Heathrow VIP press room: 'Crisis? What crisis?' At least not in so many words. That was the *Sun* headline. He may well have conveyed the impression that everyone was exaggerating the crisis and describing its impact out of all proportion to the truth. He had just returned from a meeting with world leaders where, doubtless, they were discussing the future of mankind in the way those summits always attempt to do. So what was all this fuss back home about a few strikes and the cold weather?

Of course, Callaghan gravely misjudged the mood of a nation that felt seriously beleaguered. Tom McCaffrey, his press secretary, who was with him throughout, advised against holding a press conference at the airport. 'Wait till you get back to Downing Street and are able to assess the situation,' was Tom's good advice. But Jim was not in the mood to accept that kind of caution. He simply failed to grasp the true measure of what was happening in the country. Even when, later, after he had been fully briefed, he still ducked the challenge. There was a powerful case for calling a State of Emergency, if for no other reason than to demonstrate that the government, at least nominally, was still in charge. He rejected the proposal – though he has since confessed he made a serious error of judgement over that.

The wage claims and settlements moved ahead at speed. The petrol tanker drivers, key figures in the whole crisis, finally settled for 15 per cent after much disruption; railwaymen threatened to strike unless they received a 20 per cent rise; water workers went on strike after refusing an offer of 14 per cent but finally settled around that figure. Few claims were resolved below 15 per cent. But of course the disputes that evoked most publicity and certainly did most damage to the government were the strikes of refuse workers, hospital staff and, the ultimate killer, the strike of gravediggers on Merseyside.

The merits of these cases were beside the point. Their explosion came on top of everything else that had brought public patience to a climax. Meanwhile inside the embattled ramparts of the government a Treasury paper floated across ministerial desks proposing a blanket 12-month pay freeze, full stop. The Prime Minister told the Treasury wise-heads to forget it, in pretty brusque language. Callaghan was then slumped inside Downing Street, exhausted, dejected and feeling deeply sorry for himself. He felt let down by almost everyone. Those close to him described his mood as 'worryingly lethargic'. Several Cabinet Ministers have since described to me, more graphically, that mood inside No. 10. 'It was like being on the *Titanic*' a senior Cabinet

Minister whom I still prefer not to name, told me. 'They were moving the deck chairs as the ship was sinking. But there was no music, not even a hymn to be heard.' Ministers played around with this and that idea. Yet they knew there was nothing new to come up with. The barrel was empty, scraped clean.

In March 1979 came the decisive issue that was to bring down the government – quite unexpectedly, from devolution. On 1 March Scotland and Wales went to the polls on devolution, long before Tony Blair's ideas on devolution were conceived. In truth it was a kind of referendum on the government in London. Wales voted decisively against devolution but Scotland, where support for devolution then had nothing like its contemporary force, voted narrowly in favour. But the upshot was so inconclusive that it left the Callaghan Government with a difficult problem on how to proceed. Should they scrap the whole idea or put it on ice for a time? Callaghan decided to call all-party talks but the Scottish Nationalists refused to attend and put down a censure motion, which the Conservatives supported with glee.

The vote of confidence took place on Wednesday 28 March, and Callaghan called in his ministerial team before the vote to tell them that there was to be no wheeler-dealing to ensure a government victory. He was fed up with patched up compromises, back-stage deals with the Liberals and the whole business of just keeping the government alive. The government lost the vote of confidence – by a single vote. It might have been different had two Irish supporters cast their votes as had been expected – Gerry Fitt, a life-long Labour loyalist who decided to give his prior commitment to the future of Ireland – so, perversely, he voted against Callaghan; and an Irish Republican sympathiser in Labour's ranks, Frank Maguire. There was also a range of bizarre occurrences with Liberals who were expected to support the Callaghan Government. Sir David Steel, then leader of the Liberal Party and a senior partner in the Lib–Lab pact that had kept the Callaghan Government in office during those closing stages, tells (1989) the story of how Clement Freud was tracked down to a Littlewoods' store in Liverpool while campaigning for David Alton in the Edgehill by-election. Freud was then contacted by 'someone in No. 10' and, despite Callaghan's injunction, he was confidentially offered a safe passage for his Freedom of Information (Private Members') Bill if he 'accidentally missed the train back to Westminster'. But Clement Freud, whose vote was to go against the government, decided *not* to miss the train. It was the end of the Callaghan Government.

17 1979: The Curtain Falls, Enter Margaret Thatcher

The election campaign of April/May 1979 was almost as bizarre as the events that had led up to it. Quite apart from what had been going on in Whitehall, in government, at the TUC and across the country at large, those of us at the *Daily Mirror* with any degree of influence on the paper's policy had for the previous six months experienced their own miseries. Covering the events through the 'Winter of Discontent' required all the political and journalistic skills we possessed – and many we didn't possess. We were the only voice among the national press trying to do the impossible – present a reasoned, balanced picture of an appalling state of affairs. The election announcement came as a relief – though not to our sense of deep anxiety. We had few illusions about what was going to happen, though no one I knew on the paper actually declared for any other policy than that we should give every support we could reasonably offer to help the Labour Party – even if the task seemed beyond our reach. There was little enthusiasm for the job ahead, still less much hope from even the most optimistic heart that we might be able to exert a serious influence on events.

The Murdoch *Sun* had already made it perfectly clear that as far as they were concerned the Labour Party was dead in the water and Margaret Thatcher was about to be crowned Queen. It was simply a question of her majority. Frankly, it was difficult to argue with that view. Yet, oddly enough we were helped through our misery from a surprisingly unexpected source – Reed International, owners of Mirror Group Newspapers. It was indeed almost a laughable paradox.

At the very start of the election campaign in April 1979 Sir Alex Jarratt, chairman of Reed international, held a private dinner party at the old Kettners Restaurant in Soho to which he invited about a dozen of the senior editorial executives from the Mirror Group papers. Around a large oval-shaped table in a private room were the editors of the *Daily Mirror*, *Sunday Mirror*, *The People* and the Scottish newspapers within the group, *Daily Record* and *Sunday Mail*. In addition were the political editors of the papers, Joe Haines, the *Mirror*'s chief leader writer, and myself. Tony Miles, the group editorial director, was the main executive conduit through whom Jarratt operated. Long before we sat down to an immaculately prepared table Jarratt made it quite clear that the purpose of the gathering was primarily to discuss the group editorial policy for the election campaign. We had guessed as much.

What we hadn't expected was the strength, even the vehemence of Alex Jarratt's own opinions. With great candour he declared that he wanted to see an end of the Callaghan Government. No 'ifs and buts' or 'on the one hand this ...' etc. It was straight-from-the-shoulder stuff. He, and the Reed organisation, had had quite enough of this Labour Government. They wanted it swept away as quickly as possible. He made no bones about the fact that he regarded the Callaghan Government as a complete disaster. But he then added – 'However, the policy of the papers will be decided by the editors in our normal way; you now know my view. But you are free to decide for yourselves. That's how we run our newspapers. You, the editors, must decide. But I felt it important to put my own views before you so that we can have a straightforward and honest debate.'

Despite all this Jarratt assumed that those of us round the table would be determined to continue the traditional pro-Labour policies of the *Mirror* papers. And he was correct. Jarratt's declaration, if anything, actually strengthened our resolve to back the Labour Party. It is possible – I am not sure – that there might have been the odd waverer. But if that was the case the doubts were never expressed. Everyone round the table spoke up in support of Callaghan – though there were numerous criticisms of the way the government had handled its affairs. Some strong arguments were advanced in support of Callaghan – especially the fear that a Thatcher Government might seriously damage the fabric of society.

One voice I shall always remember was that of the late Geoffrey Pinnington, then editor of *The People* and an old *Daily Mirror* man from Cudlipp's days. He rebuked Jarratt to his face. Told him that while he could understand the attitude of powerful employers wanting a Thatcher Government he suspected they had no real idea of the damage such a government could inflict. Pinnington's response to Jarratt was both powerfully courageous, as well as prescient. Many of us were encouraged to voice our own support for the Pinnington line, though it has to be said that no one expressed themselves in such vivid terms.

At the same time I felt Jarratt himself had been courageous in displaying his shop window to all of us with such candour and honesty. He accepted the consensus of support for the Labour Party with good grace and dignity, albeit with regret since he predicted that we would be greatly disappointed with the election result. 'I doubt it will do the papers much good either,' he said reflectively and quietly. Even so I admired Jarratt for his honesty. He was well aware that he would not persuade his selected guests to change sides.

There is, of course, another view to take of what may have been moving through Alex Jarratt's mind that night. He could have been preparing the *Mirror* team for what was to come in the future. There had already been evidence that Reed were tiring of running the Mirror Group and were thinking of a sale. Most members of the Reed board were known to be embarrassed at owning a left-wing tabloid. But more to the commercial point, they were already feeling the effects of nearly ten years of battle against Rupert Murdoch's *Sun* and they had no wish to continue that fight with their political hand tied behind their back. The *Sun* having gone Thatcherite seemed to have all the important cards in its favour. The financial architects at Reed House in Piccadilly saw the writing on the wall for the Mirror Group well in advance of a certain Cap'n Bob riding over the horizon with his pistols blazing.

When I now look back, once again propped up by the powerful mechanism of hindsight, I believe the election of 1979 was the turning point in determining the future ownership of the Mirror Group. From that moment until Bob Maxwell swept through the swing doors of Holborn Circus on 13 July 1984 the board of Reed International was searching for a way out. It could have chosen from a number of other options – and almost did. Certainly there were numerous people canvassed for chairmanship of the Mirror Group long before Maxwell appeared on the scene – and one man, Clive Thornton, formerly of Abbey National, was actually appointed chairman with the specific purpose of negotiating the independence of the Mirror Group. The late Sir Peter Parker, former chairman of British Rail, was another who was sounded out before Thornton.

But all this was window-dressing by Reed. Their primary intention was always to sell off the newspaper group; to rid themselves of this unruly embarrassment, this incubus that no longer had commercial attraction to them and, certainly, compared unfavourably with the immensely successful Murdoch operation. The critical watershed for the *Daily Mirror*, in my view, was the general election of 1979. As with so much else it was the great dividing, and defining, moment.

The stage was set for the sorceress herself to take her place in history: the footlights were at the ready and focus fixed.

*   *   *

During the election campaign itself I was asked by Tony Miles (editorial director) and the editor, Mike Molloy, to play a special role as the paper's link with the Prime Minister. Callaghan himself had approached them to propose this, and Miles and Molloy readily agreed. I was still expected to play a full part in covering various aspects of the election campaign for the *Daily Mirror* but, in addition, I was drafted to keep a daily contact with Downing Street and offer what help I could to the Prime Minister and his election team. So I was close to the action from day one of the campaign and worked alongside Derek Gladwin (the late Lord Gladwin), the former trade union leader who had been appointed Callaghan's chief of staff and organiser at large. In effect I became part of that Downing Street election team – a role that inescapably carried some professional disadvantages as well as political perks. But I rationalised the situation by telling myself that even without such a sensitive, perhaps even compromising, mission I could hardly have expected to be less involved or more independent in the role of a roving reporter on the election trail and away from the Downing Street hot-house. Moreover, I did get on well with Jim Callaghan; I liked him and indeed found that I could talk candidly with him. So it was that I became a kind of 'Callaghan spy' at the Tory Party's daily press conferences and, toward the end of the campaign, had my first severe brush with the Iron Lady.

I attended the news conferences of each of the parties most days, and tried not to miss the spicy press briefings at Conservative Central Office. With about a week of the campaign still to run and her confidence rising to peak level, Margaret Thatcher gave a special news briefing at Central Office. She was flanked by Willie Whitelaw, Jim Prior and Geoffrey Howe, but she did all the talking, rarely yielding a question to any of her colleagues. Mrs Thatcher described at some length her economic and industrial plans, and as she finished I jumped in with a question. I was sitting in the front row just below her. 'Mrs Thatcher, do you accept that if you are elected and go ahead with the plans you have just outlined then it will inevitably lead to a large growth in unemployment?' The Iron Lady glared down at me, turned her body in my direction, rather like a tank turning to prepare for battle with guns blazing, and she exploded: 'The trouble with you is that you aren't prepared to accept change.' The powerful emphasis was on the first 'you'.

'No, Mrs Thatcher, that's not the point,' I persisted to her visible anger. 'Could you please answer my question.' There was some uproar at this point and a BBC correspondent sprang in to back me up: 'Mrs Thatcher, would you answer Mr Goodman's question?' The uproar continued until Jim Prior tried to quell the scene with a pacifying comment. We then moved on to other issues.

My question remained unanswered. Not that I can blame her for ducking it. She probably knew what I was up to. Indeed, when I went back to Transport House across the road – then the Labour Party headquarters – and told Jim Callaghan what had happened, he laughed and confessed that he wouldn't have answered my question either.

On the Sunday before polling day I attended a huge Tory rally at the Wembley conference centre. As Denis and Margaret Thatcher arrived the scene was one of frenzied euphoria. It was almost as if the election result had just been declared, giving the lady a massive majority. The audience simply couldn't contain itself. They were already jumping for joy. Back at Downing Street the atmosphere was one of deep gloom. Nothing seemed to be going right for the Labour Party campaign, and the press was almost universal in its daily prediction that disaster lay ahead for the Callaghan Government. In the later stages of the campaign the opinion polls consistently showed the Conservatives holding a substantial lead: on eve of poll it was a clear 7 per cent. The constant theme of the pro-Conservative press – which, effectively, meant almost the lot – was 'Remember last winter ...', with large pictures of piled-up refuse just in case any reader happened to forget. The day before polling day – 3 May – the *Daily Express* called on its readers to 'help Margaret Thatcher make Britain really great again'. The same day the *Daily Mail*, not to be left behind its arch-rival the *Daily Express*, used the whole of its front page to carry a large picture of Mrs Thatcher with a huge caption informing its readers 'The Woman who can save Britain'.

Murdoch's *Sun* was loud in its backing for the Tories and called on its Labour readers to 'Vote Tory this time ... it's the only way to stop the rot'. The paper's editorial on eve of poll touched the most sensitive point of all by proclaiming 'The roots of *The Sun* are planted deep among the working class. We are proud to have a working class readership. The LARGEST [cap letters] working class readership of any daily paper ...' – a telling gibe at the *Daily Mirror*, of course.

The *Sun*'s editorial continued: 'Both young people and traditional Labour Party supporters tend to be idealists. And *The Sun* is an idealistic newspaper. We firmly believe in that system of Government which offers the greatest good to the greatest number. That is precisely why on this momentous occasion we firmly advise our readers to Vote Tory.' The paper used its entire front page and all of page two to offer this advice. It was a confident *Sun*, and one can still feel the smile that must have played across the face of the paper's leader writer as he typed that editorial. In Holborn Circus it caused no mirth at all. Labour's foes were having a field day – and so, too, were the arch competitors of the *Daily Mirror*.

There was just one stage, about a week into the campaign, when Callaghan appeared to have gained a slight initiative. He had made several very good speeches, and the impact of these were reflected in some early blips in the lead the Tories were registering with the opinion polls. Callaghan was indeed a respected figure in the country, even among Tory voters. People warmed to his avuncular style. It was also recognised that he had fought painfully hard to hold back the industrial crisis, and many ordinary voters believed he had been let down by his trade union friends – as indeed he himself believed. Yet the brutal truth and irony behind that impression was simply to boost Margaret Thatcher's campaign, rather than the Labour Party's fight-back. Callaghan knew all this. He entered the campaign with a heavy heart, and the weight of his gloom never lightened.

On the eve of poll I was with him in his room at Downing Street urging him, as had a *Daily Mirror* editorial that day, not to yield to the prophets of doom, but to go out – he was due to speak at a meeting in London that evening – with a fighting spirit to warn the voters of the dark dangers that lay ahead if the country voted for a Tory Government. But Callaghan sensed the spectre of impending defeat. He shrugged and told me, philosophically, that there 'is a time in history when outside factors take over'; when 'the people, the voters want something different ... and I believe the time may well have come for Mrs Thatcher'. He went out into the May evening on his final mission as Prime Minister.

*   *   *

In retrospect we may now be able to view that extraordinary period, the winter of 1978/9, in more rational mood. Two decades on, it should now be possible to regard it in a historic setting, although there remain questions that are still difficult to answer with any degree of clarity. Was that the watershed when the old working class was put into the margin of history? Or did that come later, with the miners' strike of 1984/5? The two dates are, of course, strongly related since it was 1979 that opened the gateway and allowed Margaret Thatcher to take control of a new political agenda. The trade union movement was changed for all time. Whatever its progress from now on into the twenty-first century the unions can never return to the influence they possessed before 1979. And in many ways the miners' strike in the mid-1980s confirmed that. These were landshifts in the terrain of history. The 1980s witnessed the dying of the old working class and the painful development of a new working class, which has yet to be effectively defined.

In my conversations with Lord Len Murray in recent years he has frequently reflected on the events of 1978/9. Lord Murray still believes that Callaghan misjudged the whole industrial picture in the summer of 1978. 'He over-reached himself. He was far too inflexible in his approach,' he told me. But Murray was equally critical of the unions and their leadership during that extraordinary period. 'It wasn't just a breakdown in wage restraint policy,' Murray reflects. 'It was the carelessness of people about what was happening to other groups. There was a fragmentation of trade unionism; all that had broken down in 1979. And all my assumptions, all the things I had always worked for, were beginning to come into question.'

From almost anyone else in the trade union movement that might have sounded like pious platitudes – but not from Lionel Murray who had, literally, devoted his life to the trade union cause. From an agricultural, poor working-class background in Shropshire he had struggled out of the farmland rut into grammar school, gallant wartime service, via an Oxford University degree, to the full-time staff of the TUC after a brief spell in the civil service. Murray was trained in the Woodcock school; and there was no better school than that. He understood, respected, loved the veins of the Labour and trade union movement. His devoutly Christian beliefs acted as an additional cord tying him to those convictions.

For Len Murray to confess what he did to me that day was in itself as profound a judgement on 1979 as I have heard from anyone. To be sure, the fragmentation Murray referred to was itself a reflection of an entire range of changes taking place throughout society and most of industry. The technological revolution was already devouring jobs, traditions, ancient habits and practices with a relentless appetite.

The whole matrix of traditional industrial, and with it political, culture was evolving into a high-tempo consumer society. The character of the workplace, and workforce, was in a process of rapid and destabilising change.

*　*　*

Ten years after his departure from Downing Street in May 1979 I asked Jim Callaghan to reflect on his final moments in Downing Street. He admitted to me then that he felt a great sense of relief when he packed his bags:

> I went back to the farm that weekend and wrote in my diary an expression of relief and also the strong desire to hand over the party leadership. I was tired, quite frankly. The burdens of office are great. I actually rejoiced at the prospect of not carrying them after that election defeat. It had been a very difficult time.

He went on to add:

> I had had enough. I came to the job too late and I was weary. I simply couldn't face the prospect of going round the country again, time after time, talking to local parties, the trade unions – going through all that over again. I couldn't face it. It was the job for a younger man. That's where Kinnock scored. He was ideal for that job and I think he did a wonderful job of reviving the Party.

That comment was in June 1989, almost exactly ten years after he lost to Margaret Thatcher. Sometime later Lord Callaghan wrote to me setting out his considered views on the trade union crisis during the winter of 1978/9.

> I never believed [he wrote] that the general run of trade union leaders stirred things up; on the contrary. But I do make an exception of Alan Fisher and I do think that David Basnett [as well as Fisher] could have shown more leadership over such things as the intolerable gravediggers' strike. As to the General Election which wasn't – i.e. autumn 1978 – what did the TUC leaders who advised an election believe would have happened? If we had lost or the result had been inconclusive [as I believe] the situation politically or economically would have been no better. Indeed it would have

been worse as Mrs Thatcher has shown. And if, by a miracle, we had won we would still have faced a 17% wage rise by Fords.

How bitterly that Ford pay deal still rankles. No one in that Callaghan Government will ever forget it. It was the final nail in the coffin. Whatever the faults of the trade union leadership at the time there is no question that it was the Ford Motor Company who provided the bait for them. And what then were they supposed to do? Refuse the 17 per cent? It was an impossible position for them, as it was for the Callaghan Government. The distinguished industrial relations academic, Lord McCarthy, has written a paper, so far unpublished, in which he sets out his views on the Winter of Discontent. He writes:

In retrospect it is difficult to exaggerate its [Winter of Discontent] immediate and long-term importance. It discredited both the Labour Government and the more lasting notion of a constructive and co-operative relationship between Government and the TUC. Labour publicly destroyed its most plausible election argument on the eve of dissolution. More important still the spectacle of doctors unable to treat patients; graveyards awaiting their dead, appeared to suggest that trade unionism itself had become a sectional and selfish movement – with little regard or concern for the comfort or sensibilities of others. Heath appeared to have been right to attempt legal constraint even if he had gone about it the wrong way.

Lord McCarthy of Nuffield College, Oxford, the university's senior lecturer on industrial relations, is a life-long Labour supporter: no one could regard his comment as being unfairly critical of the Callaghan Government or the trade unions. In that same paper he also examines comparative statistics between strikes and working days lost in Britain and industrial strife in similar countries with extensive labour laws. His conclusion is that the decline in strikes since Thatcherism has not been due to her legislation (or John Major's follow-up actions) but to a whole range of other factors, especially technology and the dramatic changes in economic conditions.

The events that flowed from the collapse of the Callaghan Government in May 1979 and the triumphant victory of Margaret Thatcher led to more than ten years of crisis for the Labour Party and, by the same token, a remarkable decade for Thatcher-led Britain. In almost every sense it was a reversal of Attlee's 1945 'revolution'. The world of Clem Attlee's 1945 Government was turned upside down. Great industries that government had brought into the public sector – coal, railways, gas, electricity, along with others to be nationalised later, like steel – were all parcelled out to private ownership. The great privatisation crusade, which began as a kind of afterthought by Thatcher's ministers, became the focal point of her policy and a brilliant new method of tax redistribution to the middle and upper earnings groups. Basic industries like coal, steel, heavy engineering, the shipyards, the traditional and older membranes of the British economy from the nineteenth century, were deliberately run down, their workforce depleted and left redundant.

The public sector of the economy, stronghold of trade unionism, came under savage cutbacks; and as unemployment rose the Thatcher Government began its step-by-step dismantling of trade union freedoms, in strikes, picketing, elections of their national officers and on issues like trade union recruitment and the closed shop. As Secretaries of State for Employment followed each other in rapid succession – after Jim Prior, first to have the job, tried to adjust the pace of trade union reform to a more moderate speed and was therefore removed – Act after new Act enforced new and seriously limiting curbs of trade union freedoms. In the end they were left with the freedom to strike in theory but found it nearly impossible to put that into practice. By the late 1980s trade union membership had been almost halved from its record level of 12,128,078, the figure registered by the TUC at its congress in 1979, a few months after Mrs Thatcher took power. Forty years of trade union growth and financial expansion was effectively wiped out in the decade of Thatcherism.

It is true that most of the 'older' institutions were to suffer from the sweep of Margaret Thatcher's handbag – BBC, the civil service, the universities, local government: but none suffered the debacle that was to hit the trade unions and, by the same token, the finances of the Labour Party. The Iron Lady was not only tearing down the old buildings of society and laying fresh foundations for her 'New' Conservative Party, she was also, consciously or otherwise, laying down a foundation for the emergence of a 'New' Labour Party. To this day the proclaimed greatest achievement of the Thatcher years is that she terminally weakened, if not all but destroyed, the old trade union base in industry and indeed for the Labour Party.

Of course, she was helped greatly by the technological revolution and the vast changes in global economics, as Lord McCarthy claims.

At the same time this sweep of destruction did seem to disprove one old canard – the persistently repeated claim that it was the growth of trade union power and influence that was primarily responsible for a distorted labour market, reduced profits, fuelling inflation and causing unemployment. The case put by the professors of Thatcherism – Hayek, Milton Friedman and the Institute of Economic Affairs – that weakening the trade union 'stranglehold' would clear the decks for a huge increase in industrial efficiency and economic prosperity, did not materialise. Removing the trade union albatross did not lead to the predicted transformation. Almost all the industrial improvement stemmed from inward investment – especially from Japan, the United States and Germany – and the immense growth in new technology.

What the assault on the unions did produce was a return to the mass unemployment levels of the 1930s; it re-empowered management, and brought back a fundamental fear into the workplace. No other group in British society had to cope with such a series of devastating blows as the trade unions suffered in that period; the wonder is that they have survived at all. It is interesting to note that despite all the draconian measures taken by Mrs Thatcher's regime the growth in productivity across the whole decade of the 1980s remained significantly lower than it was in the 1960s when the Wilson Government took such a hammering from industrial disputes. And this is in spite of the fact that large oil revenues from the North Sea helped to distort many of the statistical claims and boasts frequently made by Margaret Thatcher's ministers during that time.

It was never easy for a *Daily Mirror* political journalist to cover the Thatcher period. We all had our contacts in the upper reaches of the Conservative Party but it was a hard road to travel. In some respects I was a little more fortunate than some of my colleagues on the paper since I had already established a close relationship with several important figures in Mrs Thatcher's Cabinet, including Jim Prior, Peter Walker and Willie Whitelaw. My conversations with them were fascinating. I was always just a little bit surprised at the way they trusted me with their confidences: they were sometimes notably indiscreet and rarely concealed their doubts about the Iron Lady. Of course, I was limited in what I could then write in my *Mirror* column, but there's always a way in which one can use such information without violating confidences.

Once Jim Prior was away from the Department of Employment and safely (or unsafely!) tucked up in Belfast as Northern Ireland

Secretary he would meet me on his occasional visits to London. Conversations with Jim were invariably quite riveting as well as enjoyable. He is a very open and honest man and had little time for the Thatcher hard-liners.

Nor did Peter Walker, tucked away in Wales by Margaret Thatcher after his spell at Energy. Walker was her minister there during the miners' strike and was often in disagreement with his Prime Minister about her tactics. In particular he had no time for Mrs Thatcher's choice as Coal Board Chairman, the late Sir Ian MacGregor. Walker was always extremely shrewd about his indiscretions – but he was also shrewd enough to recognise that journalists were seasoned practitioners at reading between lines.

Yet the most interesting indiscretions of all invariably came to my ear via Willie Whitelaw. After winning the 1983 election, armed with her Falklands' 'medals', Margaret Thatcher quickly rid herself of most, though not all, of the remaining 'wets' in the Cabinet. And she tended to ignore or side-step those she retained. But Willie was the one exception. She was never quite sure how to handle Whitelaw ('every government needs a Willie'). Nor, for that matter, did Whitelaw ever quite know how to handle her. He was made a hereditary peer and replaced at the Home Office by Leon Brittan after the 1983 election victory. Whitelaw as leader of the Tories in the Lords no longer represented any kind of threat to Thatcher's leadership after that election – not that he seriously did beforehand.

Sometime after Willie had been put in the Lords we met for a long lunch. He was in a most relaxed mood as he surveyed the world at Westminster. With hardly any prompting from me Whitelaw confessed his deep reservations about the Thatcher style of government and many of her policies. 'Too abrasive – not my style.'

Nor did he like many of her closest Cabinet allies. He went on, in a marvellously indiscreet manner, to list his Cabinet dislikes for my benefit: *Nigel Lawson* – 'a most unattractive person'; *Sir Keith Joseph* – 'strange man, Keith. I admire his courage very much – he's always explaining where he went wrong in the past. Well, we all know about that. But I don't believe Keith is capable of change. He's too committed to her'; *Geoffrey Howe* – 'no sparkle'. His views about several others are, even to this day, unprintable.

He admitted to me that day that he would dearly love to be able to 'influence Margaret to change some of her policies – but frankly I don't see how this can be done. It's very difficult for me to see a way round that.' Whitelaw spoke of Thatcher in a curiously detached way. Not with affection, though clearly with respect. His method of influencing her, he admitted, had so far been by making the odd private remark but always avoiding any public criticism and certainly not trying to play off any of his Cabinet colleagues.

'I avoid making any criticisms in open Cabinet,' he added. 'It always leaks out, and there are some members of the team who enjoy leaking that sort of thing. So, I make my mark in private. She can be persuaded. She will listen and sometimes even act on advice so long as she is not seen, publicly, to be retreating.'

Yet the truth is that Willie Whitelaw's influence was far less than he assumed or hoped. He was an immensely shrewd political animal but his successes in persuading Mrs Thatcher were limited and mostly confined to smaller issues. The fact remains that the longer she remained the stronger she became – until the row with Michael Heseltine over the Westland helicopter dispute came close to de-stabilising her. In the end it was her own arrogance, and her contempt for her colleagues' views – even the views of old friends – over Europe that destroyed her seemingly impregnable position.

Yet none of this was of much help to the Labour Party. Callaghan quit the leadership of the party on 15 October 1980, one week after a gruesome annual conference where bitterness and recrimination swept away everything else. There then followed an election under the old system of choosing a new Labour leader – by a vote of the Parliamentary party, the last to be held under that traditional method. Michael Foot was elected to succeed. After two ballots he defeated Denis Healey by 139 to 129 votes, a very close-run thing. In the first ballot Healey topped the poll with 112 against Foot's 83, John Silkin's 38 and Peter Shore's 32.

So Michael Foot, an improbable leader but one of the most loved men ever to rise to the leadership heights in the Labour Party, inherited what most people by then regarded as a near impossible mandate: to revive the Labour movement. Healey became his deputy, though it was an awkward relationship, not least because Denis Healey was always convinced that he should have been leader. Indeed, there is much justification in Healey's claim – except that he was so heartily disliked in many quarters of the Labour movement that it would have been as difficult for him to lead Labour as, eventually, it became for Michael Foot. Would Healey as leader have averted the split and the formation of the breakaway Social Democratic Party by the 'Gang of Four'?

To this day Denis Healey believes he could have done so. But my own evidence suggests differently. By another of those extraordinary quirks of chance and circumstance I actually stumbled into a meeting where the plot was hatching around the formation of the new breakaway Social Democratic Party and discovered, to my amazement, that my own paper the *Daily Mirror* was playing a not insignificant role in the script. It was like this.

The *Daily Mirror* took a suite in the Wembley Conference Centre Hotel for the day of the special conference on 24 January 1981 at which the future system of electing Labour Party leaders would be finally decided. Nothing unusual in a newspaper taking a suite of that kind: normal Fleet Street practice, of course. Yet this time I was to discover a hidden motive. It is important to recall the special significance of that Wembley event – for it was here that the future 'electoral college' process was finally to be determined. By then Michael Foot was the elected leader under the old system, and the special Wembley event was his inaugural conference as leader.

The atmosphere at Wembley was one of pure Arctic. Imaginary icicles were almost visibly hanging from the sagging banners. It was also a shambles in terms of being such an ill-organised, unthought-out, singularly unplanned process. There was an eerie sense of doom and obvious despair about the entire event, as if the whole of the Labour Party, as an institution, had become petrified. The *Mirror*'s private suite therefore took on a special significance quite apart from the routine practice of providing a working base for the paper's journalists with telephones easily available, a bar and buffet for invited guests – in the usual Fleet Street style. It was in fact also a haven into which editorial executives could repair and only later, by accident, did I discover the suite contained an ante-room.

Sometime in the afternoon after various decisions had been made to replace the old system by an electoral college I went up to the *Mirror* suite looking for Tony Miles, the editorial director, and Terry Lancaster, the political editor. They were nowhere to be found. I moved toward a concealed door in the far corner of the suite, tried the handle but the door was locked. I could hear voices inside. I rattled the door and knocked. A sheepish-looking Mike Molloy, the paper's editor, came to the door, looking uncomfortable and embarrassed. I was halfway into the room before anyone could object – as I felt sure they wanted to. Inside the room were Shirley Williams and Bill Rodgers (two of the 'Gang of Four'), with others I didn't recognise but who were later identified as advisers to the forthcoming launch of the Social Democrat Party. Alongside them in the room was Tony Miles and Terry Lancaster with Mike Molloy.

The discussion inside the room was an attempt by Shirley Williams and Bill Rodgers to bring the *Daily Mirror* into line with the formation of the new party and there is no doubt that several of the *Mirror* executive team, notably Tony Miles, were in favour of the breakaway party. Miles had always been critical of Michael Foot's election as Labour leader. From the outset he was convinced that Foot would never be regarded as a credible political leader and a potential prime minister. Several other *Mirror* senior journalists shared Miles's opinion.

I do not believe it is an exaggeration to claim that at that moment the *Daily Mirror* was hovering on the edge of backing the 'Gang of Four' just prior to the formation of the SDP, which was formally launched on 26 March 1981, two months after Wembley. Nor can there be any doubt that a clear attempt was then made to keep those of us who would have opposed such a move well away from the kind of secret cabal I stumbled upon during that Wembley conference.

The idea that Denis Healey might have prevented the launch of the new party is pure self-delusion. The scene was set by Roy Jenkins once he returned from his role in Brussels. He had been convinced, for a long time, about the need for a new party of the centre-left – a phrase he used long before Blair made it common currency. Jenkins, a self-confessed Whig, could see no future for a Labour Party that remained 'chained' (as he would put it) to the trade unions and, indeed, to its historic traditions as a party of the working class. Those times were gone, Jenkins argued. Around him was built the alliance of David Owen, Shirley Williams, Bill Rodgers – the original 'Gang of Four' – as well as the others. Healey knew this – which is why, for months before the Wembley conference, he tried to dissuade Owen, Williams and Rodgers from leaving the Labour Party. But they were quite adamant that not even a party under Healey could salvage Labour. Shirley Williams made that clear in conversations with me *even before* Michael Foot defeated Healey.

There was also another factor, far more cynical. In the election of a new leader to replace Callaghan the evidence points to a significant number of MPs voting for Foot rather than Healey in order to force a final showdown and a break-up of the old Labour Party in favour of a newly formed SDP. Their reasoning was quite simple: a success for Healey would merely offer a temporary respite to a disease that they regarded as terminal. Better to precipitate a speedy crisis, with

Foot as leader, and then clear the decks for the development and growth of a new party.

There is no doubt that this *was* the strategy, and it was spelled out very clearly to me some time later by several MPs who had actually voted for Foot for those very reasons. In some ways this is what has now happened to the Labour Party, albeit in less dramatic form. The periods of leadership that followed under Neil Kinnock and John Smith were a form of interregnum awaiting the emergence of a new political phase, which many now believe to have reached its apotheosis in Tony Blair. But that is another story.

One final reflection is required at this point as the curtain falls: a word about Michael Foot. He was, as I have already agreed, an improbable figure as a potential prime minister, though, of course, he had served as Deputy Prime Minister under Callaghan and, by common consent, had done rather well. Even so the rank of Deputy Prime Minister is as empty of significance as is the label Vice President of the United States. The fact is that Michael was, and remained, almost too gentle a human being to be thrown into the snakepit of normal political life. He relishes opponents but loathes cultivating enemies; in full spate of oratory he is merciless with words, verbal abuse, brilliance of historic recall to reduce a political adversary to a whimpering hulk – akin to his hero, Aneurin Bevan. Literary destruction? Yes, indeed. Political annihilation by debate? To be sure. Destroying an opponent by guile, deception, the dexterity of dishonesty – core ingredients in the exercise of power? That is not for M. Foot. The dagger turns to melted rubber in his hands.

Someone said of him during the 1983 General Election campaign that the electorate didn't really merit such a man, sculpted as he was in the finest sensitivities of decency. The Labour Party knew all this, instinctively, as did those of us who have been privileged to be lifelong friends of a remarkable journalist-cum-political person. Maybe his critics were correct; perhaps he was not made to be a prime minister. Maybe not, I am not sure.

Michael was a great Parliamentarian whose chorus of historic and literary anecdotes spanned the gulf between political opinions and whose generosity to opponents leapt across the idiocies of shallow party points; whose capacity to demonstrate tolerance only stopped when confronted by serious evil. He was a great political figure. They have always been rare, and they might be rarer still in future.

18   Maxwelliana: Cap'n Bob and His Slippery Decks

> Mad ambition ever doth caress
> Its own sure fate, in its own relentlessness.
> – Coleridge, *Zapolya*

The building is now demolished, transformed, almost banished from memory. The Castle of Madness, no longer remembered except by those of us who still harbour the veins of times past. Perhaps, indeed, it needs the skill of a Proust to jot down those seemingly inconsequential moments when, as one wandered down the long, lost corridors of the old *Mirror* building on Holborn Circus, reflecting on a scene of utter banality, the world appeared to have taken leave of its senses. They called it the *Daily Mirror*: it might well have been labelled the *Daily Maxwell*. Since, for much of the time, that is what it was. A strange world inhabited by journalists who often seemed to be walking around the building in a kind of hazy bewilderment. And now, even stranger in a way, it all seems so long ago, far away and past its sell-by date. Life with Robert Maxwell, at least, was certainly never dull. Corrupting, absurd, sometimes even interesting in the sense that it was a collector's item part of life; and for that very reason it couldn't be described as 'dull'. Nor, in a perverse sort of way, do I regret having experienced the madness, if for no other reason than it would have been impossible to believe had I not lived through it myself.

* * *

Robert Maxwell, aka Abraham Lajbi Hoch (his original birth registration), aka Ludvik Hoch, then Jan Ludvik Hoch; aka Leslie du Maurier (which he chose impetuously from a brand of cigarettes when he joined the British Army), aka Leslie Jones ... until, finally in the midst of a battle area during the Second World War, his Brigadier and admirer, Carthew-Yourston, decided that since Hoch was about to be promoted to Second Lieutenant he had better shoulder the burden of a decent Scottish name, so the Brigadier advised Ian Robert Maxwell. Thus was Cap'n Bob born – again. Brigadier Carthew-Yourston was very impressed with young Hoch, whom he described as a most remarkable character with 'a very strong personality'. Little did he realise – or maybe he did – that he was launching a name that was to occupy, even transfix, the mind and attention of a lot of very important people in a postwar world that Bob Maxwell then tried to bring under his control.

I have already explained (in Chapter 9) the circumstances of my first meeting with Bob Maxwell at his old Pergamon Press office in Fitzroy Square. That was in July 1968, when he was offering me the deputy editorship of a newly planned national daily paper and, at the same meeting, telling me the extraordinary story of his role in the Berlin of 1945. Even with the passage of time Maxwell never forgot the Berlin story nor the manner of our first meeting. On the rare occasions we met after my departure from the *Mirror* he would usually find an opportunity, or produce one, to recall the Berlin episode and, depending on the audience available, true to character, he would adjust some of the details. Yet, to be fair to the old scoundrel, the basic elements of the story remained as he had originally recounted them. I dare say I have now reached the point where I must believe that there is truth in that remarkable Berlin episode, circa 1945, and that it is not all fantasy.

I also have to confess something even more complex: my deeply mixed feelings about the man. Of course he was mad, perhaps even clinically so; nor do we need reminding that he was a crook, a cheat, dishonest, and that his personal behaviour was appalling often to the point of being sadistic. And yet there was another aspect to this elephantine character – indeed, I would argue that there were at least twenty different personalities at war with each other, fighting to find a surface level within the Maxwelliana psyche.

Consider the scene in a remote village, Slatinske Doly, in what is now the far eastern edge of Slovakia, where Ludvik Hoch was born on 10 June 1923. He was the third child but the first son of a highly orthodox Jewish family who lived in a single room of their grandfather's house on Synagogue Street. Mechel (or Mehel) and Hannah (Chanca) Hoch produced nine children, three sons and six daughters, of whom three girls and the youngest son perished in the Holocaust along with Maxwell's parents and most of his extended family. Another son and a daughter died young. Two daughters and Ludvik survived the war – the girls came through the concentration camps and Ludvik escaped across Europe (there are numerous and confliciting accounts of how he achieved this) finally to end up in Marseilles early in 1940 where he joined the Czech Legion, picked up an Egyptian ship heading for Britain and landed in Liverpool at the end of May. He was briefly interned, then joined first the Pioneer Corps of the British Army and later the 6th Battalion of the North Staffs Regiment. That is where Ludvik Hoch became Leslie du Maurier.

The poor, deprived background from where he sprang was orthodox Jewish, stemming from a sect known as Maramaros Jews who were distinguished by their powerful physique, hard work, conservative habits and strong character. As a first-born son the young Ludvik was chosen by his grandfather, to whom he was greatly attached, as a potential rabbi, and he went to a local Yeshivo school in the village. By the age of 8 he was literate in Hebrew, Yiddish and Czech. Most influential of all, however, was his mother. Hannah was a typical Jewish mother – commanding the home from the kitchen, deciding all domestic priorities, doting on her, then only, son and providing the instinctive intellectual stimulus to protect her girls and promote Ludvik. Mechel, his father, was huge: six foot five inches tall, powerfully built, he was a hard-working peasant who scratched out a meagre living from buying cattle from local farmers and then reselling the stock to local butchers. He also sold hides to leather workers and often supplemented his inadequate income by working as a woodcutter or even a farm labourer and, occasionally, dabbling in a bit of cattle rustling, which was par for the course in that zone.

With a background of that kind, and after having travelled the cruel road to Liverpool, circa 1940, escaping the village from which most of his family were to be taken to the gas chambers by the Nazis, it is hardly difficult to identify the complex Bob Maxwell with the man I grew to know so well. His war record was also special. He was a brave, often heroic soldier on whom Montgomery was to pin the MC. The point being that to have even an element of all that on his CV placed Bob Maxwell in a different category. I have no doubt that all these factors played a significant part in persuading me to have a special regard for the old rogue. In any event we somehow managed to establish a different kind of relationship from that which so many others experienced at the *Mirror*. I put it no higher than that. We could never describe our relationship as 'a friendship', although, at times, it came close to that.

Throughout our whole relationship I always had the feeling that Maxwell was careful in how he handled me. If that sounds an immodest claim it is not meant to be: it is simply to state that he would usually show considerable hesitancy before criticising me. And I was never on the receiving end of some of his appalling personal attacks, which often resulted in sheer humiliation for the recipient. That is a far cry from claiming that I was never at the receiving end of his madness and absurd behaviour. Yet there were moments when we were together, either one-to-one or with only a handful of others, when he would defer to me. I admit to feeling uncomfortable when he did that – but there it is.

One fragment comes to mind. One lunchtime I went up to Maxwell's ninth-floor suite with the *Mirror* editor, Mike Molloy, to discuss an editorial for the next day's paper. The discussion was brief and unusually equable. Maxwell suggested that we stay on for lunch with him in the private dining room, and so the three of us sat at the large rectangular dining table where the subject crept round to the Second World War – as it frequently did. I asked Maxwell to spell out the circumstances of his escape – the story most of us had heard before but always changed a bit on repetition. So he went through the account again, and we fitted in bits of the jigsaw that had not been too clear. Then I pressed him to tell Molloy and myself about his parents: what had happened to them; how did he get the news of their eventual fate etc. Maxwell, speaking very slowly, recited how his father, Mechel, was taken to a concentration camp in North Germany, then put on a boat loaded with Jewish prisoners from the camp. The boat was then taken into the Baltic where the Germans pulled the plug, sinking the vessel with all hands on board.

As he reached the end of the story he broke down in tears. I was sitting close enough to him to know that they were genuine tears. He cried for several minutes, wiped his eyes and looked down at the table. He pushed his food away. There was silence until Molloy broke the spell with a question deliberately aimed to turn the conversation back to the next day's paper. That was no fake, no act. It was a side of Maxwell that few people witnessed at close quarters. In fact it was a side of his persona that he usually tried to protect from the outside world, although there was a public repetition of this tearful display some years later in the High Court when he was giving evidence in a libel case.

There were other brief moments when, in my presence, his emotional guard was down: fragments in the pattern of this man's extraordinary behavioural tapestry. Nothing was predictable. His mood would change from minute to minute, subject to subject, and even within a single discussion about a single item. Under the dome of his dyed thick, black hair one could sense the turmoil within the pysche; the struggle between conflicting forces, always in challenge, before one element of the personality, somehow, succeeded in overcoming the resistance of another. From Day One as he stepped into the Mirror Group building in Holborn shortly after midnight on Friday 13 July 1984 there was no point in anyone trying to predict what might happen next.

It followed on his deal with Reed International, which, in itself, was a strange business. Let us pause for a moment and reflect on Reed's own behaviour in the months preceding Maxwell's takeover. For several years Maxwell had tried desperately to get his hands on a national daily newspaper. There was the 1968 occasion, which I have already described; there were several abortive moves in the 1970s when, at one juncture, he made a bid for the *Daily Express*; then, shortly before the 1983 General Election, he made another attempt. He proposed the launch of a completely new national daily paper of the left, more downmarket than the *Daily Mirror*, to compete with Murdoch's *Sun*. Maxwell saw the 1983 election campaign as an ideal launch-pad for a new paper of the left not least because the *Mirror*'s circulation was falling while the *Sun* had become a completely Thatcherite paper.

Maxwell invited a group of people to lunch at The Gay Hussar restaurant in Soho to discuss the proposed new paper – Michael Foot, then Labour Party leader; Len Murray, then general secretary of the TUC; Sir Tom McCaffrey, Michael Foot's press secretary; Bob Edwards, then editor of the *Sunday Mirror* and an old buddy of Cap'n Bob; and myself. Maxwell set out his ideas for the launch of a new paper to coincide with the beginning of the election campaign. He calculated on a daily circulation of about half a million, which, he reckoned, would establish the paper as a credible proposition after the election. He would help to finance it by the technique he first suggested in 1968 – bringing all the trade union journals under one print production roof and using the profits from that enterprise to help subsidise the daily paper. It was a characteristic Maxwell idea – daring, novel, a dangerous gamble and dubious.

The lunch table unanimously turned down the scheme as 'half-baked' and, in any event, seriously damaging to the *Daily Mirror*, which, despite all the grave doubts, was pledged to support the Michael Foot-led Labour Party in the 1983 election.

One year later Reed International virtually handed the Mirror Group to Maxwell on a tarnished-silver platter. By then Margaret

Thatcher had won the 1983 General Election with an enhanced majority, she was stronger than ever as the victor of the Falklands war, while the Labour Party under Foot had been reduced to its lowest poll and public support since the early 1930s. Reed regarded their ownership of the Mirror Group as a greater liability than ever. Moreover the country was then in the throes of a devastating miners' strike, which still further embarrassed both the paper and its proprietors.

There is now not the slightest doubt that Bob Maxwell was tipped off to make his bid for the Mirror Group – by Reed themselves. Early in 1984, before the start of the miners' strike, Reed were in private talks with Maxwell about selling off the *Mirror's* northern headquarters at Withy Grove, Manchester. The Mirror Group was then in a state of flux, and a new chief executive had been appointed to help the flotation of Mirror Group Newspapers on the stockmarket. He was Clive Thornton, the former chief executive of the Abbey National Building Society appointed by Reed International after they had scoured the business world for a likely 'interim' chief executive.

Reed were then pursuing an each-way bet: trying to offload the Mirror Group by a stockmarket flotation and using Thornton as a kind of 'bridging man'; or, preferably, selling off the paper to someone like Maxwell in a clean-sweep deal. Thornton was used by Reed in a quite cynical manner – so much so that, as chief executive of the Mirror Group and having been appointed to that post by Reed, he was never told about the secret talks between Reed and Maxwell until the very last minute.

Leaving aside the question of whether Thornton was the right man to handle the Mirror Group at that critical period – and he probably wasn't – the manner and style of the Reed board was as cynical as one could find even in the cut-throat world of big business finance. It has to be remembered that there was a pledge on the table from the Reed chairman, Sir Alex Jarratt, that the Mirror Group would not be sold off to a single bidder. That pledge was simply brushed aside. Jarratt and the Reed board justified their sale to Maxwell on the grounds that his bid was 'almost twice that which could have been raised through an Offer for Sale in present market conditions' (Jarratt statement at the Reed AGM, 24 July 1984). Maxwell's bid was £90 million.

But what the Reed board did not disclose was that in order to push through a rapid deal Reed made available to Maxwell an astonishing interest-free bridging loan of £6 million just 24 hours before the deal was concluded. Maxwell, sitting in a suite of rooms he had taken at the Ritz Hotel, just across the road from Reed headquarters in Piccadilly, put the gun to Reed's head in the final moments of negotiation.

'I haven't got the money,' he told the Reed chief executive Leslie Carpenter. 'I am short by £6 million.' Carpenter consulted the Reed board, and the £6 million bridging loan appeared. Maxwell had played his favourite poker game to match Reed's cynicism. He now controlled Mirror Group Newspapers.

Cap'n Bob marched into the Mirror building at about 12.20 am on the morning of Friday 13 July 1984 – minutes after he had promised Sir Alex Jarratt and Leslie Carpenter that he had no intention of entering the building that night. In fact he drove straight to Holborn Circus after signing the deal in Reed House, Piccadilly. At 00.30 hours that Friday morning I received a 'phone call from Mike Molloy, who was still in the Holborn building. 'He's got it,' reported Molloy as if announcing the end of the world, which, in a way, it was for the old *Mirror* culture. Molloy gave me an account of what was happening. Neither he nor Tony Miles, chairman and editorial director of the paper, had known anything about what was happening at Reed House until a staff secretary from Carpenter's office phoned Miles to read to him the official statement issued by Jarratt and Carpenter. There was no personal contact between Jarratt or Carpenter and Miles.

Miles put the 'phone down, grabbed his jacket and told Molloy: 'I'm off home. If he comes [it was still 'if' rather than 'when'] into the building now, you can look after him.' As Miles walked to the lifts he bumped into Maxwell and his minders stepping out, smiling broadly and greeting the unwelcoming *Mirror* men with a wild sweep of his arm; 'Hello boys,' he shouted. By then Miles had disappeared, silently, into a downward lift.

The first thing Maxwell did on reaching the ninth floor of the Mirror building was to summon those directors who had remained on board. He instructed them to call an immediate meeting of the Mirror board. 'But, Mr Maxwell,' they protested, 'it's one o'clock in the morning.'

'A board meeting immediately,' he snapped back. 'That's what I am asking for, now.'

He then strode into the office of Douglas Long, the managing director, looked around, spotted Long's private bar in a corner of the room and walked across to begin handing out drinks to whoever was around ... and they included Long himself. Maxwell simply seized control of Long's office as a mere matter of routine. 'What would you like to drink, boys?' enquired barman Bob.

The room was half full of men shuffling around in a kind of sullen silence, trying to make conversation to an ebullient Maxwell who was full of his day's success. The first meeting of Maxwell's Mirror board began at 2.45 am that morning. Mirror executives had dragged themselves out of their beds, half-dressed, to attend. All but two members of the board turned up – the absentees were on holiday – and the meeting ended at 4 am – just as the last edition of the *Daily Mirror*, Friday 13 July, was running off the presses down below, carrying the announcement of Maxwell's historic purchase.

At the meeting Cap'n Bob told the board, 'I am now in charge of this great newspaper and you are all responsible to me.' The papers, he said, would retain their traditional political stand; nobody would be sacked – at least not yet – and business would be conducted normally. 'Bring all your problems to me,' he invited without conviction. He then went off for a snooze and a shower before returning to Holborn Circus at 8.30 am, where he strolled into Clive Thornton's chairman's office and sat down. When Thornton arrived Maxwell invited him to depart as soon as he liked. As Thornton left the building he complained bitterly in front of the TV cameras that had been keeping an all-night vigil on the doorstep. He denounced the Reed–Maxwell deal and, foolishly, albeit understandably, tore up a copy of that morning's *Mirror*, which contained the Maxwell takeover announcement. It was the end of Clive Thornton as a *Mirror* boss.

All day that Friday and into Saturday Maxwell busied himself with a range of meetings, walk-abouts, informal chats with the print union men, the editors of the three papers, *Daily Mirror*, *Sunday Mirror*, *The People*; and then invited the editors to lunch with him at Claridges for a celebratory inaugural. In the afternoon he returned to take part in negotiations with the print union FoCs (fathers of the union chapel/branches in the building) and thanked them for *not* stopping the paper's print run at midnight on Thursday – an action that some of the print workers wanted to take immediately they heard of Maxwell's takeover. He then warned the print union men that any repeat of that threat would be countered by his closing the entire plant. At 5pm on Friday the 13th, he called a press conference to stamp his presence on the world of Fleet Street. Then he summoned Tony Miles and instructed the former editorial director to change the slogan under the masthead of the *Daily Mirror* to 'Forward with Britain'. Cudlipp had already dropped the old postwar masthead slogan of 'Forward with the People' some years before. Maxwell now wanted something similar brought back – for all three papers.

I was called on Saturday by Maxwell and invited to meet him at the office on Sunday morning. It was a memorable occasion, to be sure. His wife, Betty, was busy arranging new furniture and carpets for Bob's new and enlarged office when I arrived. This was the room once occupied by Cecil King and Hugh Cudlipp. Telephone engineers were creeping over the floor fixing new 'phone lines and, doubtless, inserting a few new 'bugging' devices. In an ante-room where I waited for The Call into the presence there was Tony Miles, Mike Molloy, Terry Lancaster and Joe Haines. All waiting for a meeting with the new god. Everyone except Joe looked crestfallen and bewildered. Bob himself was bouncing in and out of each room, wearing an off-white suit, blue shirt and red bow tie. He was behaving like an agitated film director arranging a new set.

Suddenly amid all this bustle he turned to me and said: 'Let's have a private talk, Geoffrey. I'll get rid of the others ...' with which he shooed out the assembled pack of my friends and colleagues. He invited me to sit on a huge couch to talk, one to one, about how I saw the future of the Mirror Group. With flattery oozing from his tongue we shifted across the spectrum: how did I view the paper's development; what had been its past faults, in my opinion; what were the paper's achievements, its strong points, its weaker ones. What did I want to do – and did I want to work with him to help achieve the 'world's greatest newspaper', etc. etc. We talked for over an hour, alone.

When I agreed to continue working for the paper he told me that he was about to set up a special 'Politbureau' – his precise phrase – and he would like me to join it. It would meet weekly, probably every Tuesday lunchtime, he explained, and its role would be to decide the policy of the paper and discuss all major issues of political and company policy. 'It will be the major body running the paper,' he promised with a broad beaming smile, which spread across the whole of his vast features. Apart from the editors, Joe Haines and myself were the only two editorial executives on the 'Politbureau'. Miles and Lancaster, who were still in the ante-room when I returned, left the paper shortly after Maxwell took control.

*   *   *

Cap'n Bob's Politbureau was exactly as he had outlined – at least in terms of the day, every Tuesday at lunchtime; the venue, his private dining room on the ninth floor; an unwritten agenda, which nominally dealt with the policy issues and a cast-list of editors from the papers in the Mirror Group, which included the Glasgow contingent of editors and chief executives from the *Daily Record* and *Sunday Mail.*

To top up the Politbureau with other areas of Mirror Group management Maxwell added the managing director, the finance director, production director and advertising director. They were, in the main, just make-weight and rarely uttered a word unless invited or, more likely, provoked. In fact the actual functioning of the Politbureau turned out to be very different from how Maxwell had originally outlined it to me in our start-off Sunday morning discussion. It was a pure sham. A pretence at corporate policy-making; a piece of pure make-believe designed, principally, to demonstrate his control and managerial technique ... which was domination and, at times, control by intimidation.

Cap'n Bob's technique was to choose a subject – anything from American foreign policy to industrial relations at Ford Motor Company – and provoke a debate, which he would open with some outlandish observation. At first the unwitting member of the Politbureau would jump in with a view, which Maxwell would then invariably denounce as a 'load of cobblers'. He would play one off against another and would select one hapless victim for a dose of Maxwellian humiliation such as – 'Come on, now, Charlie [no one was actually named Charlie], where did you reach such an opinion? You've been in too many brothels recently,' etc. The most frequent victims were the poor chaps who had made the tedious weekly journey down from Glasgow. This was odd even by Maxwell standards since the two Scottish papers were then among the most successful and profitable in the group. That didn't prevent Bob Maxwell from rounding on them for the most trivial of reasons.

The peak of humiliation, in my time as a member of the Politbureau, was reserved for Maxwell's then managing director, Roger Bowes. Roger absented himself from a Tuesday lunch without warning Maxwell in advance. He was at the Savoy lunching with Finnish newsprint bosses with whom he was negotiating a new contract to supply the Mirror Group with paper. Maxwell glared round the table after spotting an empty chair and no Roger. He demanded, 'Where's Bowes?' No answer came. 'Did anybody hear my question – where's fucking Bowes?'

The production director bravely replied: 'Roger is at the Savoy, Bob, with the Finns, arranging a new paper deal.'

'Oh,' said Bob, 'is he? And who gave him permission to absent himself from today's Politbureau?' No one could answer that one.

'Bring him back,' Maxwell ordered. 'Go on – go to the 'phone now, get hold of Roger and tell him to return immediately to this table.' His instruction was directed at the unfortunate production director who had volunteered the information about Bowes. He crept out of the dining room while the rest of us shifted awkwardly from foot to foot, still holding our drinks.

Maxwell thought he would ease the tension: 'OK, boys, sit down. We might as well start lunch,' and he clapped his hands for the waiters to begin. A few minutes later the production director crept back and reported: 'I've spoken to Roger, Bob. He's on his way back.' Maxwell nodded and plunged into his hors-d'oeuvre with some savagery.

Bowes's chair remained unoccupied for about half an hour while the conversation rattled on about inconsequentials such as whether Oxford United's manager was a good or bad thing (Maxwell owned the football club), and whether it would be a good idea to buy another soccer club if the Football Association would let him get away with it; and what a 'load of wankers' the football authorities were. Then Bowes returned.

I watched him as he moved toward the vacant chair and gripped the back of it, knuckles white under the grip, face tense and looking hard at Maxwell. 'Ah, Roger,' the Cap'n began, 'how nice of you to join us. Did you have a decent lunch at the Savoy? Lousy cooks there. Tell me, Roger,' he continued, 'who gave you permission to abandon us today?'

At that point I thought – indeed hoped – that Bowes would pick up his chair and throw it at Maxwell. To my disappointment he didn't but replied, too meekly: 'I was at the Savoy, chairman, to complete an important contract for newsprint for your company. It was an important meeting ...'

Maxwell cut him short. 'Who gave you permission?'

'I didn't think I needed to get your prior approval for such things, chairman. My job as your managing director is to look after the interests of this company ....'

He was cut short again by a Maxwell cry of anger: 'Roger, how many times do I have to tell you that there is nothing more important than this Politbureau? Your business is to be here unless

I, personally, give you permission to be absent. Do you understand that, Roger?'

Bowes, of course, should have walked out of the room. His error was to reply: 'Yes, chairman, I understand.' He sat down and nibbled at a bread roll while a waiter served him a plate of food he clearly would not eat. Not long after that crazy gathering of the Politbureau Roger Bowes left the Mirror Group with a pay-off.

The humiliation was characteristic of the way Maxwell would, and did, behave to chosen victims. An example of pure tyranny – an instrument of torture that Cap'n Bob excelled in using. It was, as he would casually admit when relaxed, part of his management technique.

It was indeed my experiences at those Tuesday lunches that finally convinced me that remaining at the *Mirror* was not for me. I would have to find a way out, by early retirement or some formula. I also realised that I was in the company of someone who was evil, possibly clinically insane and yet – as I have explained – possessed an almost hypnotic quality to pull on all the strings attached to his puppets with exceptional skill, immense charm, warmth and sympathy and at times even with an element of self-deprecating humour. Here, in a nutshell, was my own dilemma about the man, and I knew it was a shared feeling among my closest colleagues, like Mike Molloy and Bob Edwards.

Even so the megalomania was on such a scale that it began to compel comparison with the great dictators – Hitler, Mussolini, Stalin, Mao. Having witnessed how Maxwell was capable of transfixing intelligent, adult men of power and experience I could better understand what probably happened round Hitler's table as he ordered his Wehrmacht generals to do what they knew was absurd, as well as in some cases impossible. They, too, were hypnotised by the Fuhrer and rolled over like sheep – with notable exceptions. As I witnessed the weekly scenes at Maxwell's Politbureau table my mind became focused on the parallel with the dictators.

I tried hard to analyse my own feelings about this: to ask myself how best to react. The obvious choice was to tell Cap'n Bob to stuff his job and walk away, even though I was not yet at the pensionable age of 65. Another choice was to soldier on trying to do the best one could for the paper, fighting to protect its old reputation and traditions from still further degeneration and trying to limit Maxwell's damage. Perhaps I should have quit at that point. I sought to rationalise my decision to stay on for a while with the comforting reflection that Maxwell had never tried to attack or humiliate me as he did to so many of my colleagues. Moreover, constantly lurking in my mind was my own ambivalence toward him: that mix of admiration and regard, even affection; the recognition that this man had been brutally damaged by his earlier experiences and was, in effect, exacting an emotional revenge on everyone – regardless. We were all being turned into Holocaust victims; we were all being asked to account for what had happened to him, Jew and non-Jew alike.

Yet none of this pyscho-analytical rationalisation could possibly excuse his appalling conduct. So I allowed the moment of my own decision to be postponed. I now believe I should not have left my point of departure so long delayed. I remained with him at the *Mirror* for nearly two years – through the terrible period of the miners' strike, when he did try to interfere with my work. There were numerous incidents following his takeover of the paper in July 1984, when the strike was four months old, where he tried, without success, to interfere and influence the way the paper covered the strike.

The most direct bid to censor me occurred within weeks of his arrival at Holborn Circus. It was about what became known widely as 'The Goodman column incident'. In my weekly *Daily Mirror* column I wrote a piece focusing on Margaret Thatcher's hatred of the miners. It contained detailed information about a Cabinet split that had developed during the previous miners' strike in January and February 1974, which led to the fall of the Heath Government. Two members of the Heath Cabinet opposed the majority decision to go to the country on a 'Who governs Britain?' ticket. A minority of two wanted to fight the miners, beat them and carry on in government without an election. They were Keith Joseph and Margaret Thatcher. And they vowed, afterwards, to return to battle with the miners. My *Mirror* article told that story for the first time.

I read a proof of the column before leaving and cleared it all with the editor. Later that evening, after both Mike Molloy and I had left the office, Maxwell returned. He had dined well and was far from sober. He asked the night editor to see all proofs of political stories including my column. He read it – or perhaps only partly read it since his attention span was very brief – and changed the content without consulting anyone. He instructed the back-bench (the production team) to delete a substantial chunk from the middle of the column, insert new cross-headings and leave more white space. In doing so he changed the whole point of the column by deleting the Joseph/Thatcher vote of 1974. In short, he left the column without coherence or any real meaning. Fortunately, because of intelligent stalling by my colleagues and friends on the back-bench, the amended, meaningless column appeared in only the late London edition. Even so it was damaging.

The night editor phoned me at midnight to explain what madness had been happening, and in turn I 'phoned Mike Molloy at home to inform him. He knew nothing about Maxwell's intervention. I told Mike that unless the column was changed back to its original form I would resign. He pleaded with me not to take any action. 'Leave it to me,' he implored. So I agreed to sleep on it and meet him next morning, when we would both go to see Maxwell. At 11 am the next day we went into Maxwell's room, and as I walked in Cap'n Bob put his arms around me, hugged me and apologised: 'How can you ever forgive me, Geoffrey, for doing such a thing? Will you please forgive me? I promise it will never happen again. I behaved stupidly ...'

There then followed a bottle-opening session to toast my 'complete independence in future' from any such interference, with Maxwell appointing Mike Molloy as my 'guarantor'. 'Mike will guarantee that I never do such a thing again,' he pledged. Bob Maxwell appeared genuinely contrite. Of course I deluded myself. Even so when the news spread of what had happened several other writers on the paper, including John Pilger and Paul Foot, sought similar assurances from the chairman and were duly given the sacred pledge, for all that it mattered.

Throughout the miners' strike I tried hard to keep Maxwell off the pitch and the paper on an even keel of sound reporting and comment, which contained both criticism of the Thatcher Government and Coal Board as well as a critique of Arthur Scargill's strategy. All along the problem was that Maxwell was far less concerned with the journalism of the most dramatic industrial story since the Second World War but almost wholly with imposing himself as the man who could settle the dispute. From the moment he took over the paper he was constantly pressing me to arrange private meetings with all the leading figures so that he could help them find a solution.

It was his pressure to do this that led to me arranging a 'secret conclave' with the miners' leaders at the Trades Union Congress in Brighton in September 1984. Maxwell pressed me to try to fix a meeting for the Sunday prior to the TUC opening so that he could bring together Scargill, Mick McGahey (NUM vice president) and Peter Heathfield (NUM general secretary), along with himself, Mike Molloy and myself in a 'mission to find a peace formula'. So, with great difficulty, I did arrange the meeting for Sunday afternoon in the basement suite of a Brighton hotel. For two hours we talked about every aspect of the miners' strike trying to find a feasible formula. Midway through the session Maxwell asked me to contact the Coal Board's labour relations director, Ned Smith, so that we could test him out about a possible solution. I phoned Ned Smith at home and brought him off a golf course to talk with Maxwell. The outcome was an astonishing burst of optimism – albeit not from the NUM leaders – when the Coal Board chairman Ian MacGregor agreed to come to a meeting the following day in a hotel halfway between London and Brighton. It all came to nothing, for sure – except that it boosted Maxwell's delusion about the potential of his peacemaking capacities.

A few weeks before that Brighton 'summit' I had also been involved in another meeting with the NUM leaders at Sheffield, the NUM's home base, at which Maxwell – accompanied by Joe Haines, John Pilger and Bob Edwards as well as myself – met Scargill and Heathfield (Mick McGahey was not present at that session) in a preliminary skirmish in search of a possible settlement. It was remarkable stuff – but it came to nought. The dialogue between Maxwell and Scargill, eyeball to eyeball across the table, was unforgettable even if pointless. On only one issue did they agree – that the police harassment of miners' families and homes had gone far beyond what was acceptable or tolerable.

Maxwell promised a *Mirror* campaign to investigate all these charges – and, to be fair, he did attempt a brief campaign along those lines, though it died away very quickly. Maxwell also agreed to sponsor holiday trips to various resorts for the children of miners' families. It was a generous gesture, and some mining communities benefited. But all the time the publicity spotlight focused on the man, Maxwell, who believed it was within his power to solve any problem. He believed, or wanted to believe, that he was within reach of a settlement to what others regarded as an intractable dispute. Of course, it was a grotesque self-delusion, but there were times when he probably succeeded in blinding most of us that even in his madness – or *because* of his lunacy – he might just pull off the sensational coup.

As I sat with him, alone, in his hotel room on the Sunday night, the eve of that 1984 TUC, he was constantly on the 'phone seeking to follow up the talks we had held in the afternoon. First he called Downing Street, where he tried to speak with Mrs Thatcher, ending up with her Cabinet secretary, Robin Butler; then he spoke with MacGregor. Again it was Maxwell's belief that he had the influence, if not the power, to move events and saw his ownership of the Mirror Group as Northcliffe or the Rothermeres had seen their control of the *Daily Mail* and as Max Beaverbrook saw his influence (even power) as controller of the *Daily Express* in its greatest days.

But this situation was very different. Neither Scargill nor Thatcher were interested in a patched-up peace by Robert Maxwell. Indeed, they would avoid such a prospect at any price. Margaret Thatcher wanted Arthur Scargill and his National Union of Mineworkers destroyed; wiped off the slate. Arthur wanted victory over Thatcher and her visible retreat from a programme of pit closures that had become, for her, a challenge as imperative as her victory over Galtieri in the Falklands. The sight of Cap'n Bob ambulating up and down the Brighton sea-front looking for peace formulae was as irrelevant to both Thatcher and Scargill as counting pebbles on Brighton beach.

None of this discouraged the intrepid Maxwell. Right to end of the strike he continuously tried to interfere; sought to use the Mirror Group papers to promote his own ego trip as a peacemaker at large; overruled his editors; sidetracked any advice that he felt failed to fit in with his own preconceived versions.

There was, of course, terrible cowardice by men and women on Mirror Group for whom I had previously had a great deal of professional respect as well as personal regard. Some collaborated willingly, perhaps even gladly. Several of them were fine journalists who had yielded to Maxwell's absurdities, his blandishments and certainly his flattery. In their defence they would argue that only by yielding to his banalities was it possible to exercise some degree of influence over potentially even worse manifestations of his madness. Of course, there may be truth in this – except that it is the argument of the courtier throughout the ages. Those who remained faithful to his whims were certainly rewarded financially, if unequally.

Yet I would not make the charge of venal corruption against any one of them: the much more plausible explanation is that they were hypnotised, caught in the glare of that extraordinarily powerful and manic pall that settled over their minds and moral judgement. But then, not to put too fine a point on all this, or paint a holier-than-thou gloss, perhaps all of us who laboured in the Maxwell marquee at that time carry some element of guilt for what happened.

* * *

Robert Maxwell MC. Died on 5 November 1991. Guy Fawkes's day. He died as he lived – an enigma wrapped in mystery. There were at least two post-mortems on his waterlogged body after it had been dredged from the ocean. The speculation about how he died remains active to this day. We have been over the ground many times – was it suicide, or heart failure in a grossly overweight body; was it an accident of fate, or was it murder? At the time of his death I was prepared to believe in the suicide theory. It fitted the circumstances. Or I could be persuaded that it was some form of natural cause – he was a sick man, used to taking medication on a substantial scale, and drugs to ease his pain and breathing problems following an earlier operation to remove part of his lung. It was even feasible, it seemed to me, that Maxwell took an overdose of drugs that left him semi-conscious as he opened the door of his cabin on his yacht, the *Lady Ghislaine*: gasping for air, fumbling toward the deck rail he slid overboard in the early hours darkness off the Canaries on that fateful morning of 5 November 1991. I have however revised my view on all this. I am no longer persuaded that he wasn't murdered.

Bob Maxwell knew he was in irreversible trouble in his business affairs. Everywhere he looked his great empire seemed to be collapsing around him – except for the still-profitable Mirror Group Newspapers. His American acquisitions were a crushing debt burden. He had rifled the entire pension funds of Maxwell Communications to try to ease that debt burden, and he mortgaged virtually all his wealth on a huge gamble with fate. By a strange irony he was again following his obsession with Murdoch – who had, only a few years earlier, also faced financial disaster by overextending his ambitions. But Murdoch was rescued. There was no one left to rescue Bob Maxwell – except one possible saviour. He still had some friends in very high political places. If they failed him then commercial disaster would swiftly turn to criminal investigations, an Old Bailey trial, abject surrender. The question that was unanswered then – and remains unanswered to this day – is: what happened to those political friends in high places, in the United States, Britain, France, Israel and even in the former Soviet Union?

Maxwell built up a tremendous catalogue of politically influential contacts with wide commercial implications. For over twenty years he had established a network of commercial and political interests in the Communist countries of Eastern Europe, which was a linchpin of his Pergamon Press company. His biographies – or, to be accurate, bland hagiographies – of virtually all the Communist leaders from Leonid Brezhnev in the Soviet Union to Nicolae Ceausescu in Romania were lucrative earners for Pergamon. The Maxwell collection also included hagiographies of Erich Honecker in the German Democratic Republic; Janos Kadar, Hungary; Todor Zhivkov, Bulgaria; Gustav Husak, Czechoslovakia; Yuri Andropov, USSR; Wojciech Jaruzelski, Poland; etc. Thrown into this pot to establish a kind of phoney balance were studies of Ronald Reagan and of Morarji Desai, one-time Prime Minister of India. Maxwell made a point of visiting them all, interviewing them, writing a foreword and editing the biographies, which Pergamon published for circulation in several languages but, most of all, for circulation in the countries over which these men ruled. Pergamon was paid in US dollars for a highly profitable operation, and the bulk of these funds went into the mysterious Lichtenstein fund which was, and remains, under secret wraps.

Yet this extraordinary quilt of commercial contacts with the East European Communist world concealed something else – Maxwell was also involved in passing intelligence to the west about the Communist rulers he interviewed and published. In fact he was almost certainly being used as – and using himself as – a two-way intelligence conduit. This Maxwell arrangement (as it was called in some circles) included a special element – passing intelligence to the Israeli security forces with whom he became increasingly involved toward the end of his life. He was highly regarded by the Israeli Government in Jerusalem. He was certainly used by the Israeli authorities to help in the process of Jewish emigration from the Soviet Union and, in return, he was seen by the Soviet Government as an important contact figure in dealings with Israel. This involved commercial interests as well, all of which linked Maxwell with secret defence deals between Israel and countries of Eastern Europe. Maxwell had important investments in the Israeli defence industry and, especially, in the defence industry trading park at Haifa.

My own speculation focuses on these aspects of Maxwell's life. The possibility that Maxwell could have ended up in the Old Bailey on charges of criminal fraud raised critical questions for a number of countries that were involved in the Maxwell triangle of international dealings, if not intrigue. Bob Maxwell in the dock at the Old Bailey was not a prospect any of the interested groups would have appreciated. Those groups certainly included the United States, Britain, Soviet Russia, Israel and France. The intelligence services in all these countries were alert to the dangers. My own theory is that any one of them – or even a combination of several – could have been responsible for Bob Maxwell's death. If, as we may assume, Maxwell was keeping open one final, despairing hope of a last-minute financial reprieve and crucial help from some of his old friends in high places then it could have come from any one of these sources. But it did not. Instead came death. Of course, it is unlikely that the truth will ever emerge. Of one thing I remain quite certain: Bob Maxwell was an unlikely suicidal figure. Indeed he believed he could walk on water ...

19   Conclusion:
A Funny Old World

It is indeed a funny old world.

When I first arrived in Fleet Street there was no television; 'the Street' was still full of a certain magic, which us romantics always exaggerated. But I can still sniff that incomparable smell of ink, a low musty oily odour, which penetrated everything. And we all knew that our minds were redolent of it. The Street was full of pubs with wonderful names and nicknames – so that the *News Chronicle*'s local at the bottom of Tudor Street was the White Swan, always known as 'The Mucky Duck'. The Fleet Street pubs were the hub of our universe because that was where gossip was traded and cunning insights gained into other people's stories. ('Hey, have you heard about the *Express* splash tonight? They're naming the woman who was murdered ...' etc.) The pubs were bazaars of information – and disinformation – with drinks thrown in.

Taxis abounded, but it was no bad thing to jump on a Number 11 bus if you wanted to reach the House of Commons quickly and cheaply – then charge a taxi on expenses!: so much so that the Number 11 bus became a Fleet Street cliché such as: 'That bloody Home Secretary ... do you think we might be lucky enough to get him knocked down by a Number 11?' Even ministers were known to catch a bus in those days. On a story, anywhere, the search for a telephone box that was vacant was by far the most important aspect of any reporter's working priorities – since getting the story back to the office speedily was always the prime test. So the wily reporter, out in the sticks, would bribe, or perhaps one should say – generously supply – a local publican, resident or hotel keeper to keep a 'phone at the ready for him to use, exclusively, of course.

Back in the office it was important to find a typewriter that worked so that if you were well briefed on typewriter maintenance in the reporters' room and knew the flawed machines it was usually sensible, albeit mean-minded, to slip a piece of unfinished copy into a good machine before you left the room – thereby 'reserving' typewriter rights. Of course, it didn't always work since most reporters eventually became alive to that trick, saw the unfinished copy in a machine and ripped it out with a muttered oath. When I first arrived at the *Daily Mirror* the typewriters in the reporters' room were chained to each desk – just in case some deprived soul felt the need to pack a machine into the boot of his car. That rarely happened – though there were some guilty cases. Reporters' pay packets then were far, far removed from the kind of pay cheques handed out today, so a typewriter was a valuable commodity.

Filing copy from abroad was based on cable and cableese – the abbreviated use of language to reduce cable costs and speed up a slow process. Radio was not regarded as a serious competitor to national or even regional newspapers since the main function of BBC radio – there was then no commercial network – was still vested in the high tide of Reithian tradition of good drama, superb music, excellent light entertainment of the Tommy Handley variety, vivid cricket commentary, especially on Test Matches by the prewar genius, Howard Marshall – and a regular sprinkling of anodyne news bulletins, which told you very little except the time of day. The BBC news readers, moreover, still had to address their microphones in evening dress. Saying nothing of importance while attired in evening dress was a prestigious occupation in those days. Maybe it still is – though no longer at the BBC.

It was good radio, often outstandingly good, but it did not impinge on the life of newspapers. It was almost unknown for the BBC to have a scoop; in fact, it was policy to avoid such embarrassment. No self-respecting news editor of a national paper bothered with BBC news bulletins. They missed nothing. On the *News Chronicle* even in the 1950s all BBC radio news bulletins were taken down by the copy telephonists whose typed notes were handed to the news editor, or night news editor, as a casual routine. The men on news desks – and invariably they were men – almost always dropped the BBC's best efforts in the waste bin without so much as a second glance.

The foreign correspondent was someone of considerable substance and status, often of renown and great authority, even on the popular national dailies, most of which were then broadsheets. The *Daily Mirror* and the faltering *Daily Sketch* were the exception – as tabloids. Great broadsheet newspapers like Beaverbrook's *Daily Express* actually made a main marketing point of claiming to have more foreign correspondents than any other national newspaper in Britain – well over a hundred staff men and stringers dotted all over the world, and they included legendary by-lines like James Cameron, Sefton Delmer, Rene McCall. Their cables – cable was often preferred to the unreliable telephone – were awaited with an eagerness and expectation resembling the excitement stimulated by messages from Antarctic explorers in earlier times.

Most foreign reporters in the early 1950s travelled by sea or even train; a flight across the Atlantic was still a novelty, and it might take anything between twelve and fifteen hours to reach New York in an old crate of pre-jet vintage air travel. Moreover, an air ticket to the United States was regarded by numerous foreign desks as an expenditure of special resort justified only by urgent circumstances – and that would certainly have excluded taking a picture of a Royal Princess basking on a foreign beach even if she was half-naked.

Around a cluster of certainties and the landmarks of authority, status, class distinction, snobbery and Ostrich-like attitudes, which even the Second World War did not easily break down, journalists operated their own code of behaviour – a kind of unwritten statute of limitations. An unwritten understanding of when and how to break the rules of convention and, it has to be said, even decency. Of course, this did not prevent excesses and frequent audacious testing of the laws of libel and defamation. Though, oddly enough, invasions of privacy forty years ago were far fewer, and where they did occur it was often, humorously, by accident rather than malign intent. Still, it must also be admitted that malign intent existed. Stumbling into an 'exclusive' was almost always a precondition for that grotesquely over-used label: some of the best exclusive stories of all time were the result of a lucky stumble; certainly a lucky gamble.

Then, at first rather slowly, things began to change. The mores of society shifted and, as I have argued in earlier chapters, somewhere around the 1960s the entire scene moved and we found ourselves – I can think of no other explanation – we simply *found ourselves* living on a different plane and even a changed planet. Everything began to explode – technology, work, sex, family life, attitudes, style, fashion, manners, ideology, religion, travel, the entire bloodstream of life moved more rapidly. So, journalism changed, too. And I can only repeat that it is an absurd oversimplification, however tempting, to blame it all on Rupert Murdoch. Certainly he exploited it, profited by it, milked it for all he could, and traded on the weakness and cowardice of his competitors. But he didn't actually invent the collapse of the old order.

*   *   *

My dear departed friend Jimmy Cameron used to say that 'journalism is a process of constant self-education'. I doubt it is possible to improve on that description of our trade. The entire canvas of this book is itself some evidence of that, not least in my own case. It is also, surely, a process of self-discovery aided considerably by the privilege of our trade – such as finding oneself, often enough, close to the focal points of power and influence with the facility to recognise the fallibility and the sophism of so many who reach the top of the greasy pole.

And then the journalist is handed the even more demanding privilege of passing on the message to others, the readers. Always there comes that final, final question: can we be sure about anything we have seen and then written about? To witness something coldly, in peace or war, still requires an interpretation, an explanation to help reach out to the truth. In the end the writer, the reporter, still has to use his subjective judgement. It is a cop-out to turn aside and say: 'No, I can't judge that' – if only because we have no other measure within us than our own subjective capacity to evaluate, to decide and then to use a moral judgement between what is right and wrong, good and evil. To pretend absolute neutrality in journalism, as in most else, is to lie to one's own conscience. Of course we can be wrong, often have been. But I have almost always felt it is preferable to have made the effort to judge, and perhaps be proved wrong, than never to have judged at all.

As a political animal I have judged, sometimes in serious error. I call myself a socialist. It is a phrase, a category of moral and political assessment that has become increasingly difficult to define with any precision. Yet I still 'feel' a socialist: the vibes are still in place despite the molestation of time. Perhaps it is an act of faith, though there is no harm in that. 'In der Beschrankung zeigt erst der Meister,' wrote Goethe, meaning that 'genius is knowing where to stop', or as I would prefer to interpret that remark, 'the beginning of wisdom is recognising our own limitations'.

The century into which I was born and have spent my life has been described as the most cruel, perhaps the most evil, of all; I do not know. History's jury is still out on that assertion and, in my view, will remain out. I am aware of Eric Hobsbawm's view that the twentieth century was the 'most murderous in recorded history'. His estimate is that it cost the lives of 187 million people – equal to 10 per cent of the world's population in 1913 (quoted from his lecture 'War and Peace in the 20th Century' in Olso, December 2001). Perhaps he is correct; I am not sure we can make such valid measurements given the extraordinary changes in the scale of human cruelty.

But of one thing I am convinced – it has been the most remarkable period for scientific and technological advance mankind has known. There has simply been nothing like the twentieth century in that respect, and if the process and speed of change continues at this pace God knows what kind of global, or cosmic, scene we will have by the year 3000. Perhaps something will snap because the human species will simply be unable to cope with such a rate of change; or maybe everything will slow down again, perhaps a comparative tranquillity will return to enable people to pause, take breath and think. We don't know and we can't know. No doubt we require a new Darwin as well as a new Marx and Freud to help us sort it out.

What we do face is a socio-industrial revolution on a global scale, which will require a completely fresh political agenda. Marx argued that capitalism will destroy itself through its own success, though, contrary to his many interpreters, he did not offer a blueprint for what might follow – he proposed an ideological concept of a dream that has so far proved a failure. His followers picked up the message and assumed it was an imperative call, a virtual instruction, to bring forward the future and impose it. That was their great error, and it has led to catastrophic failure. Yet, ironically, Marx's analysis of capitalism is, today, probably more evidently correct than ever. Even his most sceptical critic, the late Sir Isaiah Berlin, has observed: 'I think there are ideas you could find in Marx which belong to the general treasury of human ideas' (*Conversations with Isaiah Berlin* by Ramin Jahanbegloo, 1992).

It is of course quite possible that technology and science as they develop through the millennium will find their own formula to help cushion the excesses of their own innovations; this way it may be possible to sustain forms of capitalism well beyond the foreseeable future. On balance, however, that must seem unlikely, though it would be unwise to rule it out altogether. It is this doubt, this volume of uncertainty that has grown about the future, which feeds the pessimism of thinkers like John Kenneth Galbraith and Dr R.E. Pahl, the sociologist. More than twenty years ago (1982) Dr Pahl predicted that by the end of the twentieth century the social and industrial changes would be as 'cumulatively dramatic as those which took place in Britain between 1780 and 1800'. He suggested that we are living through a 'massive re-negotiation of the social division of labour' and that deindustrialisation would also have a deradicalising effect on political attitudes. Much of what Dr Pahl predicted has already happened.

Professor Galbraith is another who has predicted increasing uncertainty. In his memorable *Encyclopedia Britannica* lecture in Edinburgh, in January 1990, Galbraith said: 'Capitalism in its original or pristine form could not have survived. But under pressure it did adapt. Socialism in its original form and for its first tasks did succeed. But it failed to adapt and it nurtured an oppressive and repressive political structure ... Socialism encountered revolt because it failed to adapt.' And yet, he added: 'Capitalism does not anywhere supply good, inexpensive shelter. Health care is only satisfactory where, effectively, it is socialised ...' And his conclusion: adaptation – 'There is, sadly, no alternative.'

Well, yes, but that too, as J.K.G. knows only too well, also requires a clearer definition. Adaptation can, after all, mean anything or nothing. My own hunch is that Galbraith's concept of adaptation is meant to lead us to a set of ideas in which a socially conscious and socially responsible market system begins to combine the virtues of both capitalism and socialism; but then it might also combine their vices.

*   *   *

Let me leave a final quotation to John Maynard Keynes. He would approve of that status but in any event the exceptional mind of J.M.K. clearly deserves that accolade. In a famous essay written over sixty years ago, 'Economic Consequences for our Grand-children' Keynes suggested that already, by the 1930s, we had moved into a sphere in which the possibilities for human fulfilment were limitless – but dangerous. 'For the first time since his creation,' Keynes wrote, 'man will be faced with his real, his permanent problem: how to use his freedom from pressing economic cares, how to occupy his leisure which science and compound interest have won for him to live wisely and agreeably as well.' That proposition can be quite suitably restated today, adding technology to compound interest.

Keynes warned at the time about the dangers of another world war, which might end all such dreams of human contentment. That war came in 1939, followed again by the dreams of 1945 and afterwards by the gradual disillusioning experiences of the last half-century. It is now at least possible to believe that ultimate destruction by nuclear war is less likely than it was ten or twenty years ago -- though we cannot be sure about that either.

Keynes's other great anxiety was population explosion. Like Malthus, he was deeply exercised by the probability of a geometric growth in world population that would neutralise scientific and economic development. That threat has not been eased, in fact, it has been considerably enlarged. And it is now necessary to add a further dimension to the population issue – the environment. Indeed, there are those who believe strongly that the threat posed by environmental changes is so formidable that it exceeds any other shadow hanging over the future. So perhaps there is no answer.

Yet if we are pushed to the point of offering one, then it must lie in a convergence of freedom with control – which is not as crazy as it might sound. It is an oxymoron almost certainly waiting to develop. A permanent friction between these two forces might remain the only rational basis for a civilised society and a workable democratic system. That in order to sustain and develop human freedom and civilised behaviour it will become inevitable to extend regulation and control over the way we live and, still more, over what we consume – like fossil fuels. Maybe that is the kind of Third Way people like Tony Blair have in mind. The frontiers between freedom and control, between the market and public intervention, between capitalism and socialism, if you like, will always be moving. By definition there can be no final, absolute fixed point in this moving balance. I can only say, as an inveterate romantic, that I am drawn to the graphic design painted by Keynes in his remarkable essay of nearly seventy years ago. But in the world we are moving into it is seriously questionable whether freedom can be sustained without measures of social control.

I have a secret wish, wholly unachievable: to interview a group of those now beyond reach of the journalists' notebook – Keynes, Marx, H.G. Wells, Freud, Auden, Socrates, Byron, Shakespeare and a few more. My question: where did it all go wrong? Or did it? Mind you, I might now have difficulty finding a newspaper willing to print the answer – unless it was 'sexed up'.

References

Barnes, Denis and Reid, Eileen (1980), *Governments and Trade Unions: British Experience, 1964–79*, London, Heinemann

Benn, Tony (1989), *Against the Tide: Diaries 1973–1976*, London, Hutchinson

Bevan, Aneurin (1976), *In Place of Fear*, London, EP

Butler, David and Kavanagh, Dennis (1974), *The British General Election of 1974*, London, Macmillan

Cameron, James (1973), review of Michael Foot, *Aneurin Bevan* (London, Davis–Poynter, 1973), *Evening Standard*, 9 October

Cunningham, Valentine (1988), *British Writers of the Thirties*, Oxford, OUP

Donoughue, Bernard (1987), *Prime Minister*, London, Cape

Dorril, Stephen and Ramsay, Robin (1991), *Smear!: Wilson and the Secret State*, London, Fourth Estate

Fromm, Erich (1974), *The Anatomy of Human Destructiveness*, London, Cape

Haines, Joe (1977), *The Politics of Power*, London, Cape

Healey, Denis (1989), *The Time of My Life*, London, Michael Joseph

Heath, Edward (1998), *The Course of My Life*, London, Hodder & Stoughton

Jenkins, Roy (1991), *A Life at the Centre*, London, Macmillan

Jones, Jack (1986), *Union Man*, London, Collins

Kavanagh, Dennis (1987), *Heath Government 1970–74*, Oxford, Blackwell

Kavanagh, Dennis (1989) 'The Heath Government 1970–74' in P. Hennessy and A. Seldon (eds) *Ruling Performance – British Governments From Attlee to Thatcher*, Oxford, Blackwell.

McCarthy, Lord (unpublished), 'The Rise and Fall of Collective Laissez-Faire'

Orwell, George (1937), *The Road to Wigan Pier*, London, Victor Gollancz, New Left Book Club

Pahl, R.E. (1982), 'Looking Towards 2000', *New Society*, 7 October

Priestley, J.B. (1934), *English Journey: Being a Rambling But Truthful Account of What One Man Saw and Heard and Felt and Thought During a Journey Through England in the Autumn of the Year 1933*, London, Heinemann

Rodgers, Bill (1991), review of Jenkins (1991), *Observer*, 22 September

Snow, Edgar (1968), *Red Star Over China*, New York, Random House (first published 1937)

Steel, David (1989), in the *Independent*, 28 March

Thompson, Peter and Delano, Antony (1988), *Maxwell: Portrait of Power*, New York, Bantam Press

Vidal, Gore (1995), *Palimpsest: A Memoir*, London, André Deutsch

Wright, Peter (1987), *Spycatcher: The Candid Autobiography of a Senior Intelligence Officer*, London, Viking–Penguin

Young, Hugo (1989), *One of Us: A Biography of Mrs Thatcher*, London, Macmillan

Index

Compiled by John Goodman and Rachel Field